LOST IN TIBET

LOST IN TIBET

*The Untold Story
of Five American Airmen,
a Doomed Plane,
and the Will to Survive*

Richard Starks and Miriam Murcutt

THE LYONS PRESS
Guilford, Connecticut
An imprint of The Globe Pequot Press

Copyright © 2004 by Richard Starks and Miriam Murcutt

First Lyons Press paperback edition, 2005

The Lyons Press is an imprint of The Globe Pequot Press.

10 9 8 7 6 5 4 3 2 1

Printed in the United States of America

Designed by Stephanie Doyle

ISBN 1-59228-785-9 (paperback)

The Library of Congress has previously cataloged an earlier (hardcover) edition as follows:

Starks, Richard.
        Lost in Tibet : the untold story of five American airmen, a doomed plane, and the will to survive / Richard Starks and Miriam Murcutt.
        p. cm.
Includes bibliographical references.
ISBN 1-59228-572-4
1. World War, 1939-1945—Personal narratives, American. 2. Tibet (China)—Description and travel.
I. Murcutt, Miriam. II. Title.

D811.5.S7194 2004
951'.504—dc22

                                        2004048959

Photo Insert Credits:
Page one, top: from *China Airlift - the Hump,* Volume II, China Burma India Hump Pilots Association; **page one, bottom:** from *China Airlift - the Hump,* Volume II, China Burma India Hump Pilots Association. **Page two, top:** from *China Airlift - the Hump,* Volume II, China Burma India Hump Pilots Association; **page two, bottom:** from *China Airlift - the Hump,* Volume III, China Burma India Hump Pilots Association/Turner Publishing Company. **Page two, inset:** from *China Airlift - the Hump,* Volume II, China Burma India Hump Pilots Association; **page three, top photos:** from *A Quest of Flowers* by Harold Fletcher, Frank Ludlow and George Sherriff, Edinburgh University Press; **page three, bottom:** from *Who's Who in China,* fourth edition, Chinese Materials Center, Hong Kong. **Page four:** Ewell Sale Stewart Library, The Academy of Natural Sciences of Philadelphia. **Page five:** Pitt Rivers Museum, University of Oxford, Tibet Collections, Accession Number 1998.131.576. **Page six, top:** from *China Airlift - the Hump,* Volume II, China Burma India Hump Pilots Association; **page six, bottom:** Pitt Rivers Museum, University of Oxford, Tibet Collections, Accession Number 1998.131.167. **Page seven, top:** Richard Starks and Miriam Murcutt; **page seven, bottom:** from *A Portrait of Lost Tibet* by Rosemary Jones Tung, University of California Press. **Page eight:** Family collection of Mr. and Mrs. Wayne Perram.

Contents

PREFACE

⸺◦⸺

IN NOVEMBER 1943, at the height of the Second World War, five young American airmen took off for what they expected would be a routine mission, flying from Kunming in China back to their base at Jorhat in India. As darkness set in, a violent storm erupted that blew the men hundreds of miles off course. When their fuel ran out, the men were forced to bail out over what, to their astonishment and dismay, turned out to be Tibet.

If it had not been for the war, the five young airmen would have been home in small-town America, sipping soda pops in a drugstore somewhere, or angling for a date with their childhood sweethearts. Instead, they found themselves plunged into a harsh and forbidding land, with a strange people whose culture the Americans knew nothing about. How, we wondered, had they managed to cope?

It was clear to us that the story of Robert Crozier, Harold McCallum, Kenneth Spencer, John Huffman, and William Perram had at least two separate aspects, both of which were intriguing. On one level, their story was an absorbing true-life adventure, involving physical hardship and struggle in the face of constant danger. On another level, it was a story of cultural conflict and incomprehension, with the Americans representing a modern world in which twenty-seven industrial nations were consumed by war, and the Tibetans embodying a medieval society that was based, in part, on the benign concepts of a compassionate religion. The contrast could not have been greater.

Soon after we began our research, however, we discovered that there was a third element to the airmen's story—one that was every bit as compelling. It transpired that, while in Tibet, the airmen had become embroiled in the international political scheming that even then was revolving around Tibet's determined efforts to remain independent from China. To avoid embarrassing its Chinese ally, the United States government had apparently tried to conceal this aspect of the story, and it was this discovery that made us even more determined to see that the airmen's story was properly told.

At the time it took place, the Americans' adventure in Tibet attracted widespread attention. It was written up in *Collier's* magazine, *Newsweek, Readers' Digest* and the *New York Times*. It was the subject of a CBS radio drama documentary that was broadcast on February 4, 1944. And the publishers of Captain Aero turned it into a colorful—even lurid—comic strip. In our view, however, the story has never been given the attention or weight that it deserves.

The pilot of the plane—Robert Crozier—did cooperate on a book, published in 1965, but the book's author, William Boyd Sinclair, stated in his foreword that he took "certain liberties" with the truth. Also, he was not able to draw on many of the sources that we have used, so he could not present what we view as the full picture. One other book—a self-published autobiography—was written by the copilot, Harold McCallum, and it appeared in 1995. It gives an important account of what happened to the airmen, but as it was written entirely from the author's point of view, it again lacks what we consider are a number of important dimensions.

We have nonetheless drawn on these two books, and are grateful to their authors. We also relied on many other sources, including personal accounts dictated by other members of the crew; a selection of their private letters; interviews we conducted with members of their families and with other airmen who flew in the China-India-Burma theater; contemporary newspaper and magazine articles; and—perhaps most important of all—a now-declassified secret report, which covered the debriefing of the pilot and crew, and a series of weekly reports—also now-declassified—that were written at the time by members of the British mission in Lhasa.

These materials have been invaluable in our efforts to piece the elements of the story together.

We also received unstinting help from a wide range of American, British, Tibetan, and other research organizations, libraries, and archives, as well as the scores of individual experts we contacted in many fields, all of whom freely gave of their time. Without their assistance, this book could not have been written, and we would like to acknowledge their contributions here.

We would specifically like to thank the staffs of the Museum of Aviation, Robins Air Force Base, Warner Robins, Georgia; the National Archives and Records Administration and the Library of Congress, Asian Division, both in Washington D.C.; the U.S. Air Force Historical Research Agency, Montgomery, Alabama; the National Personnel Records Center, St Louis, Missouri; the Franklin D. Roosevelt Presidential Library and Museum, New York; the University of Michigan, Asia Library, Ann Arbor, Michigan; the Newark Museum, Asian Collections, Newark, New Jersey; the Palm Springs Air Museum, Palm Springs, California; the Allen Ginsberg Library at the Naropa University and the Boulder Public Library Inter-Library Loans Service, both in Boulder, Colorado; the India Office Records at The British Library, the Public Record Office, the Museum of Garden History, the Lindley Library and the British Film Institute, all of London, England; the Churchill Archives Centre, Cambridge, England; the National Palace Museum, Department of Rare Books and Documents, Taipei, Taiwan; the Government of Tibet in Exile, Dharamsala, India; and the Tibet Justice Center, Berkeley, California.

In addition, we are indebted to:

+ The families of the five airmen, who generously shared with us their memories, mementos, and personal records.
+ The late Jan Thies of the Hump Pilots Association, who skillfully helped us track down many of the pilots we interviewed.
+ The numerous Hump pilots and other airmen we spoke to, including Bud Albers, Jim Augustus, Dan Green, Jack Hanna, Dick Kurzenberger, Dudley Lebeau, Glen Marker, Charles Martin, Perry Raybuck and Robert Stumpf. Without exception, we found these men to be endlessly patient and courteous in their discussions with us, and it was a privilege talking to them. We were also impressed by the clarity of their memories, but as we came to appreciate, the threat of immi-

nent death, with which they lived every day, did help sear their experiences into their brains.

WE WOULD ALSO LIKE TO THANK the many Tibetan people we met in Lhasa, elsewhere in Tibet, and in the United States. For various reasons they cannot all be named, but they helped us appreciate more of their history, customs, beliefs, and culture.

We also owe a debt to the many Western travelers and writers who gave their impressions of what life in Tibet was like before the Chinese invaded. A bibliography of some of the works we drew on appears at the back of this book as an appendix.

Finally, we would like to thank Jim and Barbra Weidlein at Information Design for their enthusiastic support; as always it was a pleasure working with them. We would also like to thank Susannah Ortego, who helped produce a more consistent and readable text.

Throughout the book, we have tried to use place names that were current in 1943, but on a few occasions we have broken our own rule and abandoned consistency for the sake of clarity. Tibetan place names are notoriously hard to pin down, and frequently differ even when taken from contemporaneous sources. We do not think that any confusion will result.

Also, for the sake of simplicity, we have treated the Government of Great Britain and the Government of India as if they were one and the same. In reality, the two governments were often at odds with each other, but we did not want to bog ourselves down in internecine squabbles that were not relevant to our story, especially since the two governments' differences were eventually resolved and, whatever the issue, a single "British" position emerged.

—Richard Starks
—Miriam Murcutt

I

⸙

THE FORGOTTEN THEATER

ROBERT CROZIER STOOD AT THE EDGE OF THE RUNWAY, sure he was soon going to die. The odds against him were just too great. It would be something small that would get him—not the weather, not the mountains, not the obvious dangers that kept the other pilots awake at night—but something small that he'd never even know was there.

Like that pilot who'd taken off from Jorhat. He had been in the air for two minutes when three of his engines caught fire, each one shooting out a *whoosh* of flame that trailed back half a mile or more. The pilot decided to crash, to fly his plane deliberately into the ground so that all on board would be killed *that* way, rather than burned to a crisp, strapped into their seats like dummies. He made a turn over the airfield, and heard the tower say, "Better get the meat wagon out, we've got a flamer coming in," but then somehow managed to put the plane down, get the crew out, and bring the fire under control. It had been his sparkplugs of all things, scavenged out of another plane. Their gaps were so wide they'd let raw fuel run straight through the engines and out the turbines and *there* it had ignited, three burning tapers half a mile long. It was something small like that that was going to get him; Robert Crozier was sure of it.

He dropped the cigarette he'd been smoking and ground it out under his heel. It was mid-afternoon, the last day of November 1943—a cold, clear day, so he was able to see the mountains, a line of jagged blue peaks

etched against the western horizon. They belonged to the Santsung
Range, a spur of the Himalayas that turned south after rounding the top
of India and then pointed like a dagger at the heart of neighboring
Burma. The sky above them was bright, with just a ripple of cloud marking the route he would soon be flying. It looked good—better than
good—and that was the problem. It looked much too good to be true.

Crozier turned and walked along the edge of the runway, moving with
loose, loping strides, his eyes screwed tight to keep out the swirl of dust
and dirt churned up by a C-47 coming in to land. He passed a gang of
coolies—"slopies," the Americans called them—who were effecting some
kind of repair. The runway here at Kunming—one of the best in all of
China—was just broken rock covered by a smear of gravel. It was always
in need of repair and improvement. He watched the coolies swarm over
it the way slaves must have swarmed over the pyramids, rolling the surface flat, tamping it down, doing everything by hand, and overcoming
any problem by the sheer weight of their numbers. No one seemed to
give the coolies a thought; no one seemed to care if one or more of them
fell—dead, hurt, or exhausted. There were always more of them waiting
in the wings to take their empty places. It bothered Crozier the way the
coolies were treated like that. It both nagged at his conscience and of-
fended the tenets by which he'd been raised.

Robert Crozier was from the other side of the world, from the small
town of West in central Texas. A big, amiable man who hid his concerns
behind a friendly face and an easygoing manner, he was—at the age of
twenty-three—a member of a select group of pilots who had been chosen
to fly one of the most treacherous routes of the Second World War, a route
the pilots had nicknamed "the Hump." The Hump was a long way from
the guts-and-glory combat routes of Western Europe, but it was every bit
as important. Its purpose, quite simply, was to keep China's army supplied, and thus prevent its defeat by Japan. The route was considered vital
to any chance the Allies might have of securing victory in the Far East,
and at its heart—the hub around which its operations were focused—was
the Allied airfield here at Kunming, in the southwest corner of China.

U.S. AIRMEN HAD BEEN FLYING IN AND OUT of Kunming since General
Claire Lee Chennault had chosen it as a base for his "Flying Tigers," a

wild bunch of pilots who tried to roll back the tide of Japanese expansion in the Far East. At the time—1941—the city was considered a "sleepy backwoods," the capital of the Chinese province of Yunnan, but renowned primarily for the high altitude and mild climate that made it a refuge for French vacationers trying to escape the sweat and swelter of neighboring Indochina (now Vietnam, Laos, and Cambodia). Kunming's narrow cobbled streets, lined with pepper and eucalyptus trees, looked much as they had done when the Mongols invaded, and Marco Polo visited, back in the thirteenth century.

The city should have been attractive. Its wooden buildings could be charming and quaint—one story high, two at the most, they had red-tile roofs with elegant, curlicue corners shaped like buffalo horns. But it wasn't your eyes that registered Kunming so much as your nose, causing you to rear back as you were hit in the face by the overpowering stench of rotting waste and open sewers. Kunming was an ancient city and still had the plumbing to prove it. One pilot called it "a dirty little town." Another said it was a "cauldron of filth." By the end of November 1943, it was also a thriving military center, playing a critical role in the Allied fight against the encroaching Japanese army.

For the past fifty years, Japan had been pursuing its dream of Asian expansion, with the specific intent of taking over its far bigger neighbor. It was convinced that in every way—culturally, socially, politically, and militarily—its people were superior and therefore entitled to pluck whatever fruits China had to offer. In 1895, following the Sino-Japanese War, Japan had seized control of Taiwan. In 1931, it annexed Manchuria. And in 1932, it landed 70,000 troops at Shanghai. Finally, in 1937, it launched a full-scale invasion, sending its armies sweeping across China's eastern seaboard with a speed and ferocity that was not to be seen until Germany unleashed its blitzkrieg against Poland in the opening weeks of the Second World War.

By the end of the following year—1938—Japan had destroyed China's navy, as well as its minuscule air force, and imposed a blockade on all of China's major ports. China's army was forced to retreat, driven back as far as Chungking on the upper reaches of the Yangtze River. And there it was cut off. Supplies could reach it only through Kunming, and without those supplies, China's army faced certain defeat.

For a time, supplies to Kunming could get through via French Indochina. Ships were unloaded at Haiphong on the Gulf of Tonkin, and the goods moved onward by rail. But soon after France's ignominious surrender to Germany, Indochina came under Japanese control, and that route was quickly shut down.

Goods for Kunming then had to be trucked in along the notorious Burma Road—built, in 1937–38, by some 200,000 Chinese coolies, working with picks and shovels and sometimes with just their bare hands. The Burma Road, beginning in Lashio, was the final leg of a difficult journey that saw goods coming into Rangoon by ship, on to Mandalay by train and then to Lashio by truck. The road was of poor quality. None of it paved, it had been hacked into the sides of mountains. In the rainy season—which in Burma began in May and could run through to October—the road was often washed out, leaving deep mud that made it virtually impassable. Goods then had to be carried to Kunming on the backs of mules, a journey that from Rangoon could take as many as sixty days. But then—in the spring of 1942—Japan overran Burma, capturing Rangoon and driving the Allies across the border into India, so that route, too, was abruptly closed down.

By that time—four months after Pearl Harbor—the United States had entered the war against Japan. With the loss of Burma, President Roosevelt faced a difficult dilemma. Either he could cut China loose and leave it to its fate at the hands of the attacking Japanese, or he could keep China's army fighting by continuing to supply it via Kunming. What tipped Roosevelt's decision in favor of China was one simple fact: Japan had committed nearly one million troops—more than one-third of its enlisted men—to its struggle with the Chinese. Roosevelt did not want those troops deployed elsewhere. In particular, he did not want them freed so they could fight American troops. So he made Chiang Kai-shek, the leader of China's Nationalist forces, a personal commitment: Roosevelt promised to ensure that supplies to Kunming would continue to flow without interruption—no matter the difficulty, no matter the cost.

With Japan controlling all territory to the east, south, and west of the city, the only overland route into Kunming was from the north. That meant ferrying goods from India, through Tibet. But no road existed across Tibet, and it was unclear if one could ever be built. There would be physical problems to overcome—finding a way to carry the goods up and over the Himalayas, then across the Tibetan plateau into China. Even more challenging, perhaps, there would be political problems that had to be addressed, because just raising the prospect of a road through Tibet also raised the delicate question of who had the right to authorize such a route. Would it be the Nationalist government of China, which claimed sovereignty over Tibet? Or would it be an independent Tibetan government, ruling from the distant city of Lhasa?

It would take years to answer questions like these—years that Roosevelt did not have. So if he were to fulfill his commitment to Chiang Kai-shek, then all supplies for Kunming—everything from medicines to guns, and ammunition to fuel—would have to be *flown* in. The goods would be shipped from America—nearly halfway around the world—to Bombay or Karachi, then taken by train across the widest part of India to bases the Allies would need to construct in Bengal and Assam. And then they would be flown in to Kunming, across some of the highest and most treacherous mountains anywhere on earth—the Santsung Range that gave the Hump its name. It would be the longest and most complex supply chain the world had seen. Nothing like it had ever been tried before. It was a bold undertaking that was breathtaking in its audacity. And Robert Crozier was convinced it was going to get him killed.

CROZIER LEFT THE RUNWAY AND PUSHED OPEN the door of the mess hall, letting it slam shut behind him. Immediately, he was hit by a fug of smoke, the smell of grease, and the fusty warmth of human bodies. It was dimly lit in the mess hall, the walls bare except for poster images of Chiang Kai-shek and his immediate predecessor, Sun Yat-sen. Crozier joined the other pilots already there. They, like him, had flown over the Hump that morning, and were now waiting for their planes to be unloaded so they could make the return trip to their bases in India.

As always, the pilots were gathered in groups on both sides of the long tables that filled the hall, or they were off to one side on their own, writing letters home to Mom and Dad or first girlfriends who, as likely as not, were already moving on to someone new. Most felt as Crozier did. They just wanted the war to end, so they could get back to their families and friends, to the wide, clean streets they were used to, the thick steaks, and cool water they could drink straight from the tap. But a few affected the easy swagger of men thumbing their noses at death. They were the ones lolling in their seats, their caps pushed back on their heads or deliberately crushed, bent out of shape as an insider's sign that their wearers were pilots—men who flew, who weren't flown. Some of them sat with their feet up, showing off the soft leather boots they'd bought in Brazil when they'd deadheaded south from Miami on their way across Africa, the Middle East, and then on to their posts in India. They dangled Luckies and Camels from the corners of their mouths, and flaunted the .45s they had strapped to their hips or slung gangster-style under their shoulders.

It was all bravado, of course—an attempt to mask the harsh reality that the death toll over the Hump had recently been rising. At any time, pilots flying the Hump could find themselves caught in the sights of a Japanese Zero out on a hunting trip from enemy bases in Burma. Or they could be stuck on a runway as a wave of Mitsubishi bombers unloaded a string of 250-pounders all around them. On one recent day, six of the Americans' planes had come under attack, and a Japanese fighter had earlier been found hiding among the unarmed transports stacked over Kunming, picking them off like a fox in a henhouse until a P-40 Warhawk had been scrambled to scare it away.

And the Hump was not even a combat route. At least, not officially it wasn't. No, the real danger—the one that should have been keeping Crozier awake at night—was the weather. The weather and the mountains. The two went hand in hand. At this time of year—the beginning of winter—"the up and down drafts (over the mountains) increase in intensity," a recent weather alert warned, "and the prevailing winds approach their highest velocities. Average southwest winds of 100 miles per hour have been reported...." What that meant, if you were flying a plane and not a desk, was that hurricane winds could flip you over in midflight and toss you around like a dog would a rat.

And then there was the ice. "Icing in clouds is severe and may be accompanied by heavy snowfall and turbulence," the alert continued. What that piece of bureaucracy meant was that when you were flying the Hump, a layer of ice could build up on your wings so that no matter how much power you tried to squeeze out of your engines, you would have no other choice than to sit there, quietly praying, as the weight of the ice pushed you down like an unseen hand. The slopes of the Santsung mountains were littered with the wrecks of planes that had come to grief in ferocious weather they had never been designed to handle.

And now the death toll was set to go even higher. Colonel Tom Hardin—the Allied commander in overall charge of Hump operations—had recently issued an order saying that flights could no longer be cancelled merely because of the wind and ice. He had eliminated the problem by denying its existence. "Effective immediately," he had decreed, "there will be no more weather over the Hump."

ON HIS WAY THROUGH THE MESS HALL, Crozier waved at some of the pilots he knew, stopping for a word or a handshake, then moving on with a friendly punch on the arm, a reassuring hand on the shoulder. He fitted in well with this crowd—well known and well liked. He joined the line at the counter, shuffling forward until a kitchen coolie asked, "How you want 'em, Joe?"

No one ever asked *what* he wanted. Here in Kunming, he was going to get eggs. That was what the pilots always got. Eggs—or "egg-es," as the Chinese cooks called them. You could have them scrambled, you could have them poached, you could have them "flied"—egg-es flied hard, egg-es flied soft, or egg-es flied one side—but you were going to get eggs.

Crozier ordered, then joined Flight Officer Harold McCallum, his copilot for the day. The two men had met for the first time only that morning, when they'd been assigned to the same flight. That was normal. Crews on the Hump were often assembled at the last moment, put together like spare parts taken off a shelf. "Call me 'Mac,'" McCallum had said, when the two were first introduced. "Everyone else does." He hated the name "Harold," which only his mother was allowed to use. "I was born the day after St. Patrick's Day and the day before St. Joseph's Day," he'd often say, "so why did I have to be called 'Harold'?"

On the flight over the Hump from India that morning, the two men had taken the chance to size each other up. Pilots were dying at such a rate that they were being replaced by fliers who had never been adequately trained. No one wanted to be stuck with a novice. Many had never flown at night or in anything other than perfect weather. Others were so inexperienced that they could barely get their planes off the ground. At least one of the new pilots was known to have ordered his landing gear up while still taxiing along the runway.

At the other end of the scale, a few of the veterans had suffered so many scares that they were now likely to freeze in their seats if anything went wrong. Or they'd go "Hump happy," taking insane risks that almost guaranteed they would go down in flames. Crozier and McCallum both knew of pilots who would pull off their oxygen masks at 20,000 feet and fire up a cigarette, the air around them thick with fumes from the over-full drums of 100-octane aviation fuel they carried in the hold. Pilots like that you also tried to avoid.

On the flight over, Crozier and McCallum had passed each other's test. Now, as they waited for their plane to be readied for the return flight to India, they made an effort to get better acquainted. The two of them were a physical contrast. Crozier was six feet two inches tall and well on his way to two hundred pounds, while McCallum was half a foot shorter and forty pounds lighter. But they did have a few things in common. Both were religious—Crozier a Baptist, who as a child attended church three times a week; and McCallum a Catholic, taught by nuns and solid in his belief in an omniscient and benevolent God. Both, too, had suffered the loss of a parent at an early age.

In Crozier's case, his mother had died soon after his ninth birthday. Her cancer had forced the family to move from Post, a small farming community (population 2,400), to West, about twenty miles north of Waco, where Crozier's mother hoped to find better care. West was unusual among small Texas towns in that it was home to a mix of Bible Belt Anglos of Scottish and Irish descent, as well as Blacks, Hispanics, and recent immigrants from Germany and Czechoslovakia. However, it was also typical in that its community values were founded on a good education and strict religious beliefs.

When his mother died in 1929, Crozier, as the eldest of four children, was expected to help out at home—but only by hunting and fishing, which he anyway enjoyed, so he could put extra food on the table. His father, a teacher and farmer before moving to West, had been lucky enough to find work as a rural mailman, a good job as it was a government job and therefore secure—no small matter in the

"Dirty Thirties" when towns like West were about to be decimated by the Depression.

The family moved into a rented clapboard house with chickens, a cow, and a large vegetable patch in the back yard. About half their food came from there. On weekends, Crozier would play pick-up games with neighborhood kids on vacant lots. And in summers, he visited a ranch near Fort Worth, where one of his cousins worked as a foreman. It was a simple life, but a good one, with the family enjoying memorable times they could look back on together, and with just enough money for Crozier to be able to enroll at Baylor—a university in nearby Waco with a mandate to blend academic excellence with Christian commitment.

He spent two years at Baylor, studying geology and physics and working nights at the Tiger Malt Shop to help pay his way. But in 1940, he could see that war was coming, decided to enlist, and joined the U.S. Army Air Corps, where he trained as a pilot—mainly because he "did not like to walk." After two years instructing at Kelly Field near San Antonio, he transferred to Air Transport Command, which first had him flying the world delivering aircraft, and then sent him to Jorhat in India to fly unarmed transports over the Hump. Crozier was a long way from being a veteran, but he did have twenty-one missions under his belt, and was now entitled to wear the silver bars of a First Lieutenant.

McCallum had had a much tougher deal. Born in Quincy, then a small town in Massachusetts not far from Boston, he was fourteen when he lost a parent. One day, his father just upped and disappeared, and was neither seen nor heard from again. McCallum, like Crozier, was the eldest of four children, so he, too, was expected to help provide for his family. But with no breadwinner at home, the family didn't just need additional food, which often was in short supply; it also needed money coming in. McCallum was forced to leave school and take a job with a local pharmacy, the Quincy Drug Company, where he worked hard for the princely sum of three dollars a week. It was a twist in his life that was to cost him the chance of a higher education, and that, in turn, nearly cost him the chance to pursue the "first love" of his life—which was flying.

One day, when McCallum was still a boy, he had looked up at the sky and watched a small biplane flying loops and whorls. As he stood transfixed—gazing up, his mouth open and his neck craning—he saw a stream of smoke come billowing out from under the airplane's wings, the pilot twisting and turning in a complex pattern of aerial rolls, leaving behind a trail of smoke that eventually spelled out "Lucky Strike" in huge letters across the sky. From that day on, McCallum had been hooked. Then and there, he had determined that he, too, was going to fly.

As only a high school graduate, however, McCallum was not qualified to train as a pilot. But he was a lot smarter than most who had been through college. And he was driven. When war broke out in Europe, he transferred from the National Guard to the U.S. Army Air Corps, where he worked for a year in photo reconnaissance. The Air Corps would soon be needing extra pilots, and when it lowered its educational requirements to attract more recruits, McCallum immediately applied. One year later, he qualified, and two weeks after that—with the rank of Flight Officer and a propeller and wings newly tattooed on his arm—he was sent to India to fly the Hump.

Not as experienced as Crozier—McCallum had flown just twelve round-trip missions from India to China—he was nonetheless convinced that he could take off and land just about anything that wasn't screwed to the ground.

As the two men ate their eggs together, McCallum would have learned that Crozier's amiable manner wasn't a front—he really was as loose and relaxed as he appeared. McCallum was noticeably different. He enjoyed a good time as much as the next man, and certainly he liked to indulge his second passion in life, which was girls. At his base in Jorhat, he was considered unusually good-looking, with strong features and a striking head of thick black hair that he combed straight back. Pilots there saw him as "a guy who wouldn't have trouble finding the ladies." But while they sat around—relaxing over a beer and bragging about "Indian wrestling" with the girls in the Calcutta brothels on Kariah Road—McCallum would put his time to what he considered was much better use. Each day he religiously performed a grueling program of calisthenics, which included fifty push-ups he did on his thumbs. And since arriving in India five months before, he had been teaching himself Hindustani—figuring that if he was going to be talking to the locals, he might as well do so in their own tongue.

For his part, Crozier would have been aware of McCallum's sense of commitment. He would also have noted the take-charge manner that was in marked contrast to his own easygoing style. That—plus the fact that at twenty-four, McCallum was one year older but two ranks lower—had the potential to sow a seed of discord between the two men.

As they finished eating, a G. I. runner approached their table. "Your plane's ready, sir." Crozier nodded and stood up, McCallum rising with him. The two of them followed the G.I. out, McCallum checking his .45, at the same time shrugging into his A-2 jacket. Although neither man knew it, the jacket—a standard-issue leather flying jacket—was about to play a pivotal role in events yet to come. It had a large "blood chit" sewn on the back, a piece of cloth the size of a dishtowel, which featured a flag—the white sun on a blue square and red background of Nationalist China. The blood chit also carried a message—in sweeping Chinese characters—which said in effect, "The wearer of this jacket is a friend of China's. He's fighting for China, so he should be your friend, too. If you help him, you will be rewarded."

Chits like this were aimed at any Chinese national who might find a flier who had bailed out and landed on Chinese soil. The chits were not required, but they were in general use. Often, the chits were run up by local tailors, with the airmen deciding what their chits should say, and in how many languages. Some pilots sewed them on the insides of their jackets, or carried them loose, stuffed into their pockets. McCallum, however, had his chit prominently displayed on his back.

The two men walked beside the runway, back the way Crozier had come. Their plane that day was a C-87, serial number 42-107270. Like all Hump pilots, they were both all too aware that priority in the war had been given to the struggle in Europe, and that here, in the China-Burma-India theater—the so-called "forgotten theater"—they were forced to make do with substandard planes, hand-me-downs and rejects that no one else wanted, and that more often than not were poorly serviced and badly maintained. But the C-87—a modified version of the B-24 bomber—was better than most. It had its faults. Crews didn't like its poor instrumentation, its leaky fuel tanks, or the unnerving tendency its engines had to burst into flames. But it was a marked improvement on the C-47 and C-46—twin-engine planes that were more often employed to fly over the Hump. And it was certainly better than the C-109, a sister plane that had been specially adapted to carry fuel. Little better than a flying bomb, among pilots the C-109 would later be known as the C-one-oh-BOOM.

At least the C-87 had four engines. And better still, the engines—each a Pratt & Whitney R-1830-43—were fitted with exhaust-driven turbo superchargers. That meant the higher the plane went, the greater its power, so flying one was like driving a sports car that was so engineered it could accelerate faster from sixty to seventy than it did from zero to ten. The C-87 also had a modified Davis wing, producing a larger lift-to-drag ratio than other, more conventional wings would have done. That helped increase the plane's range as well as its speed, so it could comfortably fly some 3,200 miles at a height of 25,000 feet and a cruising speed of 175 miles per hour.

That morning at their base in Jorhat, Crozier and McCallum had run the plane through a detailed inspection. Now, in Kunming, they joined their mechanic for the day, Corporal William Perram, and gave the plane just a cursory check—peering inside the wheel wells, testing the struts, examining the tires, and studying the propellers for nicks and the nacelles for leaks.

Perram—solidly built with heavy features and a prominent chin—was a twenty-two-year-old aerial engineer from Tulsa, Oklahoma. Almost as big as Crozier, he stood six feet tall and weighed in at 185 pounds. He had stayed with the plane while Crozier and McCallum had been in the mess hall, since saboteurs, in the pay of Japan, were known to be active among the coolies. Someone had to guard the plane, and Perram had seemed the obvious choice. Also, it was Perram's job, while the plane was being unloaded, to make sure the ground crew left enough fuel in the tanks for the flight back to the base at Jorhat.

Three weeks before—on November 9, 1943—an "instruction to all pilots" had been issued saying that C-87s, on their return flights to India, could carry a maximum of 1,200 gallons of fuel. Anything above that must be siphoned off and left in Kunming. The whole point of the Hump operation was to ferry goods—especially fuel—over the mountains from India. It made no sense to fly it back in the C-87s' half-full tanks. But inevitably, the November 9 instruction to pilots created a conflict between the ground crews trying to take, and the aircrews trying to keep, as much fuel as they possibly could. A C-87 needed a minimum of

800 gallons to fly back to Jorhat, so there wasn't much room for error. If anything went wrong—even something as small as an unusually strong headwind—pilots could find themselves "flying on fumes," or maybe just "on their reputations."

When Perram was satisfied that they had enough fuel, he, Crozier, and McCallum climbed on board, Crozier squeezing himself into the cramped space on the left of the cockpit, while McCallum dropped into the seat on the right. Perram took his place immediately behind McCallum—next to the fourth and final member of the crew, Corporal Kenneth Spencer, who was already sitting at a small table aft of Crozier. Spencer was the radio operator. Tall and scrawny, with light brown hair and a freckled skin his parents were always telling him he should keep out of the sun, he was also the baby of the bunch—just nineteen years old, not long out of high school and with little more than a year of training behind him.

Spencer looked up with an open expression, as eager and guileless as a puppy's, then continued running through his checks, making sure they had taken on the right-colored flares, and turning on the IFF—the Identification Friend or Foe—black box, which alerted other American forces that he was on the Allies' side. No one wanted to be shot down—and certainly not by friendly fire.

At the last moment, the four men were joined by a fifth, Private First Class John Huffman. At twenty-seven, Huffman was notably older than the others. Also, he wasn't a flier. He was a mechanic, assigned to the base motor pool at Jorhat. He had been curious to see—just once—what crossing the Hump was like, so he'd arranged through McCallum to fly over on another plane. Now he was hitching a ride back. Crozier had said he could tag along, and agreed that for the duration of the flight Huffman should be given the nominal title of assistant engineer. Huffman—lightly built with a quiet, contained manner that said he liked to control his own space—eased himself into the gap between Perram and Spencer. As they nodded "hello," Perram and Spencer couldn't help noticing that Huffman appeared immaculately turned out, with a pressed shirt, knife-edged creases down the front of his pants, and a neat, thin, dapper moustache.

Crozier ordered the engines started and watched as the propellers became whirling silver disks. He gave a signal to the ground crew, meanwhile

checking the gauges and looking for the flicker that would tell him the aux-
iliary-power unit had been pulled away. From the tower, over the radio and
above the clatter and roar of the engines, he heard "Clear to take runway,"
and taxied the plane into position, feeling it bump and bounce over the
gravel. He held the plane steady—flaps at twenty degrees, turbos on, mix-
tures rich, gyros and instruments all in green—then heard "Clear for takeoff," and eased the throttles forward. The pitch of the engines rose another
notch. He released the brakes, and the plane rumbled down the runway,
taking its time before lifting off into the thin air. He touched the brakes to
stop the wheels spinning and ordered, "Gear up," meanwhile keeping the
plane in a long, lumbering climb. Then he settled into his seat.

It was nearly 1600—a few minutes before four o'clock. A late afternoon sun shone into his eyes, and up ahead, the ripple of cloud he had
earlier seen stood out high above the distant peaks. It did not appear to
pose any kind of threat.

2

HITTING THE SILK

THE STORM WHEN IT HIT WAS WHOLLY UNEXPECTED. From Kunming, Crozier had turned the plane onto a course of two-eight-zero—almost due west—and for nearly an hour had flown through clear, open skies with the earth unrolling smoothly beneath him. For any pilot flying the Hump, this was as good as it could get: no real weight in the hold, good visibility in all directions, the serrated peaks of the Santsung Range still a long way ahead. Even so, Crozier couldn't relax. The tension of flying lay deep within him. It was always there, in the tautness across his shoulders and his neck. On the flight deck around him, there was little in the way of conversation, just a few jokey remarks tossed back and forth over the intercom. Most crews liked to keep it that way. Light and impersonal. They didn't want to invest time and emotion in men they might not see again, men who might soon be dead.

They circled the airfield at Yunnanyi, one of the smaller Allied bases in China, 130 miles west of Kunming. Crozier peered down at the thin strip of the Burma Road, which sliced across the terrain like a scar. He waited for clearance, then put the plane down, with McCallum beside him logging the time of their arrival. It was 1650—ten minutes before five o'clock. Not yet dark.

Their cargo that day—on the return trip to India—was a small consignment of food. They watched as it was unloaded, then once more prepared to take off, this time planning to fly nonstop over the mountains to their base at Jorhat. But first, Crozier and McCallum checked in with "Operations" to study the latest weather report. They read it in silence: "Ceiling unlimited. Visibility unrestricted. Sky clear." The two of them looked at each other. The weather report could not have been better, but they both knew it was not to be trusted, as it was based, like all such reports, on what the weather had been like the last time someone had flown over the Hump; it made no attempt to forecast what future conditions might be. Crozier shrugged. Maybe this one would be different. Maybe the weather would hold, and the report, for once, would prove to be true.

By the time he and his crew took off, at a few minutes past 1800, the sun was below the horizon but still washing some of the peaks of the Santsung Range in a delicate shade of pink. Crozier set a course just north of the one he had earlier been following, and for the next fifteen minutes again flew through clear, open skies.

Already, the airmen were beginning to look ahead to their arrival at Jorhat. Not that there was much to look forward to there. Jorhat was a dismal place—one they endured rather than enjoyed. With no real entertainment, it mainly offered endless games of bridge or poker, played night after night in the thatched-roof barracks—or *bashas*—where most of the men were billeted. When you landed at Jorhat, the routine was, you checked in with "Operations," then with "Intelligence," and then with the "Dispensary," where you'd be given a two-ounce shot of whiskey or raw South African brandy. The alcohol was supposedly intended to drive the bubbles out of your bloodstream after you'd been on oxygen—or so people said. In reality it was dispensed as a way of helping you steady your nerves. A shot of whiskey and a two-beer chaser, and most of the men would begin to unwind.

Pilots were allowed two cases of beer—real, imported American beer—every month. There were no refrigerators or coolers at Jorhat, so the beer was invariably hot—or it would have been hot, had it not been for the fact that crews had long ago realized that beer could be chilled to perfection if it was taken up to 20,000 feet, over and back across the Hump. As a result, there were few planes returning to Jorhat that did not have at least one case secreted somewhere in the hold.

WHEN THEY REACHED THE WALL OF THE SANTSUNG MOUNTAINS, Crozier gave the order to climb, and before long they entered the bank of cloud he'd earlier seen. It had thickened considerably, and with the sun now gone, visibility was close to zero. Crozier and McCallum immediately switched to full instruments. As they gained height, clawing their way up through the overcast, they knew that a thick layer of ice was beginning to coat the plane like a second skin. They could feel it through the suddenly heavy controls.

Crozier would have liked to switch on the wing de-icers—thin rubber patches called "boots," which normally were attached to the wings' leading edge. They could be inflated like tiny balloons, breaking up the ice that invariably formed there. But on C-87s—the ones used over the Hump—the de-icing boots had all been removed, in spite of their obvious importance. Officially, the boots were hacked off because otherwise they would have rotted in the heat and humidity of India. Or perhaps it was because they would have been damaged by stones kicked up from the rough Chinese runways. Stories varied. As far as the crews were concerned, the boots had been cut off solely to save weight—so that even more goods could be ferried across the mountains.

As they continued to climb, Crozier ordered the prop de-icers to be switched on, at the same time varying the pitch of the engines. That broke up the ice coating the propellers, sending chunks shattering against the fuselage, hitting it hard as buckshot. He could sense that ice was also sheeting the fins of the high twin tail. But there was nothing he could do about that. The entire tail had an unnerving tendency to buckle and twist if ice built up in a thick enough coat. But then it would shake and shudder like a dog shedding water, and the ice would all be thrown clear.

Crozier's main worry was that ice would start to smother the carburetors, covering them in a thick, white crust. If that happened, the engines would die, no longer able to get any fuel. He ordered more power, and he and McCallum pushed the throttles forward, keeping the plane in a steady climb until reaching a height of 20,000 feet. At that altitude, no more ice was likely to form as the air around them would be too cold to retain much moisture. To be on the safe side, Crozier kept the plane climbing, slowly adding more height.

The C-87 was not pressurized, so all five men were now on oxygen and bundled up against the cold. They were also strapped in, although not wearing their parachutes. Instead, they were using the chutes as seats, with the attached survival packs, or "jungle kits," serving as backs. Few airmen wore their chutes in flight. There were too many straps, too many buckles. Also, there was a lot of dysentery in both China and India, and it was bad enough rushing to the rear of the plane to use the bucket the engineer would have placed there, without having to do so wearing an unwieldy chute.

When the storm suddenly struck, they had topped out at 24,000 feet and were just beginning to level off. The first sign of trouble was a sudden hole in the sky. They fell into it, dropping like a stone, but were then caught in an updraft that sent them once again soaring. A hurricane-force wind then grabbed them. It seemed to blow out of nowhere. Crozier and McCallum needed all their strength to keep the plane flying, to stop it from flipping over and spiraling down, out of control. The wind tore at them, finding every gap and hole in the fuselage. They could hear it whistling even above the roar of the engines. No one spoke—there was nothing to say. The clouds around them pressed tightly in against the windshield. All they could see was a dull opaqueness like gray cotton wool. So they sat, like blind men, strapped into their seats—and listened. Not to the wind, but to the sound of the engines, hearing each one individually, alert to any change in tone.

On the flight deck behind Crozier, Kenneth Spencer—the radioman—sat braced at his table. Part of his job was to help the pilot and copilot make sure the plane stayed on course. Under normal conditions, a C-87 would have had a crew of five, including a navigator. But on flights over the Hump, the navigator's job had been dispensed with—another way of saving weight—so the radioman was often required to assist. On clear days, keeping the plane on course was easy. You just followed the "aluminum trail" of wrecked aircraft that littered the mountains all the way from China to India and back. But in bad weather, or when flying at night, you had to rely on radio signals beamed up from the ground.

The theory was that you used dead reckoning—flying a known course at a fixed speed for a certain period of time—to get from your point of departure to the first of the nondirectional radio beacons that marked the course you intended to fly. When your plane came within range of the beacon, you listened for the signal sent up from below. It told you whether you should fly more to the left or more to the right. Alternatively, you could use one of your onboard radio compasses, or Automatic Direction Finders—the C-87 was equipped with two of those—which, if tuned to the right frequency, would pick up a signal for you. In response to the signal, the needle of the compass would swing slowly around until it locked onto the beacon you were trying to find. Either way, you would arrive at the first of your beacons, and then—again using dead reckoning—you would set a course for the second. It was like joining the dots. You flew from one beacon to the next, until you arrived at your destination.

In practice, of course, it was seldom that simple. You could, for example, stray so far off track that you missed one or more of your beacons. Or you could be lured far from your route by siren signals sent out by the Japanese. You could also lose your way if you failed to detect any signals beamed up from the ground. The signals might be buried in static. Or they could be blocked by the side of a mountain. If that happened, you would get no clear sound through your headset—and the needle of your radio compass would continue to turn uselessly around.

As the plane flew on, the wind raging outside, Spencer—like the two pilots in front of him—strained to detect the first of their signals. It should have come from a beacon set up at Fort Hertz, a base the Allies controlled in the northern tip of Burma. But Spencer could not hear it. Part of his problem was that he had never wanted to be a radioman in the first place. The year before, when he'd graduated from South Side High School in Rockville Centre on Long Island, New York, Spencer had decided to be a pilot. That was where the glamour was. But his Methodist parents said "no." A pilot's job was much too risky. Spencer tried to bring them round, pleading his case like a kid asking for permission to stay out late, past his bedtime. But his parents insisted. Finally they compromised by allowing Spencer to train as a radioman, sold on the idea that somehow that would involve fewer hours spent in the air.

Spencer kept searching for the Fort Hertz signal. He could hear nothing through his headset, and the needle on his radio compass was spinning in meaningless circles. Crozier held the dead reckoning course for five minutes beyond their ETA—their estimated time of arrival—at Fort Hertz, then swung onto a new course, due west, which he hoped would take them to the next of their beacons at Chabua. They flew on in tense silence, Crozier and McCallum fighting controls that were bucking and pitching, threatening to tear loose in their hands, both men focusing on their instruments. Without accurate readings, it was easy for them to lose their orientation, even to the point of no longer knowing which way was up. The wind outside—the *hurricane* outside—continued to rip at the plane, tossing it around like a leaf, sending the rate-of-climb needle all over the dial.

At their ETA at Chabua, Crozier once more shouted into his intercom. "Any signal?"

"No, sir," Spencer said. He was sure the radio compass was set to the right frequency, but its needle was still uselessly turning. Crozier had personally checked the onboard compasses that morning, and knew they had been in good working order. With nothing to show him the route he should take, he had no choice other than to continue to hold his course.

They had now been in the air for two-and-a-half hours. They should have been over Chabua; they should have been able to pick up its signal. Crozier flew on, then, once more beyond his ETA, turned onto a new heading, more to the south, which was intended to take them down the Assam Valley towards their base at Jorhat. They should definitely have crossed the mountains by now, and be losing altitude as they approached their destination. It was tempting to circle, to hope they'd come within range of a beacon, but they all knew that was the worst thing to do. You had to know the course you'd been flying—and for how long—if you were ever to be able to establish your position. You could not fly a random pattern. Already, Crozier had dropped to 20,000 feet, but with no idea of where he might be, he could not risk going much lower.

"Try contacting the ground," he told Spencer. It was an order he had not wanted to give, as it was a sure sign that they were in trouble. Crews were expected to find their own way home, not rely on controllers on the ground.

"Yes, sir," Spencer said. He called, using his command radio set, and was relieved when he raised the tower at Jorhat. He asked for a heading. The tower needed a continuous transmission that would allow it to take a bearing on the plane, so Spencer began "the long count"—slowly counting from one to a hundred, and then down from a hundred to one. Fly three-three-zero, he was told.

Spencer relayed this message to Crozier, who gave it some thought and decided it didn't make sense. A heading of three-three-zero would take them north, almost due north. But surely, to reach Jorhat, they had to fly south. If the storm had been running true to pattern, it would have come up from the Bay of Bengal. If it had been pushing them far off course—and Crozier was convinced it had been doing just that—then it would have been blowing them north and east. That meant they should now be flying south and west. He told Spencer the bearing was "evidently wrong," and ordered him to double-check it.

Spencer called back. The tower at Jorhat took another bearing, and confirmed the original course. Three-three-zero. Spencer told Crozier, who shook his head. He still didn't like it, but he and McCallum swung the plane round, heading north, struggling to get onto the bearing they'd twice been given. They had no alternative. In the thick overcast, one direction was like every other. You couldn't fly off on some random bearing, just because it felt right.

After another hour of fighting the controls, they were relieved to sense that the storm around them was beginning to fade. They were still in thick cloud, but at least they were no longer being tossed around. The wind speed had dropped; the storm was moving on. But then Spencer reported he was no longer able to reach the tower at Jorhat. Crozier told him to switch from his command set to the liaison set, a more powerful radio with a much greater range. Spencer did so, but still wasn't able to raise the tower.

"Try Tommy King," Crozier ordered, using the radio code for Kunming.

Spencer called, and was able to reach the tower there. It could not take a bearing, but said that if Jorhat still could, then maybe the bearing could be relayed to the plane via Kunming. Spencer passed this suggestion along to Crozier, who told him to give it a try. Spencer started another long count, and Jorhat managed to take a bearing and give it to the tower at Kunming. Kunming relayed the bearing to Spencer, who passed it on to Crozier. "Two-seven-eight," he said. Almost due west.

Crozier liked that heading better, but again told Spencer to check. Spencer did, once more speaking to Kunming, and getting the same bearing, taken by the tower at Jorhat. "Two-seven-eight," he confirmed.

Crozier changed course. He had another problem nagging at him now. Since taking off from Kunming, they had been in the air for nearly four hours—on a flight that should have taken only three. They had to be running low on fuel. He ordered Perram, the flight engineer, to check the tanks. Perram read the gauges—thin, vertical glass tubes, each about twelve inches high, which were set at the rear of the cockpit. They were fed directly from the tanks, so they could be relied on to give an accurate reading.

"Thirty minutes to dry," he reported.

Crozier pressed on, still flying west on a heading of two-seven-eight. He decided to climb, to try to get above the cloud. He ordered more power and the plane plowed its way up through the overcast, from 20,000 feet to 25,000 feet. And suddenly it broke free. For the first time since reaching the Santsung Mountains, the five men on board had something approaching clear visibility. The night was still dark, and the earth below remained hidden beneath a blanket of cloud. But at least, in the moonlight, they could see their wingtips, as well as flashes of reflection from their spinning propellers.

The overcast below angled down, and they followed it lower. Spencer reported he still couldn't raise the tower at Jorhat, and now, more worryingly, he was also beginning to lose Kunming. Crozier had just made the decision to turn around—heading south, so he would come back within radio range of Kunming—when McCallum beside him pointed off to the right.

"Look!"

Crozier peered through the windshield and saw a strange shape sticking up through the overcast. It looked like the top of a big cumulus cloud, but there was something odd about its shape. He was still studying it, when Spencer shouted over the intercom. "There's another. Off to the left!" This cloud, too, had a strange shape, like the twisted top of an ice-cream cone.

It was McCallum who realized what was wrong. "That's not a cloud," he shouted. "It's a mountain!"

Crozier immediately threw the plane into a one-eighty-degree turn. "We're getting the hell out of here," he said.

As they banked sharply left, Spencer caught sight of another mountain. Then another. And then a whole range of them. He had never seen mountains like these. But what struck him most was, he wasn't looking down at them, instead he was looking straight out at them. At something close to 20,000 feet.

"Get Tommy King," Crozier ordered.

Spencer called, and managed to raise the tower at Kunming. But it still couldn't give him a bearing. And now, neither could Jorhat. "Try Chabua," Crozier ordered. Spencer did so, and this time he was given a course. One-six-eight. Since making his sudden U-turn, Crozier had been flying one-five-zero. Now he swung onto one-six-eight—still south, but not as far east.

Perram had again been checking the fuel tanks. "Fifteen minutes to dry," he now reported.

Spencer called Chabua, and was given yet another bearing—one-five-four. Crozier started to bring the plane around. But then Spencer reported he had managed to raise the tower at Tinsukia, a town—like Chabua—in the Assam Valley, but to the north and east of their base at Jorhat. Crozier found a break in the cloud, and looking down, thought he could see the outline of a city. At the same time, the Tinsukia tower told Spencer it could hear an unidentified plane circling overhead, and asked him to flash his lights. Spencer passed this message on, and Crozier blinked his wing lights—on, off, on, off. Tinsukia reported it had seen a flash, so Crozier decided he must be over the town and should rapidly go down for a closer look. He might just have time to find somewhere to put the plane safely on the ground.

But even as he began his descent, a part of Crozier's mind was telling him something here was wrong. Tinsukia was only about 500 feet above sea level. Yet here he was at 20,000 feet, and looking down only 8,000 feet, maybe 10,000 feet at the most. The numbers didn't add up.

He steepened his dive, but the cloud closed in around him, and once more he was flying blind through dense overcast as thick as smoke. He held the descent as long as he dared, then with McCallum's help, pulled back on the controls and started to climb. They were going "back upstairs," he said. They rose quickly, the four propellers chewing through the clouds until finally they broke free and once more leveled off at 20,000 feet. They again turned south, still hoping to reach Jorhat, but a few minutes later one of their superchargers started to torch—a sure sign that they were running out of fuel. On the starboard side, the outside engine spluttered and died, followed almost immediately by one of the engines on the port side.

Spencer was still talking to Tinsukia when Crozier gave the order they'd all been dreading. He stayed hunched over his radio, but immediately changed his call to "Mayday, Mayday, Mayday." Spencer's worst nightmare was being confirmed. They were going to have to bail out. They were going to have to jump—or, in the deliberately casual parlance of the day, they were about to take "the big step," and then "hit the silk."

WHEN PERRAM HEARD THE ORDER TO JUMP, he reacted with something approaching horror. Bailing out was reckoned to be the most terrifying event a flier could face—much worse than being shot down or crashing into the side of a mountain, where at least the end, while being the same, had the virtue of being quick. Some fliers refused to jump no matter the circumstances, preferring instead to go down with their planes.

The irony was that Perram didn't even think of himself as a flier. It was true he spent long hours in the air. But at heart he was a ground person, an engineer. He fixed planes, and the best place to do that was inside a hangar or out on a runway. Yet here he was being told to step into a hole that was 20,000 feet deep. He didn't know how to do that. None of them did. They had never jumped before, not even in training from a hundred feet up. The only instruction they had ever been given was along the lines of, "Here's a parachute, there's the door." All of a sudden it did not seem much by way of preparation.

For Huffman, the order to jump was even more distressing. Like Perram, he had trained as an aerial engineer. But then, in one of those strange quirks of military thinking, he had been assigned to work in a motor pool. He had never received any training as a flier. He didn't even know how to put a parachute on. And, of course, he wasn't even meant to be here. He was a hitchhiker, cadging a lift home. He could have chosen any number of flights heading back to his base at Jorhat. *So why did he have to pick this one?*

But when the order came, it somehow brought with it a sense of release. At least there was something positive they all could do. They sprang into a frenzy of action, knowing they had only a few minutes of flying time left. Crozier told Perram to get to the rear of the plane and get the door open. Huffman, too. Spencer was still transmitting, "May Day, May Day, May Day." Crozier ordered him through to the back. Spencer tied down the key to keep a transmission going, then he, too, scrambled to the rear. McCallum was still in his seat, trimming the plane so it was nose-heavy. Crozier set up the automatic pilot, confident that, with two engines working and nothing in the hold, the C-87 would still be able to fly. But already it was losing height. As the two pilots left the cockpit, Crozier looked back and saw the altimeter reading 18,500 feet.

When he reached the rear of the plane, he found Huffman wrestling with the straps of his chute, trying to figure out how they fitted together. Perram was helping. Then Crozier noticed the door. *Why wasn't it open?* He couldn't understand it. It was their only way out; they *had* to get it open. Spencer had pulled the emergency release, and the door had shifted. But now it was stuck. It was the hinges, Crozier thought. They were too rusty to let the door open. For one horrible moment, his deepest fears seemed about to be realized. Something small *was* going to get him.

He and McCallum ran for the door. Perram joined them. They kicked and pushed at it, trying to force it open. But then they realized. The problem lay not with the hinges, but with the slipstream. The door was designed to open outwards, towards the rear of the plane. That meant it had to open *against* the slipstream. It would never do that. To Crozier's mind, it was as if someone much stronger than they were was standing outside, pushing against it and holding it shut.

"Pull out the pins," one of them shouted.

The door's hinges were held in place by two metal pins, attached to a cable. By pulling the cable, they could force out the pins. Then they kicked the *front* of the door where the hinges had been, and the door cracked open there—just enough for the slipstream to catch the lip of the door and tear it loose, sending it tumbling into the night.

A third engine then died. Huffman still couldn't get his parachute on. Unlike the others, he had, at the start of the flight, wrapped himself in a bulky winter jacket. The parachute wouldn't fit over the top. He had also twisted his leg straps so that they were too short to reach the harness at his chest. McCallum went to help him. Of the five airmen, McCallum knew most about putting a parachute on, having once worked as a rigger, stuffing parachutes into their packs. He freed Huffman's leg straps and tried to fit them into the harness. But they still wouldn't reach. There was nothing else for it. Huffman would have to lose his jacket.

Huffman threw his parachute to the floor, tore off the jacket and started again. "Take it easy," McCallum said. "We've still got plenty of time, so don't get excited." Part of the problem was that Huffman's chute was one of the older kind. It had a male-female fastener at the center of the chest harness, not the large snap-hook the newer parachutes had. Also, as McCallum could see, Huffman was becoming "half groggy" from a lack of oxygen, and was no longer able to properly think.

As McCallum struggled to help him, the last of the four engines died, and the plane gave "a terrific lurch" onto its side.

"Let's get out of here," McCallum shouted. "It's going into a spin."

He and Huffman moved to the door, where the others were ready to jump. They saw Crozier go first. Spencer was right behind, his hand resting on Crozier's shoulder. Huffman still couldn't get the male-female fastener on his harness done up, and was about to jump, just holding the straps closed with his hand. It would have been suicide. He made one last desperate try, forcing the two parts together—then he, too, jumped. He was followed immediately by McCallum, and then finally by Perram.

AS SOON AS CROZIER LEFT THE PLANE, the slipstream caught him. He saw the high tail fin go past and tugged on his ripcord. His chute flared, opening with a crack like a rifle, dragging him back almost horizontally. He hung in the air for a moment, then started to swing. After all the noise and shouting in the plane, it was suddenly eerily quiet. He looked up at the huge mushroom of his chute, billowing above him, and expected to swing back and forth like the tip of a pendulum before settling into a steady descent. He guessed he had about 15,000 feet to fall, before landing somewhere in the Assam Valley. But he swung back once, tracing an arc in the air, and then slammed into the side of a mountain.

The impact stunned him. He'd been in the air for less than forty-five seconds, and he'd hit a slope so steep it sent him tumbling and rolling fifty feet until his shroud lines snared on a rock and pulled him to a painful stop. He lay still, just concentrating on trying to breathe. From somewhere in the distance, he heard the dull *whoomph* of an explosion, and turning to look saw a bright burst of flames, several thousand feet away. He hoped the others had managed to get out of the plane in time.

He tried standing, pulling himself up by his shroud lines, but something was wrong with his knee. It didn't seem able to take his weight. He dragged himself to a flattish rock and hauled in his canopy, which had collapsed on the ground above him. He wrapped himself up in the nylon. He was shaking with cold, his knee hurt, and he was still finding it hard to breathe.

When Spencer's chute opened, it felt as if two giant hands had grabbed him by the shoulders, yanking him back. He looked down and saw Crozier's parachute below him, then was momentarily blinded when the loose end of his chest strap suddenly swung up and hit him across the chin, slicing the flesh down to the bone. He, too, was expecting a drop of several thousand feet, but fell for only forty-five seconds before crashing into the mountain. He rolled to a stop and lay still. Like Crozier, he could do nothing more than pull his parachute towards him and curl up in it, hoping the canopy would help keep him warm.

Huffman, coming down close behind, suffered the most. When his chute opened, he was upside down, so the full force was borne by his shoulder. He thought he might have broken his back, or maybe had an arm torn off. As he swung in the air, his feet somehow became tangled in his shroud lines. He was dimly aware of a mountain flashing by, and had just enough time to free his feet so that when he hit, he was able to absorb much of the impact with his knees. He rolled a few times, smashed into a rock and was immediately knocked unconscious.

McCallum, too, was in the air for just thirty or forty seconds. The fall knocked him out, and when he came round he could not figure out where in the world he was. His head throbbed and he could feel blood congealing on his scalp. He groped around, found his shroud lines, and reeled his canopy in.

Perram, the last one out of the plane, landed on the other side of the mountain. He fell less than 500 feet, before his shroud lines caught on a rock and threw him into the face of a cliff. He dropped to the ground and lay still, trying to adjust to the numbing cold. Like the others, he wanted to use his parachute for warmth, but the canopy had fallen too far away for him to reach. He huddled inside his leather jacket, and silently prayed for an early dawn.

3

INDIA OR CHINA?

CROZIER HAD NEVER EXPERIENCED SUCH COLD. He lay, violently shivering, in the nylon of his parachute, waiting out the night. When morning came, a pale glow brightening the eastern sky, he sat up stiffly and examined his knee. A jagged cut ran diagonally across it, starting just below the kneecap and angling up onto his thigh. He rooted around inside his jungle kit and found a needle and thread. The cut on his knee was wide and deep. He threaded the needle, blowing onto his hands, and then—like a careful seamstress—he began to sew the cut closed, stitching the edges together into a ragged, bloodstained line. It didn't hurt much; he could barely feel the pierce of the needle. He was much too cold for that.

When he had finished, Crozier pushed himself to his feet, testing the knee for weight, and looked carefully around. It would be a long time before the sun rose above the peaks he could see on every horizon, and until then the temperature would remain many degrees below zero—as many as twenty by Crozier's estimate. He peered into the shadows of the valley below, where he could see the strand of a river winding its way through terrain that was as bleak and desolate as the moon. It certainly didn't look like the Assam Valley. In fact, it didn't look like India at all. But it *had* to be India. Unless, of course, he was still in China.

He turned and looked up at the craggy peak of the mountain above him, figuring from the distance he'd jumped, and the height at which he had started, that he must now be standing at something close to 15,000—maybe 16,000—feet. No wonder he was so cold. And no wonder he was finding it hard to breathe. He stood for a moment, sucking in air, then made his way to a nearby ridge. He let out a holler, and was surprised and relieved to receive an immediate response.

"Spencer? That you?"

Spencer stood up so Crozier could see him, little more than three hundred yards further up the mountain. He was wrapped in his parachute, like an apparition in the dim early light. A few moments later, Crozier heard another shout, and looking higher up the mountain, close to the summit, saw a second parachute bundled on the ground, with McCallum standing and waving beside it. The three men called back and forth. They could not link up because the mountainside was scarred with rocky crevasses too wide and deep for them to traverse.

"We have to find the others," Crozier shouted.

They split up, searching around, yelling out for Huffman and Perram. McCallum managed to clamber around to the other side of the mountain, but could see no sign of the other two there. McCallum knew Huffman had jumped, but he wasn't sure if Perram had even made it out of the plane.

McCallum himself had landed at the top of a cliff. A few feet more and he would have gone over. When he finally accepted that he had survived the night, he offered up a silent prayer, promising God that he would say his rosary to the Holy Virgin every day for the rest of his life. McCallum also wanted to thank the rigger who had packed his chute. If the chute hadn't opened the way it had, McCallum would certainly have been killed. From his own experience of stuffing chutes, McCallum knew the rigger would have signed a Form 64, then tucked the paper into the pack. McCallum dug out the form to see the name of the person he should thank, and was astounded to find his own initials there. The chute was one he had packed himself, earlier that month.

After an hour of searching, Crozier was forced to call off the hunt for the two missing men. As loath as he was to leave Huffman and Perram—assuming both were alive and still on the mountain—he was all too aware that he, Spencer and McCallum could no longer stay where they were. It was far too cold, and in the thin mountain air, even the search they had mounted had left them feeling weak and exhausted. They agreed to meet down by the river that Crozier had seen, and one by one they set off, carrying their bundled-up chutes, which they knew they would need later for warmth.

AT THE BOTTOM OF A CREVASSE, close to where the others had landed, Huffman had spent a long, bitter night. He had tumbled down a steep slope before being knocked out, and when he came to, he was stiff with cold and groaning in pain. In the dark, he warily explored the extent of his injuries. His left shoulder was definitely broken, he had a deep cut above his left eye, most of the skin had been raked from his left cheek, and his nose was bleeding as if he'd been in a fight. He lay still, unwilling to move, but could see the canopy of his parachute billowing above him, so he pulled it down and wrapped himself in it. During the night, the canopy kept sliding off, the smooth fabric slithering over its own folds, so only his feet were relatively warm, encased in the thick over-boots he had worn for the flight.

When dawn came, he saw that the slope he had rolled down was more like a cliff, and he was now at the bottom. Immediately in front of him, another wall of rock rose almost sheer; and off to the left—about five feet away—was a hole in the mountain as deep and straight as an elevator shaft. If he'd gone in there, he would never have been able to pull himself out. He looked to the right, along the V formed by the cliff behind and the rock face in front, and could see a river glinting in the distance. He studied it for a moment, searching for a possible route down, then sank back against the cliff.

Huffman hailed from Indiana. He'd grown up on a 220-acre farm there, a few miles south of the town of Straughn—a tiny place with a population of about 100, which locals boasted rose to 150 on market day. It was flat around Straughn—flat and open. Huffman knew nothing about climbing down mountains. As a kid he had shinnied up trees and splashed around in the local creek. He'd dangled a homemade line in the water, and walked miles with a gun tucked under his arm, searching for rabbits or squirrels to shoot for the pot. But he had never climbed down any mountains.

He looked up at the sky—now a pale, cold blue—and thought he could hear someone calling his name. He tilted his head, straining to listen, then struggled painfully to his feet. He shouted back. He was sure he could hear other voices farther away. They bounced off the rocks so it was hard to tell where they were coming from, but he was sure there were people up there, calling his name. He thought one of the voices might be McCallum's, saying something about going around to the other side. But Huffman was here—down here, on *this* side of the mountain.

For a while, the voices receded, and Huffman stopped shouting. But then the voices came back. Huffman could hear every word McCallum was saying. *So why couldn't McCallum hear him?* Huffman kept yelling, his voice growing hoarse. He heard the others planning to meet down by the river, and he called out again, saying he was too badly hurt, too badly injured, he didn't think he could make it, not to the river, not on his own. But no one called back, and slowly he had to accept that the others had gone, leaving behind a silence, which was the loneliest he had ever heard.

CROZIER HAD TROUBLE MOVING DOWN THE MOUNTAIN. He had never been fond of physical activity, his size and bulk working against him, but part way down he met up with Spencer, who helped him negotiate the more difficult slopes. Spencer was lean and agile, still not properly filled out. At school, he had always been keen on sports, trying out for the basketball team, then settling for track when he wasn't quite able to make the grade. His overall fitness and youthful resilience were now a considerable asset.

The two of them took four-and-a-half hours to scramble down to the river, doubling back whenever they came to a cliff or rock face they couldn't descend. They stopped frequently to rest, breathing heavily as if they'd just run a grueling race. Crozier was grateful for the help that Spencer provided, while Spencer was glad to have the company. He would not have fared well if he had been left to fend for himself.

When they reached the valley floor, they found a sandbank among the rocks and boulders—the winding bed of the river was still some distance away—and sank to the ground, waiting for McCallum who was making his own way down, slipping and sliding over rough scree as he dropped nearly 3,000 feet. McCallum joined them on the sandbank, greeting them both "like long-lost brothers."

It was now late morning, and the sun had risen over the peaks, filling the valley with an unexpectedly harsh heat. The three men sat with the sun on their backs, absorbing its warmth, as they took stock of their situation and their surroundings. The valley they were in was bleak as a desert. Except near the river, it held little in the way of vegetation. There were a few spindly trees and some wispy grasses, as pale yellow as the sandy soil, which blew in whorls stirred up by the wind. McCallum was convinced that they were somewhere in India—an idea that Crozier was still willing to accept. If so, there was a chance that the strange valley around them was that of the Brahmaputra—or the Brahma*putrid*, as the Americans called it—which flowed past their base at Jorhat. At two or even three miles across, the valley was certainly wide enough, and if the river running through it *was* the Brahmaputra, then perhaps the airmen were not that far from home. It was an encouraging thought, and one on which the three of them were happy to agree.

They decided their best plan of action was to walk west—the direction in which the Brahmaputra flowed—as it was standard practice, if you were lost, to follow a river down from its source. That way, you were more likely to come into contact with civilization. Before setting off, they checked their jungle kits, a process that did not take them long. Jungle kits were meant to be stocked with a range of items, including fishing lines, matches, string, maps, language books, medicines, knives—and maybe even a machete. But they were often the target of petty thieves, especially in China. Crozier's kit was almost empty. He had his needle and thread, a handful of candies, and a single magazine of bullets. McCallum had a knife, a bar of chocolate, some maps of India, and an anti-bacterial drug called sulfanilamide. Spencer's jungle kit yielded some chocolate, a few extra bullets, and a bottle of iodine that he had already applied to the cut on his chin.

They rested until one o'clock, then started walking, keeping to the sandbanks and avoiding the boulder fields that split the river into numerous meandering courses. The sun, which earlier they'd welcomed, was now high in the sky and bearing down on them with a fierce intensity that soon had them wishing for shade. The wind, too, had changed its nature, and was now blowing hard into their faces, carrying dust and grit that filled their eyes and scoured their skin.

As evening drew in, they followed a spit close to the water, and there they discovered that the river did not flow west, as they had assumed. Instead it flowed east. All that day they had been walking in the wrong direction. With night coming on, and feeling disheartened, they decided to find shelter. They hunted around and finally hunkered down behind a sandbank, where they ate a little chocolate while watching the shadows spread like spilled ink across the valley floor. As the temperature again dropped below zero, they laid out their parachutes and wrapped themselves up, huddling together with only the one in the middle able to savor anything like warmth.

AFTER THE VOICES FADED AWAY, Huffman sat for a long time, leaning back against the cliff, nursing his broken shoulder. Then, slowly, he rose to his feet. With his high forehead and wiry hair, rippling back in crests of waves, Huffman had the look of an academic—or maybe that of a young executive on the way up. His self-contained manner gave him a gentle, almost sensitive air that went well with his dapper moustache and notable fondness for starched shirts and creased pants. But his appearance—like his dress—was deceptive. Huffman was a lot tougher than he seemed.

Growing up on the farm in Indiana, he had been forced to toil long hours, doing backbreaking work—planting, hoeing, weeding, and reaping. And if his chores weren't done, and done on time, then as likely as not he would find himself on the wrong end of a whipping from an irate father. The second eldest of nine children, Huffman had been born into a family that, throughout the Depression, was "poor, poor, poor." He hated the farm and everything about it—the lack of running water, the absence of electricity. At the age of sixteen, he made his escape, going to live with an uncle and aunt. He still worked hard—baling hay for anyone willing to take him on—but at least now he was being paid and able to say he was his own man.

Huffman knew that no one was going to come and get him, not here at the base of a cliff on the side of some unknown mountain. He cut a strip of nylon off his chute and fashioned it into a sling, tying his left arm close to his chest. Under his shirt, he found his watch, which must have been ripped from his wrist during the jump, yet somehow had managed to lodge itself inside his clothing. He also discovered that he had lost the bracelet he had taken to wearing—one he had bought in India and had engraved with his own name.

Once more, he studied the way down, deciding that the shortest route was to follow the course of a stream he could see in the distance. He cut his parachute free from its pack and started down. He missed the winter jacket he'd abandoned in the plane, yet—after an hour of scrambling—he took the rash decision to discard his over-boots, too. They were too heavy, and were quickly tiring him out. He found the stream and followed it lower, but it soon dead-ended, the flow disappearing under a pile of rocks that he couldn't get over or around. He was forced to climb all the way up, close to the cliff from where he had started, and begin again.

By the time Huffman reached the valley floor, it was mid-afternoon. The descent had taken him seven hours, far longer than he had expected. He climbed a hillock and looked around. No one was in sight, but he could see footprints, snaking across a patch of sand. He walked towards them and found another set of prints, which he followed to a sandbar. And there, he found the two sets of prints were joined by a third. Burnt matches stuck out of the sand, along with the butt of an American cigarette, which he gratefully smoked. The three sets of tracks headed to the west—downstream, Huffman assumed—but when he scrambled over the boulders to reach the river, he found the water flowed in the other direction, towards the east. The others had gone *up*stream.

Huffman mulled things over and decided to follow the others west. For the next nine hours, he walked parallel to the river, his left arm tied to his chest, meeting no one, but following the tracks where they showed in the sand, stumbling on until dusk turned to night and he was no longer able to see. At ten-thirty, long after it was dark—and long after the tracks he'd been following had disappeared—he found a sheltered spot out of the wind and wrapped himself up in his parachute, resigned to spending what he already knew would be "another miserable night."

PERRAM, MEANWHILE, HAD STAYED HIGH ON THE MOUNTAIN. As the last man out of the plane, he had fallen, not further up the peak, but on the other side. He had not heard the other men shouting; nor had he seen

McCallum coming around the summit to look for him. Peering down in the morning from the ledge on which he had spent the night, Perram was not sure what he should do.

Perram came from a restless family. His grandfather had been born in London, England, and then emigrated as a young man to Cape Town, South Africa. He later tried his luck in Canada, where he met his future wife, and then moved on to the United States, entering the country at Port Huron in Michigan on September 5, 1914. Seven years later, after attesting to the fact that he was neither an anarchist nor a polygamist, he renounced his allegiance to the crown of Great Britain and successfully applied to become an American citizen.

But Perram himself had never strayed far from home. By the time he was born, his family had settled in Tulsa, running a "tire, auto, and accessory business." Perram planned to go into the business, too, and after graduating from Tulsa's Central High School, moved briefly to Stillwater—seventy miles away—where he attended the Oklahoma Agricultural and Mechanical College. When the war started, he enlisted in the army—on September 3, 1942—and after six months of training in Las Vegas, New Mexico, and Kansas City, Missouri, he was sent overseas. He had been in India for less than three months.

On his application to join the Air Corps, a neighbor who had known him "since he began walking in pants" had described Perram as "a man with a character above reproach—honest, dependable, and trustworthy." Well, maybe so. But as he looked down from his ledge near the top of the mountain, Perram felt too sore and too drained to work out what action he should take now. He thought he could see a village off in the distance, but was not sure if he could climb down towards it. So he sat for a long time—cold and stiff so he could "barely move"—then set off instead for the summit, hoping to secure an all-round view that might reveal an easier way down.

As he started his climb, the summit appeared well within reach, but as he struggled towards it, he began to realize that he had badly misjudged the distance. He had also failed to take into account the debilitating effects of the altitude. Forced to stop after nearly every step, he needed several hours of strenuous scrambling to get to the top. And when he arrived, he was disappointed to see there was no clear route for him to take. Everywhere he turned he saw slopes too steep for him to tackle.

He decided to try for another village he could see in the valley, but after several more hours of difficult climbing, he came to a rock face that he couldn't descend, and began to search around for somewhere sheltered to spend the night. He could feel the cold beginning to grip him again, and the leg he had injured was now hurting him "more than a bit." Perram had already spent one night stranded on the mountain. He was not sure he could survive another—not without his parachute to help keep him warm.

MCCALLUM, TOO, WAS WONDERING if he would make it through a second night. Even on the valley floor, down by the river and wrapped in a parachute, he suffered from the cold as well as the dearth of oxygen in the air. Several times, he found himself fighting for breath, forced to sit up and consciously make his heart and lungs work properly again. At first light, he roused Crozier and Spencer, and the three of them ate the rest of their chocolate, meanwhile discussing what they should do. They decided that their best option was to follow the river downstream as they'd originally intended, even though that meant retracing the steps they had taken the previous day.

They started early, but it was still past noon by the time they came to the sandbank where they had first met up. They sat down to rest, Mc-Callum pulling out his pistol and firing a shot at a bird that landed not far away. He missed—so the only food they would have to sustain them was the handful of candies that Crozier had. They continued walking downstream, occasionally climbing over boulders to go to the river to drink. The water was murky, full of sand and yellowish clay, so for the most part they sucked on pieces of ice they broke off from the sheets that formed near the bank.

After another hour of walking, they saw in the distance a caravan of animals—"like buffalo, but with a lot more hair." They frantically shouted and waved, but the men who were leading the animals "took fright and put on a spurt." Another hour later, they rounded a bend and saw a second caravan, which this time they managed to keep in sight. The caravan led them along a trail near the river, past untended fields, until finally it brought them to the edge of a village.

The three Americans stopped. It was getting dark. They had covered thirty miles that day and were now close to exhaustion. They had no idea what kind of welcome they might expect, but as they walked on, entering the village, they were willing to admit they were all three "scared stiff."

4

---ꝏ꙳---

NO SHANGRI-LA

AT FIRST, THEIR RECEPTION WAS MUTED. Villagers gathered in groups outside their houses, standing and staring with unsmiling faces at the strange beings who had suddenly appeared in their midst. But as more "natives" emerged from their homes, the atmosphere took a turn for the worse and became distinctly hostile. The murmur of voices that had greeted the airmen became a menacing growl. Crozier saw swastikas painted in black on some of the houses, and for a wild moment thought they had stumbled into "some kind of German-controlled territory." As the three men walked slowly on, in line abreast like lawmen in a Western movie, the villagers massed in a crowd up ahead.

The three men stopped. Crozier could see that some in the crowd had unsheathed knives hanging from their belts. For a moment, nobody moved. Then unexpectedly the crowd began clapping, giving the men what seemed to be an enthusiastic round of applause. But from the villagers' expressions, it was clear to the airmen that the standing ovation was not one of appreciation. Without warning, the crowd suddenly surged towards them, swirling around, pushing and shoving, jostling against them. Someone grabbed Crozier's arm and hung on. Others reached out, tearing at his clothes. McCallum became especially alarmed, as he felt himself being swept away. He pulled out his pistol and fired it once in the air, the shot resounding as loud as a cannon. The effect was immediate. The crowd fell back, with many of the villagers dropping to the ground.

The three Americans backed slowly away, edging out of the village. But as they retraced their route, running along by the side of the river, they heard voices behind, and looking back saw the crowd of villagers streaming towards them. They stopped again, McCallum checking his gun. He had two bullets left. Crozier and Spencer had seven bullets each in the magazines they carried. The three men agreed that if they were cornered, they would make a stand, "getting as many natives" as they could. They were too drained, too exhausted, to run any farther.

They lined up again, facing the villagers. The crowd slowed, and the babble of voices died away. After a brief moment of silence, a man in a heavy fur cloak, with long sleeves that fell over his hands, pushed his way forward and advanced towards them. McCallum held his gun by his side. The man stopped a few feet away, put his hands together and raised them to his forehead. He did not look Indian—but nor did he appear to be Chinese.

"As salaam alaikum," the man said. McCallum recognized the greeting—"Peace be with you"—from the Hindustani he had learned, and immediately responded, "Alaikum as salaam." And peace be with you.

The man bowed, and in halting Hindustani asked McCallum where he was from. McCallum told him. He and his two companions meant no harm, he said; they were airmen who had crashed their plane, and now they were in need of food, shelter, and warmth.

"Ask him if this is India," Crozier said.

McCallum did, and the man shook his head. He pointed to the ground. "Tibet."

"Tibet?" Spencer said. "Did he say 'Tibet'?"

McCallum nodded.

"Oh, my bare bottom," Spencer said. "Tibet."

THE MAN SAID HIS NAME WAS SANA ULLAH, and that he was a trader who had been several times to India. He had seen English people there, so he did not find Westerners as alien as the other villagers did. The people here were friendly. They had not meant to scare the three airmen. They were merely curious, never having seen Westerners before.

Ullah invited the airmen back to the village. They could stay in his house, he said, where they would be given food as well as a place to rest.

McCallum bowed in acknowledgement, but as the three airmen trailed after Ullah, the crowd again gathered around, the villagers gazing up into their faces, reaching out to grab their arms and tug at their clothes. They still seemed hostile, and the Americans continued to harbor deep suspicions of their intentions. But Crozier soon found that if he gave the villagers a smile, their faces would break into wide grins, their teeth gleaming against the burnished copper of their skin. A few of them even stuck out their tongues, in a gesture he later learned was one of friendship or respect.

By the time the Americans entered the village, wending their way through narrow, dirt streets, the atmosphere had radically changed. At times, it seemed almost festive. Crozier couldn't quite believe it. He felt like the Pied Piper, surrounded by people no taller than his shoulder, jabbering and gibbering, and excitedly pointing out aspects about him they found especially funny or strange. But as they pushed and shoved up against him, Crozier couldn't help thinking the villagers were not only curious; they were also the dirtiest people he had ever encountered—the children barefoot, their hair in tufts, the adults looking like bundles of rags, dressed as they were in animal-skin coats that exuded a stale, musty odor.

To Spencer, the villagers just looked old. Old, wrinkled, and gnarled. This was no Shangri-la, he thought. This was no heaven on earth.

As the three airmen followed Ullah along the streets, Crozier studied the houses they passed. Most were two stories high, with tattered flags lining their roofs and animal skulls mounted like trophies over their doorways. Their mud-brick walls were washed a pale white, while their empty windows were outlined in black. And yes, there were a disturbing number of swastikas around. As he looked more closely, however, he saw that the swastikas were the wrong way round—mirror images of the German ones, their arms rotating counterclockwise. But what struck Crozier most was not the swastikas but the fact that everywhere he looked, he just saw mud. Mud walls lining mud streets, and mud courtyards in front of mud houses.

Ullah led the airmen through one of the courtyards and into a house, ducking low as he went inside. The first floor was a windowless stable, with hay on the ground, a trough for water, some fluttering chickens and a mule tethered against one wall. Ullah climbed a wooden ladder to the floor above, and the airmen followed him up, emerging into a smoke-blackened room that was not much brighter than the stable below. A dozen or more villagers swarmed up the ladder behind them, packing the room until no more could squeeze in.

Ullah lit a lamp to dispel some of the gloom, and then invited the airmen to sit while McCallum retold his story. McCallum obliged, addressing the crowd, while Ullah roughly translated. McCallum managed to elicit "oohs and aahs" in all the right places—especially when he told of how he and his companions had flown over the mountains from China. The villagers looked at one another. Only gods were able to fly. A few of them shook their heads, and one or two checked behind the airmen's backs as if expecting to see angel wings there. All of them seemed greatly disappointed when the three Americans failed to fly in tight circles around the room.

When McCallum had finished, Ullah hustled the villagers out, but a new audience pushed its way in and McCallum was forced to tell his story again. After the fifth such telling, McCallum thought he was getting across how it was possible for humans to fly, but he still couldn't make the villagers understand the way parachutes worked. He began leaving that part of his story out.

Ullah finally cleared the room, and arranged for the airmen to be given a meal—a kind of stew washed down by rancid, yellow tea they could barely swallow. Blankets were spread over the floor, and the three men lay down, immediately falling into an exhausted sleep.

When they woke the next morning, they discovered that several of the villagers had stolen back during the night and were crouched beside them, staring into their faces. The Americans found it unnerving, having so many strangers staring at them like that, especially while they were sleeping. After more stew, Ullah told them to follow him, and led them downstairs and into the street.

A crowd of villagers immediately swarmed around, as Ullah took them to a large building, which looked as if it were some kind of assembly hall. Cushioned seats had been lined up in rows, which were divided, one from another, by brightly painted wooden columns. Red light shone from a lamp, and red rugs had been casually draped across the seats. Even so, the overall impression was one of shadows and gloom. A smell of incense hung in the air, but did not quite mask the musty odor that rose from the crowd of villagers who had followed the airmen in. At the far end of the room, a group of men sat cross-legged on a row of other cushions that were positioned slightly above the rest. The three Americans were swept towards them by the crowd, then deposited at their feet. The villagers drew back, subsiding into a respectful silence.

The group of men—elders of some kind—were dressed in maroon robes they had wrapped diagonally around them so as to leave one arm and shoulder bare. On their heads they balanced tall, saffron-colored hats that angled back like dorsal fins. The three Americans were asked to sit. Salty tea, filmed with grease, was served from a wooden urn. And McCallum was invited to tell his story yet again, with Ullah translating—although by now, Ullah knew the tale almost as well as McCallum did.

During the subsequent exchange, McCallum managed to learn that the village they were in was called Tsetang, and the river they had followed was named the Tsangpo. Then he moved on to his main point of concern.

There were, McCallum told the elders, two other men who had been in the plane when it went down, and now both were missing. So could the elders help organize a search? The elders conferred, and then graciously nodded their consent. McCallum scribbled a note the searchers could take with them, but said he and his two companions wanted to take part in the hunt, too. The elders again conferred, but said that was out of the question. McCallum and the other two airmen could remain in Tsetang, and they could continue to stay in Ullah's house. But under no circumstances would they be allowed to leave the confines of the village.

McCallum was forced to accept this restriction, and for the next two days he, Crozier, and Spencer waited anxiously for news. When it finally came, brought back by one of the searchers, it could not have been worse. Huffman and Perram, the other airmen were told, had been badly injured during the bailout—and now both of them were dead.

HUFFMAN, FOR ONE, WAS FAR FROM DEAD. After following the tracks of his three companions, he had hiked beyond them, passing them in the dark about fifty yards from where they were sleeping. The following day, Huffman continued to make his way upstream, his left arm still in a sling, his face and hair matted with blood. Several times he met up with "natives," but when he asked them for help, they just stared blankly back. He tried to mime the flight of an airplane—complete with sound effects that included the cough and stutter of a dying engine—but the only response he was able to get was a "sad shake of the head and a gentle cluck of the tongue." When he pointed to the ground and asked one man, "Is this India?" he was given a nod in reply. But when he then asked, "Is this China?" he again received the same humoring response. All he knew for certain was that he was in a land "where a white man wasn't common."

Not until the following day—after a third night sleeping rough—did he come within sight of a village. He slowly approached it, and at three o'clock in the afternoon, limped warily in. Immediately, he drew a large crowd pushing and bumping against him. Huffman singled out one man who looked better dressed than the others, and by motioning with his one good arm, indicated he needed food. The man left, but soon returned with three others who, Huffman decided, were village officials. They cleared a way through the crowd and took him to a house, the "whole village following along."

Huffman was handed a cup of goat's milk and a bowl of potatoes, and when he had finished eating he had the presence of mind to mime to the crowd that he now wanted a smoke. A pack of English cigarettes—Guinea Golds—immediately appeared, and Huffman lit up, the tobacco so dry he thought it had to be twenty years old.

His next move was to try to establish a measure of trust, so he began to lay out his meager possessions, displaying them on the spread-out canopy of his parachute. Each item he produced—a knife, a compass, his watch—was picked up, passed around and examined in minute detail. As the items went from hand to hand, Huffman noticed that the three officials were taking more interest in the nylon canopy than in his other possessions, so he cut off a few of his shroud lines and handed them around. The effect was immediate. The three officials held the lines to the edge of their clothing "like a woman does a piece of ribbon," and nodded and laughed like teenage girls. Huffman grinned back, and cut off some more of his lines.

The next morning, he decided to retrace his steps and head downstream. If the three other airmen he had been following had come this far, then they, too, would have been in the village. They must, he thought, have gone some other way. Huffman, however, could not face the prospect of walking back the way he had come, so to the assembled crowd he made the motions of riding a horse. Within minutes, two guides appeared, with three mules "all saddled up and ready to go."

They set off at a steady trot, the two guides leading Huffman to another village, which they reached early that evening. Again he was given food and a place to sleep, and again he showed off his possessions and handed round a few of his shroud lines. He was bedding down under the watchful gaze of the whole village, when two men elbowed their way in and handed him a note. "We are in the village of Tsetang," Huffman read. "Tibet is the place. How we got here, God only knows. These fellows will bring you here, where there's plenty of food and drink. Chin up, and when you get here, we will start back." The note was signed "Mac."

Huffman jumped up, eager to leave right away, but the two new arrivals insisted he wait until morning. At first light, they set off—Huffman on a fresh mule, his two guides traveling on foot. He almost "ran them to death" in his keenness to get to Tsetang, but it was still late afternoon by the time he arrived. He was taken before a council of "half a dozen important men," given a bowl of tea with a scum of butter on top, and, at his request, another dry cigarette. He was briefly questioned by one of the men who spoke "a kind of broken English," and then he was allowed to join his companions already there.

The other airmen saw him coming, climbing the ladder to Ullah's house, and rushed to greet him. A few hours later, the four Americans were able to hold another reunion when Perram managed to stagger in.

PERRAM HAD SURVIVED THREE NIGHTS OUT IN THE OPEN, close to the top of the mountain where he had landed. With no parachute to wrap himself in, he had endured such intense cold that he had lost all feeling in his toes. His "bruised" leg continued to hurt, so although he could still see a village far in the distance, he made no attempt to reach it. But on the third day, with no sign of rescue coming his way, he resolved to get off the mountain no matter how hard it would be.

He started down, and after several hours of difficult scrambling saw four men, whom he thought were Chinese, walking along the crest of a ridge. He gave a shout and the men stopped. When he caught up with them, he found they had no food or water, and when he sought their help, they motioned for him to stay where he was.

Perram waited all that day, but no one appeared, so he spent another night on the mountain. In the morning, he pulled off his shoes and examined his toes. They lacked all feeling, and when he prodded the skin, it felt as stiff and lifeless as leather.

He was trying to decide what to do next when he heard a shout and saw the four men climbing towards him. This time they had food—a little rice mixed with flour—as well as some water. They also carried his parachute, which they had somehow found higher up the mountain, close to the summit. They led the way down, moving with ease as Perram slipped and slithered along behind them. They could not make it as far as the village, so Perram was forced to spend a fifth night sleeping rough. When he looked at his toes the following morning, he found they had turned an alarming shade of yellowish gray.

The four men made an early start, but it still took another full day of painful walking before Perram reached the edge of the village. He was taken straight to Ullah's house, where he was given a rapturous welcome, and that night the five Americans, once more united, held a noisy celebration—"the happiest bunch of guys" in all of Tibet.

It was, however, a celebration that was to prove short-lived, as the American airmen did not understand the nature of the country in which they had landed—nor did they appreciate the dramatic impact their sudden arrival was about to have.

5

THE LAST BLANK ON THE MAP

THE TIBET INTO WHICH THE FIVE AMERICANS had so unexpectedly jumped was a barren land shrouded in mystery and intrigue—a strange, inhospitable place where time had stood still at least since the Middle Ages. It was one of the last great blanks on the map, an empty space the size of Western Europe or the U.S. states of California, Nevada, Utah, Arizona, New Mexico, Colorado, Oklahoma, and Texas combined. Yet it had a population of about two-and-a-half million, smaller than that of modern-day Chicago. To Western eyes, its people seemed as alien as the land. Nomads, monks, lamas—maybe even yetis—they were outlandish beings about whom anything could be believed because very little was actually known. Tibet was Conan Doyle's "Lost World," an elevated plateau, alone and cut off, which few outsiders had ever seen.

Partly it was the terrain that kept people away. Bleak and windswept, it had been carved eons ago when the Indian tectonic plate bumped into its Asian neighbor, gouging beneath it like the shovel of a snow plough, scrunching up the Himalayas and forcing the Tibetan plateau to rise to an average height of some three miles—more than 15,000 feet—above the sea level at which it had once rested. Except in the Tsangpo and a few other valleys, the land was harsh and desolate—a high desert with barely a tree or shrub to be seen. With its vast distances and unforgiving climate, Tibet was a country that was almost impossible for outsiders to penetrate.

But of course, the harder the challenge, the greater the allure. So as early as the seventeenth century, and as late as the nineteenth century, Tibet had been the coveted goal of some of the most resolute explorers the world had seen, determined men—and sometimes women—who pushed on, their heads bowed against the incessant wind as they struggled to be first to cross the plateau and then to enter the Forbidden City, the *fabled* city, of Lhasa. For them, Lhasa was the ultimate goal, as fascinating as Timbuktu, as elusive as the source of the Nile. Many of the early explorers were Jesuit and Franciscan priests, bent on converting a people so clearly wedded to religion, albeit to the wrong one. Others were spies, intent on unlocking Tibet's many secrets for the benefit of their imperial masters. Those who came later were often in search of personal glory or personal gain—and sometimes both. But with rare exceptions, the Westerners who tried failed to reach the Forbidden City, because it was not just the land they had to contend with, but also the people.

Tibetans may have been Buddhist in their faith, and therefore imbued with compassion and love, but deep down they still nurtured the belligerence of the conquering warriors they had once been, as well as a streak of cruelty that was almost medieval in its ferocity. Would-be trespassers were caught, beaten, sometimes tortured, and then—if still alive—sent back along the routes by which they had come. As for the Tibetan officials who were careless enough to let the intruders in, they were arrested, flogged, and imprisoned—sometimes for decades—while their servants, in one case at least, had their eyes gouged out and their hands and feet lopped off. For more than one hundred years—from the end of the eighteenth century to the beginning of the twentieth—Tibet was, as a result, a closed society, isolated from the rest of the world. Tibetans liked it that way. They had learned to be self-sufficient or, more commonly, to do without. They had no wood, no machines, no power, no medicines, and no wheels other than prayer wheels.

When they finally yielded, revealing their country to Western eyes, they did so not at the behest of a hopeful explorer traveling alone, but at the point of a gun wielded by an invading army.

IT WAS PERHAPS INEVITABLE THAT THE BRITISH should have been the ones to batter down Tibet's defenses. Britain may have been a small island, many thousands of miles away off the coast of Western Europe, but to the Tibetans it was a next-door neighbor, just the other side of the Himalayan fence. At the beginning of the twentieth century, Britain controlled all of the territory that ran along Tibet's southern border—more than 1,300 miles of it, stretching from Kashmir in the west to Burma in the east, with just a break in the middle where the still-independent, mountain states of Nepal and Bhutan intervened.

Not surprisingly, when the British overran India, they could not resist peeking over the fence to see what Tibet had to offer. Not much, by the look of it—and certainly not enough to warrant the trouble and expense of mounting an invasion. Of all the countries in the world, Tibet was probably the one most blessed with natural defenses. Its high, central plateau was protected by a ring of some of the most forbidding mountains on earth—the Kun Lun Range in the north, the Karakorum in the west, and, of course, the towering Himalayas that ran in a sweeping arc in the south. These ranges functioned much better than any castle walls. Soaring far above the plains of India, they even possessed built-in crenellations in the form of passes, which, when not entirely blocked by snow, could be defended by a few small bands of determined men. Only in the east, where Tibet pushed up against China, were there any breaches in Tibet's natural defenses. There, the great rivers of Asia—the Yellow, the Yangtze, the Mekong, the Salween, and the Brahmaputra—had gouged deep cuts through the mountains, leaving that flank exposed.

As for the Tibetan plateau, it was nothing like the horizontal plane its name might suggest. It tilted from top left (the northwest) to bottom right (the southeast). And as the five American airmen had already discovered, it was crossed by soaring ranges that, had they been located anywhere else, would have been known in every schoolroom around the world. These unnamed mountains dwarfed their counterparts in the Alps or the Rockies, and stood shoulder to shoulder with all but the highest peaks of the Andes. The Tibetan plateau was not the kind of terrain over which to maneuver an army. So the British just looked, and then they withdrew—coming back only when India, the richest jewel in Victoria's crown, seemed to be threatened by their archenemies, the Russians.

FOR MORE THAN ONE HUNDRED YEARS, Britain and Russia, then the two most powerful nations on earth, had been locked in a cat-and-mouse struggle—the so-called "Great Game"—that was fought back and forth across the plains of central Asia. A succession of czars had looked out from their wintry palaces over the various "stans"—Kazakhstan, Uzbekistan, Turkmenistan, and Afghanistan—and seen opportunities for trade and expansion, as well as a route through to the warm-water port they coveted. They had also seen, glittering in the distance, the prize of India, which they had long hoped to wrest from British control. Its gain would be Britain's loss—a double win for the czars.

For their part, the British were determined to protect India at any cost, and to that end they needed a buffer that would keep the Russians at a safe distance. Tibet was a central part of that buffer, and when, in the opening years of the twentieth century, Britain thought Lhasa was about to fall under Russian influence or even control, it panicked.

Lord Curzon, the Viceroy of India, was especially aggressive in his response to the apparent threat. He was a committed Russophobe as well as a firm believer in Britain's "forward policy"—which held that the best way to deal with the Russians was not to wait for them to act, but instead to get Britain's "retaliation in first" by taking preemptive measures. Curzon was convinced that Russia was trying to wrap Tibet in a series of treaties the way a spider would entrap a fly. He therefore dispatched a force under the political command of Francis Younghusband—and the military command of Brigadier General J. R. L. Macdonald—with the aim of "showing the flag" in Tibet and countering any initiatives the Russians were taking there.

The Younghusband campaign was intended to be little more than an uninvited visit. But when the Tibetans resisted the foreign soldiers on their soil, the British advance quickly became a full-scale invasion that was far bloodier than anyone had intended. At Guru, high on the Tibetan plateau near the town of Tuna, seven hundred Tibetans were slaughtered in a matter of minutes when their outgunned army—largely consisting of monks—refused to lay down their antiquated arms. Although Younghusband was sickened by the massacre, he allowed his forces to push on, inflicting another defeat on the Tibetans at Karo-la—a pass at more than 16,800 feet, and site of the highest battle in Britain's long imperial history.

Younghusband finally reached Lhasa on August 2, 1904, eight months after he had entered the country. His arrival there was a momentous event, full of historical significance and meaning. It brought an end to Tibet's isolation, and it forced the Dalai Lama to flee to China. It also proved to be a false alarm. The Russians, it turned out, had never had any serious designs on Tibet. Nor had they established a meaningful presence in Lhasa. The Great Game was apparently over, but Britain hadn't heard the final whistle. It had rushed in determined to put out a fire that wasn't even smoldering. Younghusband hemmed and hawed, imposed a treaty that was to have a profound and unforeseen effect on Tibet's long-term future, and then, seven weeks later, quietly withdrew, taking his soldiers with him.

Since then, few Westerners had penetrated far into Tibet. And only six Americans had ever made it as far as Lhasa. The first was Dr. William McGovern, an anthropologist who traveled to Lhasa with a British mission that reached the capital in 1922. The second was Charles Suydam Cutting—a globe-trotting naturalist and investment banker, who was also an avid sportsman (he was the 1926 U.S. Amateur Singles Court Tennis Champion), a glittering socialite, and the man credited with introducing the Lhasa Apso, a Dalai Lama favorite, to the dog-loving American public. Cutting reached Lhasa in 1935, returning two years later with his wife, Helen, the first American woman to enter the city.

The Cuttings' visit overlapped that of Theos Bernard, a lawyer-turned-Buddhist who later became the first American lama. Bernard was followed by the fifth and sixth Americans—Ilia Tolstoy and Brooke Dolan—who, in a sign of the changing times, were the first of many American spies to enter Lhasa. Sent there on a secret mission by Franklin D. Roosevelt, Tolstoy and Dolan arrived in December 1942, setting off a series of events that would later embroil the five American airmen.

In 1943, when the airmen themselves arrived on the scene, Tibet—like Greta Garbo—wanted only to be left alone. But in a world that was now committed to war—one in which every country had some strategic advantage to another—that hope had become an impossible dream. When the Japanese invaded China, and later defeated the British in Burma,

Tibet assumed a geopolitical importance that forced a number of foreign governments—particularly that of the United States—to sit up and take notice. Forces were gathering that soon were to engulf Tibet, and although they did not know it, the five American airmen waiting in Tsetang were about to be drawn into the complex struggle involving Tibet's desire to be independent, its centuries-old conflict with China, the future of the Hump that the airmen had been flying, and the prickly question of how best to get war goods through to China from Allied bases in India.

IF THE FIVE AMERICANS HAD THOUGHT ABOUT TIBET at all, they had done so in terms of caricatures. The average American saw Tibet the way Spencer had done, as a kind of mythical Shangri-la, a country that existed more in the mind than in reality. It was a place they might enjoy reading about, but not one they would actually want to visit.

Unlike the early explorers, the five Americans had never intended to come to Tibet, and now that they were here, they wanted nothing more than to get out again. (*Yes, and the sooner the better*, Spencer thought.) The Tibetans, however, had different plans. They were every bit as perplexed by their uninvited guests as the Americans were by them, and until they came to terms with the airmen's arrival—and more importantly, with their objectives—they had no intention of letting the men go. It took the Americans several days to realize it, but in the nicest possible way they were now prisoners.

The Tibetans continued to give the airmen food, at one point laying on a banquet of yak stew, boiled potatoes, and sour, yak-butter tea, and they generously offered a meager selection of much-needed, if somewhat soiled, clothing that included boots, shaggy coats, and fur-lined Cossack caps. But the council of elders in Tsetang was adamant. The five Americans must remain where they were. They would not be allowed to leave the village.

McCallum was particularly irked by this restriction. He was eager to return to the base at Jorhat and wanted to start right away. Like the others, he knew that word of their disappearance would have been sent to their families back in the States, and he was keen to let people know he was alive. He pushed Ullah to persuade the elders to change their minds, but Ullah insisted the council had ruled and was not about to reconsider—not until it heard from Lhasa. News of the airmen's arrival had been sent to the capital the day after they'd appeared in Tsetang, and until Lhasa responded, the Americans were free to explore the village. But they were not free to leave.

How long would it be, McCallum wanted to know, before word arrived from Lhasa?

A few days, Ullah told him. Perhaps more, perhaps less.

Time in Tibet, McCallum was learning, had a flow of its own that was not responsive to human demands—or to American impatience.

Huffman used the delay to clean the cuts on his face and re-bandage his broken shoulder, hoping the bone might set in a way that would not be disabling. He rarely complained, although it was clear to the others that he was often in pain. Perram tried to do what he could to heal his own injuries. His toes were clearly frostbitten, but he had wisely resisted the temptation to roast them over a fire, preferring instead to soak them in water that was only just warm. The gradual heating seemed to have helped. At least it had cured the numbness, and for a while Perram thought it had cured the frostbite, too. But his toes were now an angry, swollen red, and the source of constant discomfort. He could no longer wear shoes, not even the soft-sided boots the Tibetans gave him; instead, he was forced to hobble around in multiple pairs of borrowed socks.

As the other airmen explored the village, they continued to rouse great curiosity wherever they went. As soon as they left the relative sanctuary of Ullah's house, crowds would stalk them as if they were film stars—men and women reaching out to touch them, children trying to hang from their arms. The villagers were willing to watch them for hours, staring at them with an intense fascination normally reserved for the rare and exotic.

As he wandered around, Crozier began to play a game with them. He would stare stolidly back, then—just as he'd done the first day in the village—he would suddenly flash them a smile. The Tibetans would immediately step back with the startled joy of someone who had been studying a statue that unexpectedly burst into life. And then they would grin back. Crozier delighted in their reaction. He still thought they were the dirtiest people he'd ever seen, but increasingly he was coming to value their charm and lack of guile.

At first, he and the other Americans found the constant attention mildly amusing. At worst, it was simply annoying. But then came the problem of what to do about a latrine. There didn't seem to be a toilet anywhere in Tsetang. That hadn't mattered when they had first arrived, but as the airmen continued to consume a diet of Tibetan stew and yak-butter tea, it became an issue of pressing importance. At one point, Mc-Callum walked to the edge of the village, hoping to find a quiet spot, but the crowd that pursued him was so large he couldn't even "pull down his pants." Crozier wasn't much help, telling McCallum to hold out until dark. But that night, when Crozier and Spencer snuck out on a similar mission, the crowd that followed them was as big as ever—even holding up lanterns so it could get a much better view. The problem was finally solved when McCallum managed to broach the subject with Ullah, who led them to a first-story roof and pointed to a slit that dropped into a crawl space sealed from below.

As the days passed, the Americans came to appreciate that Tsetang was much more important than they'd supposed. To them it was a village—and a squalid one at that. Dogs, goats, donkeys, and mules roamed the streets, scavenging for whatever scraps they could find. The people, too, seemed to live on the edge, subsisting at a hand-to-mouth level that even Huffman viewed with dismay. On the farm where he'd grown up, there had been no amenities of any kind. But there'd always been food on the table and an ironed shirt to put on his back. Here, the people had nothing. Yet somehow they seemed to want for nothing. They were happy to believe that their needs would be met by a prayer set loose on the wind.

To the Tibetans, however, Tsetang was a sizeable town, one that was important to the country's present as well as to its distant past. It lay at the heart of many of the trade routes that crisscrossed the country and ran over the mountains as far south as Gangtok and Darjeeling in India. It attracted merchants from Nepal and Kashmir, who had set up market stalls and small shops selling mutton, barley, yak meat, butter, and tea. It was also located near the Tsangpo river, which flowed more than 1,200 miles across the southern half of the country, cutting it in two and, with its tributaries, providing Tibet with most of its fertile soil. Most significant of all, however, Tsetang was important because it lay in the sacred Yarlung valley, the birthplace and cradle of Tibetan culture and civilization.

The Yarlung River ran south to north, at right angles to the east-flowing Tsangpo. Legend had it that the Tibetan people were descended from a monkey who had dropped from Heaven onto the slopes of the Gongpo Ri, a prominent hill next to the river. It was also in the Yarlung valley that the first Tibetan king had apparently come down from Above, arriving on the summit of the Lhabab Ri, dangling at the end of a magical sky cord. And it was here in the Yarlung valley that the Buddhist religion had first taken root when a sacred text fell out of the sky, fulfilling the requirements of an ancient prophecy.

Each day, as they wandered around, the Americans witnessed how vital a role legend and myth played in the villagers' lives. It was not just the murmur of prayer that constantly pursued them like the hum of bees; it was also the ritual: the touching of stones, the sprinkling of offerings, and the lighting of butter lamps and candles. Everything was symbolic, everything had significance. And yet it was the Tibetans who thought the Americans were religious—because they were seen to wash so much. Surely, no one would scrub his face and hands—not every day—unless he was performing some kind of sacred rite.

For the most part, though, the Americans focused on trying to keep warm. During the day, that was easy. The sun was so fierce that Spencer, for one, was forced to avoid it as much as he could—just as his parents had always nagged him to do. But at night, when the temperatures dropped ten or twenty degrees below zero, the airmen were never able to get warm—not even when they huddled around the yak-dung fire and wrapped themselves in "three blankets apiece."

They groused constantly about the cold, until one morning they looked down into the courtyard and saw a child, completely naked, playing in the dirt. From that point on, they decided they must all be "sissies" with no further rights to complain.

One evening when they were sitting around, Spencer told Huffman, "Go on, tell them about the girl."

"What?"

"The girl," Spencer said. "Tell them about the girl."

Huffman looked down at the floor. "Oh, that," he said. "It was nothing. Just that the first night I was in a village, I was stretched out trying to sleep, when one of the men brought a girl into the room. She was about sixteen, I would say. And...well, the man motioned for me to scoot on over so the girl could get into my bed."

"And did you?" Crozier asked.

Huffman shook his head. "The whole village was looking on. She would have got in, but I had to say no." He scowled at Spencer. "The whole room burst out laughing."

Spencer grinned at Huffman's discomfort. But he was having his own problems with the Tibetans. They could not believe that someone so young could be so far from home. The women—and many of the men, too—wanted to mother him, to make sure he was eating enough and being well looked after. Their fussy concern had started to annoy him, so much so that he had lost all patience; he was now threatening to punch out the lights of the next Tibetan who tried to tuck him in at night.

Inevitably, as they sat around talking, the airmen would relive their escape from the plane and the precious few seconds they had spent in the air before hitting the side of a mountain. All of them knew how lucky they'd been. Bailouts nearly always resulted in major trauma or in death. But they had beaten the odds twice—first by getting out of the plane and then by managing to regroup on the ground. It had been a close call—or as Spencer liked to say, in a convoluted twist of reasoning, "The Army always tells us 'count to ten before pulling the ripcord.' But if we'd counted to ten, we'd never have gotten as far as five."

But sooner or later, the conversation would invariably turn to the problem of how the airmen could get back to their base in India. They discussed the possibility of walking out, following one of the trade routes that had to lead south to Sikkim and the rest of India. But Ullah warned them against that idea. Even if they were allowed to leave Tsetang, they would soon discover that the passes were closed at this time of year, and the mountains were so full of bandits they'd need an army to protect them if they hoped to reach India alive. McCallum was keen to float down the Tsangpo, which flowed east to the far end of the Himalayas, before swinging round in a tight hairpin and dropping down to the Indian plain. But again Ullah warned them of the dangers. There were rapids and waterfalls where the river plunged off the Tibetan plateau. No one had tried to run the river—at least no one who had ever been seen or heard from again.

So the airmen waited—like the prisoners they were—until word finally came from the capital. It was brought by a strange delegation of diverse nationalities. And it was not what the Americans wanted to hear.

6

⟨∘∘∘⟩

A WHOLLY ERRONEOUS CONCLUSION

UNKNOWN TO THE FIVE AIRMEN, news of their plane crash, when it first reached Lhasa, had thrown the city into a state of turmoil that, in some quarters, bordered almost on panic. The Tibetan capital was already on edge following an unfortunate incident in which a water god in the Jokhang, or cathedral, had started to drip from its mouth. Whenever that had happened before, it had been a portent of bad things to come—the death of a Regent, or even a Dalai Lama. Now, here was news of an airplane, one that had flown low over the city scaring the people who'd heard it, and then fallen out of the sky to crash and burn close to Tsetang in the sacred Yarlung Valley. There were many in Lhasa who were unsure how to interpret this latest omen, but no one doubted that it was a clear sign of troubled times ahead.

At the highest levels of the Tibetan government, however, there was widespread agreement on what the downed airplane meant. Its sudden arrival was viewed in the context of an international political storm that had been building for months—one that threatened the country's existence, as well as the unique culture its people had developed over the past 1,300 years. The fact that Tibet's main leaders were entirely wrong in the conclusions they drew was not to be known until long after the events they triggered had been played out in full.

In 1943, when the five airmen bailed out of their plane, Tibet was under the absolute rule of a child—the fourteenth (and current) Dalai

Lama, who, like his thirteen predecessors, was the undisputed head of state as well as the nation's spiritual leader. He had been born eight years before as Tenzin Gyatso, and was still an infant when the leading lamas of Lhasa proclaimed him to be the reincarnation of Avalokiteswara, the Buddha (or more accurately, the Bodhisattva) of Compassion. Tenzin Gyatso exhibited many of the qualities that marked him out as the new god-king. He had the sign of the conch imprinted on one of his hands. His eyes, and his eyebrows, sloped back at the correct angle—upwards. And his ears were both of the requisite size—large. Furthermore, when he was shown a selection of apparently random household objects—a teacup, prayer wheel, and bell—he was able to pick out those that had belonged to his immediate predecessor, the thirteenth Dalai Lama, because, of course, the objects had once been his, during his previous incarnation.

Unfortunately, Tenzin Gyatso was found in Amdo, in Ch'inghai—a near-autonomous fiefdom on the Sino-Tibetan border nominally under the control of China—and the lamas from Lhasa were rash enough to announce the child as their new leader before they were able to smuggle him into Tibet-proper and install him in the Potala. Their haste, and the intense interest of the watching Chinese, was to cost them dearly. The local warlord who ruled Ch'inghai—a Muslim general named Ma Pu-fang—refused to let the god-child go until he received a godlike ransom of some 400,000 Chinese dollars, most of which was destined to go to the Chinese government.

Until he came of age, the new Dalai Lama, like his predecessors, was guided in his decisions—and his education—by a Regent. The Regent, in turn, was advised by a cabinet, called the Kashag, which consisted of four counselors, or *Shapes*—three of whom were members of the Tibetan nobility, while the fourth, and usually the most senior, was a monk. The Shapes, in their turn, were appointed by the Dalai Lama and advised by the *Tsong du*, or National Assembly, which, to come full circle—an important symbol in Tibetan culture—was responsible for choosing the Regent. Like the Kashag, the National Assembly comprised both monks and laymen, but it mainly reflected the views of the abbots who ran Tibet's many monasteries, especially the big "three seats" in Lhasa—Drepung, Sera, and Ganden.

At first, Tenzin Gyatso was advised by a Regent named Reting Rinpoche, who, in addition to his many other duties, was responsible for developing his young charge's moral fiber. Reting himself was known for so-liciting bribes—bribes being the grease on which the Tibetan government ran—and for spending much of his time in the company of women of ill repute. This did not sit well with the Dalai Lama's other advisors. But nei-ther did it prevent Reting from remaining in his post, until the day, in 1941, when he was required to receive the Dalai Lama's vows of celibacy and his renunciation of carnal pleasures. The irony was too much even for the tolerant Tibetans, who were often willing to turn a blind eye to other people's indiscretions. Reting was forced to resign—no doubt helped on his way by the state Oracle who predicted, correctly as it turned out, that Reting would have a much-shortened life if he didn't take more care with his devotions.

Reting was replaced as Regent by a lama named Taktra Rinpoche, who was a very different character. Taktra was old, austere, and conservative, and he was possessed of a high moral character that made him determined to reverse the decline of the Reting years and to reinstate the discipline that had prevailed during the reign of the much-respected thirteenth Dalai Lama.

At the end of 1943, when the five American airmen bailed out over Tibet, the young Dalai Lama and his old and austere Regent were strug-gling to deal with a new threat from an ancient enemy—China. China had been a problem for as long as anyone in Lhasa could remember. In-deed, it had been a problem since Tibet had been unified, back in the sev-enth century, by the great Songsten Gampo, one of the three towering figures in Tibetan history, who not only brought his countrymen together, but also introduced them to writing, a code of law, and the even-then-an-cient Buddhist religion, which he hoped would displace the shamanistic faith of Bon.

In the long struggle with China, it was Tibet that had first gained the upper hand. Its armies managed to carve out a huge empire that not only covered Nepal and parts of Burma, but also extended as far east as the Chi-nese capital of Chang'an (now the city of Xi'an), which the Tibetans seized in 763. One hundred years later, Tibet was still dominant enough to im-pose a treaty on China that set the border between the two countries and obliged each one to respect the other's independence. To seal the bargain, the two nations literally had parts of their treaty carved in stone, erecting three stelae—one of which stands in the center of Lhasa today—that were engraved with an optimistic inscription: "All to the east (of the border) is the country of Great China; and all to the west is the country of Great Tibet....Henceforth, on neither side shall there be waging of war or seizing of territory.... All shall live in peace and share the blessing of happiness for ten thousand years.... Tibetans shall be happy in the land of Tibet, and Chinese in the land of China."

The harmony, however, did not last as long as the stelae. In the ninth century, Tibet entered a dark period, and China was able to retake most of the territory it had lost. Both countries then fell under the control of the Mongols, whose mounted armies swept like locusts across the face of Asia, but they reemerged as separate nations when the Mongol empire later collapsed. By then—the fourteenth century—Tibetan aggression had been subdued, and the neighboring Chinese no longer saw the country's once-feared armies as a meaningful threat.

The Tibetans, however, were still able to fight among themselves, and their many monasteries—newly created and richly endowed—went to war, both with one another and with the lay nobility that ruled in Lhasa. After years of struggle, one particular order—the Gelugpa—was able to prevail. It was founded in the fifteenth century by a monk named Tsongkhapa—the second great figure in Tibetan history (who also founded the monasteries of Sera and Ganden, and began construction of the Potala)— and it was from this order that future Dalai Lamas would be drawn.

Chief among these was the fifth Dalai Lama—the so-called "Great Fifth," and the third towering figure to leap from the pages of Tibet's long history. He cemented the Gelugpa grip on power and, for the first time, united Tibet's secular and spiritual authority, bringing them together in his own person. By the time he died, in 1682, the Great Fifth had transformed his country. But he had also bequeathed the Tibetans a problem—one that still plagues their country today. It was the problem of succession.

Celibate rulers like Dalai Lamas do not leave natural heirs, so when one of them dies, a search must be mounted to find a successor. But because a Dalai Lama is not just a secular leader, but also a spiritual one, Tibetans must first discover his reincarnated spirit in the body of a child, and then wait up to eighteen or so years while the infant matures. Only then can the country once more enjoy legitimate, temporal rule. Inevitably there is a gap—filled by a Regent who might not be suitable, or who might not be willing to surrender his powers once his charge comes of age.

Since the time of the Great Fifth, Tibet has been ruled more by Regents than by Dalai Lamas, and many of those Regents have been thoroughly corrupt. During one 125-year period, until the thirteenth Dalai Lama came to power in 1895, Tibet was ruled almost entirely by Regents, and during that time a suspiciously large number of young Dalai Lamas met premature deaths before they were able to assume their thrones.

Of course, it is also possible for the Dalai Lamas to be wholly corrupt. Selected as infants when their characters are unknown, they can—and do—develop into adults of questionable merit. When the Great Fifth died, Tibetans waited fifteen years for his successor to mature, only to discover that their new leader not only had no interest in his temporal duties, but also preferred to express the spiritual side of his nature by way of alcoholic binges and sexual orgies. This did not make him any less popular with his people, although there were official attempts to remove him from office. But it did give the watchful Chinese an opportunity to reassert their waning influence.

Four times during the eighteenth century, Manchu emperors sent their troops into Tibet. And when they withdrew, they left behind powerful agents, or *ambans*, who were able to exert considerable influence over Tibetan affairs. During the long period of Tibet's isolation, the Chinese ambans remained firmly entrenched. But then, gradually, their authority declined. By the opening years of the twentieth century, Chinese influence in Tibet had all but disappeared, and Tibet was once again at peace with itself and with its neighbors.

It was, however, about to become entangled in a complex web of international agreements and treaties, which, by 1943, had created a delicate political balance that the arrival of the five American airmen was soon to disrupt.

WHEN FRANCIS YOUNGHUSBAND HAD WITHDRAWN his troops from Lhasa, the British had imposed on the Tibetans the Lhasa Convention of 1904—the treaty that was to have a profound effect on the country's long-term future. Nominally, the treaty gave the British a face-saving presence in the country in the form of trading posts, which they could set up in the towns of Gyantse and Gartok to complement the one they already had in Yatung. Other than that, the British had agreed to leave the Tibetans more or less free to get on with their lives as they had been doing before.

However, one clause in the Lhasa Convention was particularly significant. Under its terms, Lhasa was prohibited from allowing any other power to take a political or commercial interest in Tibet, unless it had first obtained British consent.

Two years later, without consulting the Tibetans or even bothering to inform them of the result, Britain signed a separate treaty with China—the Anglo-Chinese Convention of 1906—which contradicted some of the terms of the agreement it had reached with Tibet. In particular, the treaty with China allowed Peking to deal with Lhasa without obtaining British approval.

A year later, Britain went one step further when it concluded the Anglo-Russian Agreement of 1907. It committed both signatories—Britain and Russia—to deal with Tibet only through China.

Britain at this time was still playing the "Great Game"—trying to protect its holdings in India by keeping the Russians out of Tibet. It thought that the 1904 Lhasa Convention would prevent Tibet from dealing directly with the Russians, while the 1907 Anglo-Russian Agreement would stop the Russians from dealing directly with Tibet. What Britain didn't appreciate was that Russia wasn't the threat. China was. Britain was facing the wrong way. Once again, it had seriously misread the situation, and was trying to slam the front door in the face of the Russians (who weren't trying to get in anyway) and inadvertently allowing the Chinese to come in through the back.

China was quick to take advantage of the inherent conflicts built into the various treaties. In 1910, it invaded Tibet, entering Lhasa with a force of arms and causing the Dalai Lama to flee. (This was the same Dalai Lama, the thirteenth, who had been forced to flee to China when the British had invaded in 1904. Now, having just returned to his capital, the Dalai Lama was obliged to flee from the Chinese and seek sanctuary with the British in India. Along the way, his royal party was intercepted by two British ex-army sergeants, one of whom uttered the immortal words: "So which one of you blighters is the Dalai Lama?") Britain was horrified by China's action—mainly because Tibet was in turmoil, which left the northern border of India exposed, but also because the political landscape had been radically changed without Britain's involvement or consent.

Events then took a quantum jump sideways when, in 1911, the Manchu dynasty collapsed and China fell apart, politically. Its troops were expelled from Lhasa. The Dalai Lama returned from exile in India. And in 1913, Tibet was once more able to declare itself to be a free and independent state, with its own government, its own civil service, its own set of laws, its own army, its own currency, and its own ethnic uniformity.

But it was still not a settled country. Border disputes with China persisted. And Britain continued to fret over Tibet's ongoing failure to provide the stable buffer it wanted for India. The British government decided to intervene. In 1913, it held a tripartite meeting at Simla—a summer resort in the Himalayan foothills, which was a miniature version of the England the British in India so badly missed—where it hoped to establish once and for all Tibet's main borders and its true political status.

The meeting did not go well, but negotiators for all three countries—Britain, Tibet, and China—nevertheless initialed a treaty that would have seen Tibet divided into an Inner Tibet (as seen from the viewpoint of Peking) that was adjacent to China, and a much bigger Outer Tibet that covered most of the land to the west of the upper reaches of the Yangtze River. Both Tibets were to come under the suzerainty, or paramount control, of China; but Outer Tibet—essentially the Tibet the Dalai Lamas and their Regents had been ruling for centuries—was to be an autonomous, or self-governing, state.

In article 2 of the initialed Convention, the Chinese negotiators agreed that China would "respect the territorial integrity (of Tibet) and to abstain from interference in the administration of Outer Tibet... which shall remain in the hands of the Tibetan Government at Lhasa." China would also undertake "not to convert Tibet into a Chinese province." But when the initialed agreement was submitted to the governments of the three countries, China—unhappy with the way the Tibetan-Chinese border had been delineated—refused to sign. So the Simla "agreement" fell apart. The various issues that the three countries had tried to resolve were left unsettled, and remained as a festering source of conflict and strife.

In 1943, just months before the American airmen arrived in Tibet, China was again threatening to invade. It was supposed to be locked in a life-or-death struggle with Japan, but in April of that year, Chiang Kai-shek, leader of the Chinese Nationalist government, ordered the governors of three Chinese provinces to move troops up to their borders with Tibet. In response, the Tibetan National Assembly vowed to fight, if China tried to launch an attack.

Reports of an imminent conflict were sufficiently alarming that Britain's Prime Minister, Winston Churchill, took time out from waging the broader world war to raise the matter with the Chinese government. On May 20, 1943, at the Pacific War Council held in the Cabinet Room of the White House in Washington, Churchill told China's foreign minister, Dr. T. V. Soong, that "a disturbing rumour had reached him that China (was) massing troops on the borders of Tibet, and that he hoped that it was in error, both because the borders of Tibet had been secure for so many years, and also because it would mean diverting forces away from the true enemy, Japan."

Soong responded by claiming "emphatically that there was no truth whatsoever to the rumour, either that troops were being massed on the border or that China had any present intention of attacking Tibet."

In spite of these (false) assurances, in October of that year—only one month before the American airmen appeared on the scene—reports reached London confirming that "the Chinese continue to increase their forces on the Eastern Tibetan Frontier." China had already let it be known (again falsely) that Tibet was offering aid to Japan, giving it a pretext for an attack. Now, in another ominous sign, it began broadcasting propaganda into Tibet, hoping to undermine Tibetan resistance.

It was against this background of tension that word of a plane crash near Tsetang reached the Tibetan government in Lhasa. The news could hardly have come at a worse moment. With its nerves on edge, the Tibetan government overreacted. It immediately jumped to the understandable—but wholly wrong—conclusion that the downed plane must have belonged to the Chinese. In fact, the government suspected that the plane's unannounced appearance—and the fact that it had flown low over the capital—might even be the start of the expected invasion.

These suspicions were apparently confirmed when it was learned in Lhasa that one of the airmen from the plane had a Chinese flag stenciled on his back. Not only that, but he also had prominent Chinese letters under the flag proclaiming him to be a friend of China, fighting for China. The Tibetan government was left in no doubt. The plane's crew had to be working for the Chinese. As such, the five airmen could not be allowed to leave the country as, apparently, they wanted to do. Instead, they must be brought to the capital and made to account for their aggressive actions.

To that end, the Tibetan Regent—Taktra Rinpoche—acting in the name of the Dalai Lama, told the Kashag to issue an order. A two-man delegation would be sent to Tsetang as quickly as possible. In good Tibetan tradition, it would see that the airmen were treated well and given adequate food. But then it would escort the men over the mountains—bringing them back for interrogation and possible censure here in Lhasa.

7

---◈◈◈---

POLITICAL QUAGMIRE

ON THE OTHER SIDE OF TOWN, in a house overlooking Lhasa's main square, news of the plane crash was being digested with equally intense—but differently motivated—interest by Dr. Kung Chin-tsung. Kung was China's envoy to Lhasa—officially the head of the Resident Office of the Commission on Mongolian and Tibetan Affairs of the National Government of China in Lhasa, Tibet.

Since the fall of the Manchu dynasty and Tibet's declaration of independence in 1913, China had been trying to reestablish its influence in Lhasa. In 1934, it managed to squeeze a foot in the door when it opened a small office there, using the occasion of the thirteenth Dalai Lama's recent death. China sent a "mission of condolence," as well as a substantial sum of money that was ostensibly intended to help construct a suitable tomb for the (temporarily) departed god-king, but was also aimed at greasing the palms of the influential abbots of Lhasa's "three seats" and, of course, the corrupt and opportunistic Regent, Reting Rinpoche. Somehow the mission never got around to leaving again. Most of the Chinese did depart, but they left behind two representatives as well as a radio, which the Tibetans—foolishly and naively—later came to rely on as an easy way to communicate with the outside world.

Kung arrived in 1940 under a similar pretext. He was part of the Chinese delegation sent to Lhasa to observe the enthronement of the new

Dalai Lama—the fourteenth—and he simply stayed on. At first, he enjoyed a good relationship with the Tibetan government. He was given ac-
cess to the higher levels; he had a place of honor at official banquets; and
he was escorted wherever he went around town by an armed guard. But
Kung soon made himself unpopular, and before long the Tibetan government was asking China to have him recalled. As the chief representative
of a country that was threatening to launch an invasion, Kung was never
likely to win many friends. But the animosity and resentment he managed
to stir up went considerably further than that.

Kung's problem was that he shared the sense of overwhelming superi-
ority that nearly all Chinese nationals felt towards the Tibetans. To him,
Tibetans were not just dirty, unwashed, and unkempt. They were also
unworldly, lacking in grace, and—as far as their diplomatic skills were
concerned—woefully unprofessional. They would not deal with major
issues, preferring instead to bury their heads in the sand and hope those
issues would go away. And when handling the minor ones, they would
base their decisions on silly superstitions and the State Oracle's deliberately vague and ambiguous predictions. At times, it seemed, the Tibetans
lacked sufficient sense even to know what was good for them.

Kung himself was the exact antithesis. He was urbane and sophisti-
cated, and, at the age of forty-five, most comfortable when moving in
high political circles, having served his country in a number of overseas
posts that included Denmark and Belgium. He had a B.A. in economics
from the National Peking University and a Ph.D. in political science
from the University of Bruxelles, and his curriculum vitae included a
stint as professor at the National Szechuan University and the National
Central University in Nanking. He was the author of several books on
the ominous-sounding "border-territory administration and coloniza-
tion," and had written an academic tome, *The Five Power Constitution:
Its Theory and Application,* which he had published in French. In appearance—with his soft, smooth features and round, owlish glasses—he
seemed both gentle and benign. But he nonetheless possessed a strong
personality, and was determined to get what he wanted.

Kung's difficulties with the Tibetans began when he tried to prevent a
"half-caste," or "Koko," from being given the one hundred lashes to which
he'd been sentenced by the City Magistrate in Lhasa. The Koko, who was

half-Chinese, had been brawling in public with his wife, and then made the mistake of assaulting a policeman who tried to intervene. By his actions, Kung was accused of attempting to meddle in Tibet's internal affairs, and was advised in no uncertain terms to direct his attention elsewhere.

But Kung's most taxing problem with the Tibetans stemmed from one of Lhasa's other attempts to assert its independence from China. In July 1942, the Tibetan government—in a typically tangential way—set up a new department that it somewhat grandly called its Office of Foreign Affairs. Nominally, the new Office—it was a resurrection of one that had briefly existed during the previous century—was meant to serve as a conduit between the Kashag, or Cabinet, and the foreign powers with which it dealt. That basically meant Britain, as well as Nepal, both of which maintained missions in Lhasa. But did it also include China? The Tibetans said "yes," because China was clearly a foreign power. The Chinese said "no." China could not be a foreign power because Tibet was an integral part of the Chinese republic.

The three countries—Britain, Nepal, and China—could easily have continued to deal with the Tibetan government as they'd been doing before, but Britain and Nepal were happy to go along with the new arrangement. For Britain, the change meant little, since the head of the new Tibetan Foreign Office was, as a rule, also one of the four members of the Kashag with whom Britain was already dealing, so there was not even a change in personnel. For Nepal, the new setup meant even less. As a result of various treaties, Nepal had won the right to communicate with the Tibetan government through something called the Gorship Office. That right had not been revoked, so Nepal was able to bypass the new Foreign Office altogether. That left just China—the obvious target of the Tibetan government's initiative. If it agreed to deal with the Office, then it would be admitting that it was a foreign power, and that was something that China adamantly refused to do.

Kung rebelled against the new arrangement and took his complaints to the Kashag. But the Kashag said its hands were tied, as the new Foreign Office had been created by the National Assembly. For its part, the National Assembly told Kung that it did not talk to foreign powers, and suggested he take his concerns to the Kashag—or better still, to the new Office of Foreign Affairs. To the watching British, this was "an excellent

illustration of passing the baby, the popular method of procedure in Tibetan Government circles."

Since Kung's own government prevented him from having any dealings
with the new Office, this meant that he was officially cut off, unable to
have formal contact with any representative of the Tibetan government.
This was a stricture that Kung took so much to heart that on one occasion he went so far as to refuse to accept a letter that had been sent to him
from China, merely because it was delivered via the new Office. The letter was handed back, passed to the Kashag, and then returned unopened
to the original sender in China.

In spite of his official isolation, Kung still had other contacts in Lhasa.
He was, for example, in regular touch with the British, and had his own
sources within the capital's sizeable Chinese community. As a result, it was
not long before he, too, heard the news that a plane had crashed somewhere near Tsetang.

Right away, Kung jumped to the same—wrong—conclusion as the Tibetans had done. The plane must have belonged to the Chinese, as it appeared to be too far inside Tibet to be from any other nation. Kung did
not know what the plane had been up to (although he knew its appearance did not signal the start of any invasion), but he was just as determined as the Tibetans were to find out. He did not possess the authority
to order the crew to come to Lhasa, and he did not know that the crew
would soon be heading his way. So independently of the Tibetans, Kung
dispatched two of his countrymen—a Mr. Tsao and a Mr. Chas—and
sent them secretly off to Tsetang. He wanted to intercept the airmen
there, and see if he could turn their arrival to his advantage in his increasingly bitter struggle with the Tibetan government.

THERE WAS ONE OTHER PERSON IN LHASA who was also taking a keen interest in the plane's unexpected appearance, and that was George Sherriff,
head of the British mission there, and thus Kung's counterpart and rival in
the battle for influence over Tibetan affairs. The two men were well known
to each other. They frequently met at the elaborate lunches, dinners, and
parties that were the mainstay of life for the rich and powerful in Tibet,
during which, among the reveling, they would scheme and intrigue
against one another while maintaining the politest of diplomatic fronts.

Like China, Britain had opened a mission in Lhasa during the 1930s. It had watched with growing concern as China reestablished a presence in the capital, and it had seen how the Tibetans were trying—unsuccessfully—to resist the Chinese encroachment. The two countries—Britain and China—were in fierce competition to gain influence with the Tibetans. Both had resorted to bribery to help sway official opinion their way, and when one took an initiative, the other immediately countered the move. The relationship between the two countries appeared to be cordial, but beneath the surface it was a far cry from that of the allies they were supposed to be in the common struggle against Japan.

When Tibet sought help to counter the pressure it was feeling from the Chinese, Britain moved quickly to oblige. It dispatched a delegation, first under the leadership of Frederick Williamson, who died soon after arriving in Lhasa in 1935, and then under Basil Gould. Gould was keen to transform his delegation into a permanent British mission, but rather than ask outright for Tibetan agreement that might not be forthcoming, he resorted to a neat political trick. The day before his delegation was due to leave, he raised a number of issues with the Kashag. As anticipated, the Tibetans were dismayed. They could not possibly deal with so many questions, not in one day. So Gould suggested that perhaps he should leave a representative behind, supported, of course, by a wireless operator who could keep the two governments in touch. The Kashag agreed, and thus—in September 1936—the British mission was born.

When George Sherriff arrived—in April 1943—the mission had grown modestly in size, but still did not have the diplomatic stature that would have implied British recognition of Tibet's assertion that it was an independent country. Tibet may have been claiming it was a sovereign state, and China may have been claiming that Tibet was part of its republic, but Britain was sticking to the delicate balance it had tried to secure at Simla. As far as it was concerned, Tibet was neither independent, nor a part of China. It was, instead, an autonomous state under Chinese suzerainty.

A few years before, in 1935, the British government had spelled out its Tibetan policy. "Our interests in Tibet," it said, "are the maintenance there of an autonomous state under a stable and friendly government, able to preserve order and keep the peace beyond the northern frontier of India.... It follows that the exclusion of Chinese administration is also desirable, be-

cause its unpopularity and inefficiency would lead to disorder...." Five
years later, that approach was still current: "Our primary interest contin-
ues to be the maintenance of Tibet as a buffer state from which any influence hostile to India should be so far as is possible excluded...."

The best way to achieve this goal, the British government believed,
was to maintain Tibet in the confusing and unstable state of autonomy-
plus-suzerainty.

In 1943, just four months before the American airmen appeared,
Britain's Foreign Secretary, Anthony Eden, had sent his Chinese counterpart, Dr. T. V. Soong, a memorandum. Britain, Eden wrote, "had always been prepared to recognise Chinese suzerainty over Tibet, but only
on the understanding that Tibet is regarded as autonomous." This policy, which the government in London had steadfastly maintained for
thirty years, was, from one point of view, a shining example of British
diplomacy. It used the flexibility of the English language to mask a yawn-
ing gap between the two irreconcilable positions taken by Tibet on the
one hand and China on the other. The key words—"suzerainty" and "autonomy"—were hard to define. Who knew what they really meant? Not
only were they fuzzy at the edges, but they also overlapped, blending into
one another so they could be given any interpretation that either party
wanted. From another point of view, however, they were just a form of
words, and the reality behind them was as wobbly as a stupa balanced on
its point. As Sherriff well knew, that balance could easily be disrupted by
something as small and apparently insignificant as the sudden arrival of
five, unknown airmen.

Fortunately for Sherriff, Britain's relations with Tibet were as good as
China's were bad. In large measure, this was due to the diplomatic skills
of Sherriff's immediate predecessor, Frank Ludlow, who—by building on
the foundation of *his* predecessors, notably Hugh Richardson—had
made friends with many of the senior officials in the Lhasa government.
The two men—Sherriff and Ludlow—were themselves long-time friends
who had lived unconventional lives as explorers and naturalists in some
of the remoter parts of Britain's far-flung empire. They complemented
each other in just about every respect.

Sherriff—a professional soldier and skilled mechanic—was a Scot,
born in 1898, the same year as Kung. The son of a family that distilled

Scotch whiskey, he had been educated at Sedburgh School in England, where he excelled at sports, then enrolled in the Royal Military Academy in London. Sent to fight the Germans in the British trenches in France, he was almost immediately gassed, and forced to spend the remaining months of the First World War in a hospital. The following year, he was fit enough to ship out to India, where he served in a mountain battery on the Northwest Frontier, distinguishing himself as a gunner and being mentioned in dispatches, a quaintly British term meaning he had performed above and beyond the call of duty. He then joined the Consular Service, and in 1928, at the age of thirty, was appointed British Vice-Consul in Kashgar in Chinese Turkistan. It was there that he first encountered Ludlow.

It was fitting that the two men should have met in Kashgar. Built around an oasis at the western edge of the Taklamakan Desert, Kashgar was one of the more exotic cities in Asia, home to a rough-and-tumble mix of races and religions, and for centuries a welcome stop for merchants wending their way along the Silk Road. Ludlow had been invited there by Sherriff's boss, who had once been the British Trade Agent in Gyantse—the Tibetan town where Ludlow had set up an English school intended to give the sons of well-to-do Tibetans the benefits of a British education.

Ludlow was forty-three years old—thirteen years Sherriff's senior—when the two men met, and he was already established as an outstanding naturalist who collected specimens of plants and birds for the British Museum in London. Like Kung—but unlike Sherriff—Ludlow was an academic and scholar, who had graduated from Cambridge with a BA in natural sciences. After the First World War, he joined the Indian Education Service as Inspector of European Schools, before leaving to take up his post as headmaster of the school in Gyantse. By that time, he was also known for his love of poetry, and for his ability to recite large chunks of Shakespeare and Tennyson, as well as the lighter ditties of Gilbert and Sullivan.

The two men—Sherriff and Ludlow—even looked their different parts. Sherriff, the practical soldier, was the shorter of the two, with a round face, hard as a cannonball, while Ludlow, the distracted academic, was more angular, with a high forehead supposedly indicative of an intellectual bent. Both men, however, were excellent marksmen—Sherriff with a rifle and Ludlow with a catapult, having discovered that bringing down ornithological specimens with a silent slug was an essential skill in countries like Tibet, which theoretically banned killing.

In spite of their superficial differences, the two men hit it off, and over the next several years, they embarked on a series of expeditions that were to bring them a kind of lasting fame. They explored some of the least-known areas of the Himalayas, mainly in Bhutan and parts of Tibet, overcoming formidable obstacles that their unshakeable confidence didn't allow them to see. They were both members of that select group of wool- and tweed-wearing, British colonial officers—a reserved, all-male, pipe-smoking breed, with formal manners and impeccable behavior. Wherever they went, they took an eccentric interest in all aspects of the lands and cultures through which they passed. And after each trip, they returned to England with literally hundreds, if not thousands, of specimens of birds, butterflies, plants, and flowers.

It was, however, for their expedition of 1936 that they are best remembered. That year, they brought to London sixty-nine species of rhododendrons, of which thirteen were new to science, as well as fifty-nine species of primulae, of which fourteen were previously unknown. In garden-crazed England, that was enough to turn them into celebrities. "L&S," for Ludlow and Sherriff, became one of the better-known abbreviations on the labels of new, Asiatic plants exhibited before the Royal Horticultural Society, and grateful gardeners throughout the empire— and the United States—were able to plant exotic flowers that were hardy enough to survive the northern winter.

Although their names were so closely entwined, and they spent years traveling together under trying and dangerous conditions, the two men never quite managed to cross the threshold of intimacy that would have put them on first-name terms. To each other, they were never "Frank" and "George," but always "Ludlow" and "Sherriff."

The outbreak of the Second World War saw the two men back in Scotland staying at a shooting lodge in Perthshire with Sherriff's brother, Christopher. On hearing the news, they both rushed to London in the hope of giving further service to their country. Sherriff tried to join the army, but was turned down by several medical boards (he had "strained his heart" on one of his Himalayan expeditions while helping a coolie carry a load over a pass), and was only able to reenlist when he returned to India and passed one of the boards there. Ludlow followed a political route. He returned to Kashmir, was appointed Joint Commissioner in Ladakh, and then Additional Assistant Political Officer in Sikkim. Finally, in April 1942, he was sent to head the British mission in Lhasa—only to find himself replaced one year later by his old friend, Sherriff.

At the end of 1943, Sherriff was, of course, fully aware of the Chinese buildup of troops along the Tibetan border and of the threat of a possible invasion. It had been his reports that had helped alert London to the danger Tibet was now facing. When Sherriff heard that a plane had crashed near Tsetang, he, too, assumed that it was Chinese. But it also occurred to him that it might be British. Or even American. If the latter—if the plane was really American—then Sherriff would have a problem on his hands, because that would bring a fourth country into a political picture that was already crowded and complex enough with just the existing three.

Until recently, the United States had shown little interest in Tibetan affairs. But the previous year, President Roosevelt had ordered an American expedition to travel from one side of Tibet to the other. Its goal had been to determine if a road could be built across Tibet, linking India to China—a road intended to be a ground alternative to the Hump, allowing China's beleaguered army to be more easily supplied and thus better able to pursue its fight against Japan. The issue of the road had since developed into a running sore—one that was putting an unwarranted strain on British, Tibetan, and Chinese relations. It was, in fact, the fuse that seemed likely to ignite the expected Chinese invasion.

Sherriff, too, therefore wanted to know what the plane had been doing and exactly what mission it had been on. He could see that its arrival represented a threat to the delicate structure of autonomy-plus-suzerainty that he was charged with maintaining. So not knowing that the plane's crew had been ordered to Lhasa, Sherriff, like Kung, decided to send his own representative to Tsetang.

IT WAS THUS A MIXED GROUP OF PEOPLE who independently set off from Lhasa, all intent on making contact with the airmen in Tsetang. Each had its own set of motives and its own agenda to follow, but each was keen to see the airmen and be given a full account of their actions and their intentions. As for the airmen, they just wanted to be allowed to leave the country as soon as they could and make their way over the mountains to India. They had no inkling of the political quagmire into which they had jumped, and no understanding of the role they were about to play in Tibet's ongoing efforts to assert its independence.

8

GOKAR-LA!

IT WAS THE TIBETAN DELEGATION THAT ARRIVED FIRST—two officials on horseback, wearing maroon robes tied at the waist, their hair cropped so short it was little more than five-o'clock shadow. Crozier heard them coming—or thought he did. He and the other members of his crew were upstairs in Ullah's room, squatting around a yak-dung fire and smoking Tibetan cigarettes that were dry as sawdust.

For the past several days, they had been confined to the close quarters of Ullah's house, growing increasingly frustrated by their inactivity and the Tibetans' lack of any sense of urgency. The airmen were still free to roam the village, but the muddied lanes and fetid back alleys had lost whatever appeal they might have had. Also, the novelty of being the focus of so much attention was beginning to wear thin—especially for Spencer, who was finding the villagers' constant intrusions more than a little annoying.

Crozier attempted to soften the mood by abandoning the concept of rank. There seemed little point in maintaining distinctions—not when they were all trapped in the same boat. When Huffman tried to address him as "sir," Crozier told him to call him "Bob," "Chief," or maybe "Skipper," then added, "We'll be calling each other a lot worse names than that before we get ourselves out of here."

Several times, while they sat around waiting for word from Lhasa, the airmen found themselves holding a kind of court. Word of their presence had spread far beyond the Yarlung valley, and large numbers of curious Tibetans continued to show up, climbing the ladder to Ullah's room and silently staring, sometimes for hours. Many of the visitors were monks from Samye, the oldest monastery in Tibet, which stood on the opposite bank of the Tsangpo River. Samye was home to several thousand monks, and to the Americans, it sometimes seemed as if every one of those monks wanted to see for himself the alien beings who'd dropped into their midst, apparently dangling at the end of sky cords in much the same way their first king had done, back near the beginning of Tibetan time.

One monk who turned up—a moody Bhutanese who spoke some English—had traveled more than one hundred miles, a journey lasting nine or ten days, just so he could see the airmen. He set up a tent at the edge of the village and invited the Americans to visit, serving them barley-flour dough, or *tsampa*, which they rolled into balls and dunked in their tea. The Bhutanese morosely told them the many reasons they would never make it back to their base in India, and the Americans were willing to listen. Whenever they could, the airmen badgered their hosts for information. Was it possible to cross the mountains? Were there really that many bandits hiding in the hills? The answers were never encouraging.

But then one day Crozier heard hooves clattering in the courtyard below, and peering out saw with relief that the long-awaited Tibetan delegation had finally arrived from Lhasa. It didn't take him long, how-ever, to realize that it wasn't the two, maroon-robed officials who were the source of the commotion he had heard. It was a third member of the party—a large, potbellied man with a drooping, Mexican bandit-like moustache—who was causing the disturbance. He was struggling to dismount from a pony that seemed too fragile to bear his weight. The pony stood with its legs braced as the man slid to the ground, his large stomach pushing against it, causing the animal to take several skit-tish steps to the side. The man shouted for someone to take his reins, then marched across the courtyard, into the stable downstairs and up the trembling ladder.

As he entered the room where the Americans were gathered, the new-comer all but elbowed Ullah aside, banging on the floor with a cane he was carrying, and issuing orders that had Ullah and his household scurrying to produce yet more tea. Then he introduced himself.

His name, he said, was Rai Sahib Bo Tsering, and he was not Tibetan, but came from India. Since he worked at the British mission in Lhasa, where he was employed as Sub-Assistant Surgeon in the hospital there, he spoke excellent English. He had been ordered to come to Tsetang, he told the men, by the British representative, George Sherriff, and he was instructed to offer whatever assistance he could to airmen who—he could now see—were not the Chinese nationals that everyone had assumed them to be, but were, in fact—

"—American," Crozier said.

Bo nodded and bowed in greeting. The two Tibetan officials, who had followed him up the ladder, slipped into the room and took up positions close to the fire. Crozier ignored them. There seemed little doubt about who was in charge. Bo was issuing so many orders that Crozier was starting to feel embarrassed. Ullah had treated the Americans well, showing them kindness as well as respect. Yet Bo was ordering Ullah around as if he were some kind of servant. When he had the chance, Crozier took Bo aside and asked him to show Ullah more consideration.

Only then did he learn that Bo was not the one in command. The two Tibetan officials were. Bo had met up with them on the trail from Lhasa, where he had learned the purpose of their mission. If it had been left to him, Bo confided to Crozier, the Americans could return immediately to India. But the Tibetan officials were under orders. They had been told to escort the airmen directly to Lhasa—and that was where the Americans must go.

The news caught Crozier by surprise. It also filled him with considerable dismay. Lhasa lay to the north and west, in precisely the opposite direction from the one in which the airmen wanted to go. To make the journey to Lhasa would be to advance even further into Tibet. It would also mean crossing the Gokar-la—one of the highest passes in the world, and one that few Westerners had even seen. Crozier tried to argue, but there was never any opportunity for real discussion. As the five Americans had already discovered, they had little hope of returning to India without official Tibetan blessing.

Reluctantly they agreed that they would take the difficult route to Lhasa—leaving first thing the following day.

THAT EVENING, IN HIS ROLE AS SUB-ASSISTANT SURGEON, Bo took a look at Huffman's shoulder and Perram's frostbitten toes. It was a cursory look at best, with Bo proclaiming the shoulder would heal and the toes recover by themselves. At the British hospital in Lhasa, Bo was mainly required to treat bites rendered by the vicious Tibetan dogs, and to give injections for syphilis and the other sexually transmitted diseases that were frequently rampant among the often-promiscuous Tibetans. For their other medical problems, the Tibetans preferred to rely on cures they had developed themselves. They would, for example, cure aches and pains by branding the affected part with a red-hot piece of iron. Or they would write prayers on pieces of paper, then burn the paper and eat the ashes—or swallow the dried excreta, in the form of a pill, of an honored abbot or Dalai Lama. That latter treatment was a surefire cure for any ailment or complaint.

Crozier told Bo that Huffman would probably prefer to stick with his sling and Perram with his multiple pairs of socks. He did not think the Sub-Assistant Surgeon had any medical training, but was happy to give him the benefit of the doubt, honoring him with the dubious title of "Doc."

As they packed up their few possessions in readiness for the next day's departure, Crozier wondered how to thank Ullah for his generous hospitality. But Ullah was one step ahead of him. After that night's stew, he handed Crozier a large sheaf of papers on which he had scrawled a list of words and numbers. The list made no sense to Crozier, but Doc Bo explained that Ullah was presenting him with a bill covering every item the Americans had consumed since they'd arrived in Tsetang nine days before—right down to the individual matches they had used to light their dusty cigarettes. Crozier had no way of paying, but Doc Bo said he could sort the matter out later—as Ullah intended to accompany the airmen to Lhasa.

THEY LEFT AS PLANNED THE FOLLOWING MORNING. The two Tibetan officials, in spite of their quiet demeanor, had proven both influential and efficient. They organized food and the other supplies the party would need, as well as mules for the Americans to ride. As the airmen prepared to set out, they were astounded to see the entire village gathered together to watch them go. Every man, woman and child had turned out to give them a rousing farewell—including the shopkeepers and stall owners who knew they would see no customers until the Americans had gone.

Women served butter tea and candy, while the men sang Tibetan folk songs. When they demanded a song in return, the airmen were forced to warble their way through the first two verses of "God Bless America." With Ullah translating, Crozier made a brief speech to express his gratitude to all who had helped them. The villagers responded by bowing and sticking out their tongues, and in return the Americans introduced them to the "Western handshake." It was approaching noon before the airmen were allowed to take their leave.

It was a bizarre procession that wound its way along the trail by the river. Leading the group was Ullah, followed by Crozier on a mule so small that both his feet could touch the ground on either side. Then came McCallum in his A-2 jacket with the blood chit stitched to the back, Huffman with his arm tightly bound in a sling, and Perram with his feet wrapped in many pairs of woolen socks. Spencer brought up the American rear, and behind him came Doc Bo, burdening his mule as much as Crozier, and, right at the back, the two quiet Tibetans who nominally were the party's leaders.

Spencer had difficulty accepting that this scene was real. Of the five Americans, he was the one most used to cities. Rockville Centre on Long Island, where he'd grown up, was a quintessentially small American town where, in true Norman Rockwell style, it had been safe for his ten-year-old sister to go off on her own all day, riding her bike, with no one even thinking she might come to some kind of harm. But Rockville Centre also boasted two modern theaters—the Fantasy and the Strand—where Spencer would go to take in the latest movies. And it was close enough to New York City for him to catch a train into Manhattan to watch a show at Radio City, shop at Macy's, or dance to Glenn Miller's "In the Mood" or Benny Goodman's "Goody Goody." He could not believe that he had often strolled down Broadway and now was riding a Tibetan mule out of Tsetang.

At first, the trail they followed was relatively flat, giving the airmen a chance to adjust to the quirks and foibles of their different mounts. The mules seemed to have one speed only—a lively gait faster than a walk but slower than a trot—which McCallum thought was maliciously designed to give maximum discomfort to the riders. As the party approached a bend in the river, Ullah reined in his mule and waited for the others to catch up.

The river here was wide and shallow—a pale-yellow flow clouded with silt. Several wooden boats lined the shore, their owners standing beside them, before rushing forward as Ullah dismounted and the rest of the group followed suit. In less than an hour, the airmen and their Tibetan companions had been ferried across to the other shore.

Their trail again turned west, climbing over promontories and crossing streams—tributaries of the Tsangpo—that flowed in from the north. Out of the sun, slabs of ice as big as hockey rinks covered fields that in summer might have been meadows. In places the trail broadened out, but for the most part, it was a thin, single track over sandy soil that was as barren as the Sahara desert.

As they came round a bend, Crozier was astounded to see something he'd never expected to clap eyes on again. It was the burned-out wreckage of their C-87. After its engines had died, the plane must have glided over the Tsangpo Valley, crossed the river and crashed onto the northern shore. Charred, unrecognizable pieces were strewn all around—a grim reminder of how close the airmen had come to dying.

Drawing nearer, Crozier saw one of the wings, blackened by fire, sticking up out of the ground. Not far away lay the plane's nose wheel, upside down with its tire, amazingly, still inflated. A number of Tibetans were peeling metal from the chunks of fuselage that were lying around. And Spencer saw one man hauling away part of a radio. When the part proved too heavy, the man dropped it to the ground and hacked it in two, taking away the smaller piece.

The Americans took some souvenirs, then silently watched as a group of Tibetans tussled with the blade of a propeller that was poking up through a patch of ice. The Tibetans were pulling the blade from side to side, trying to pry it loose—unaware that beneath the ice there were several hundred pounds of engine attached to the other end.

The Americans carried on, following Ullah as he led them north, away from the river and past the monastery at Samye. As they began to climb into the mountains, the trail quickly steepened, and their mules settled into a steady plod. Each man sat on his mount, alone with his thoughts, surrounded by silence except for the rhythmic creaking of their wooden saddles. Steep cliffs fell away on one side, so they could hear rocks, kicked over the edge by the mules' hooves, clicking and clacking into the valley far below. A strong wind blew, and the air became noticeably colder.

With darkness falling, Ullah led them into the village of Chanda, where once again the Americans found themselves the focus of attention. The two Tibetan officials found all of them shelter—an upstairs room suffused with the smell of rancid butter and ancient smoke—and they settled in. A meal was served, with each man—including Ullah, the two Tibetans, and Doc Bo—dipping into a central pot, passing around a single spoon.

As the men finished eating, they heard a flurry of noise and activity below. It was the two Chinese—Mr. Tsao and Mr. Chas—whom Kung had dispatched; they had finally caught up. They pushed their way into the room, and immediately made themselves welcome by unpacking a saddlebag that revealed five bottles of South African brandy. They lined up the bottles in a row like skittles, opened one, and offered it around.

Crozier took a sip. The liquor was raw and burned his throat, but it was a welcome change from the rancid tea, which at this altitude was invariably served cold. By his estimate, each bottle contained a fifth of a gallon, and as first one and then another made its way around the room, he kept an unofficial tally. By his best guess, Ullah, Doc Bo and the two Tibetans had worked their way through half a bottle before retiring early. The five Americans did somewhat better, drinking one-and-a-half bottles before calling it a day. As for the two Chinese, they were just warming up. They had already consumed one bottle each, and now they proceeded to down what remained of the others.

The next morning, when the Americans awoke, they made the painful discovery that alcohol and altitude do not mix. But Doc Bo showed them no mercy: he had them up and back on their mules well before dawn, the whole village again turning out to see them depart, a group of children running alongside them until the trail narrowed and once again turned steeply upwards.

IT WAS NOW DISTINCTLY COLDER. Crozier could feel it, seeping into his bones. The airmen continued to climb all that day, finding shelter for the night in another small village, where the two Chinese immediately set off in search of further refreshments. They came back a short time later with three gallons of barley beer, or *chang*, which they poured into cups and heated over a yak-dung fire. They again offered the drinks around, but the Americans all silently shook their heads; hot chang was the last thing they wanted. But when Perram announced that today—December 13—was his birthday, they forced themselves to take a few sips.

The beer—looking like watery milk—reminded Crozier of the "white lightning" he had seen distilled in Texas. It was equally strong, too. As he raised his glass in a toast and looked around at his companions, he could not help thinking it would be hard to imagine a more dismal place in which to celebrate a birthday—16,000 feet up, crouching around a smoky fire, in a mud hut on the cold slope of an unnamed mountain, with little to look forward to other than the dirty blankets spread out on the floor when they were ready to sleep. Perram, though, seemed happy enough. He was twenty-three years old that day. He would not live to see twenty-four.

THEY LEFT EARLY THE FOLLOWING MORNING, climbing still higher in the face of a wind that was blowing so hard they could barely stay in the saddle. By midmorning, they were forced to dismount and walk up the trail; it was the only way to keep their blood moving. Perram suffered the most, as he was still unable to walk properly and had to remain on his mule. The others took turns walking beside him, rubbing his feet to stop them from getting frostbitten again.

As the Americans continued to climb, their stops became longer and more frequent. They were now above 18,000 feet—a height where the amount of oxygen available to breathe was just half that to be found at sea level, and where what little air was available was hard to absorb because of the much-reduced pressure. In an ideal world, they would have been climbing no more than 1,000 feet per day, giving their bodies time to adjust. Instead, they were climbing at a rate that was three times faster than that, so inevitably the Americans experienced the physical decline that always sets in, even in someone who is fully acclimatized. All five of the airmen had trouble just eating and sleeping, and all five suffered from pounding headaches and continuous waves of nausea.

But they were most worried about Perram. Stuck on his mule, he sat still as a statue, his hands frozen like claws around his reins. He was no longer shivering, but that, they all knew, could not be taken as a favorable sign. It was, instead, an indication that Perram was suffering from hypothermia—a potentially lethal condition in which his body had become so frozen that it was now shutting down. Superfluous movement like shivering could no longer be afforded, as he fought to keep his core temperature above a critical minimum.

At the front of the American group, Crozier kept looking ahead, hoping to detect signs that the trail he could see snaking above them might soon begin to level off. But each time he looked up, he saw the trail continuing to climb. At one point, Doc Bo—far ahead of the Americans—turned and called encouragingly, "Just one more mile." They plodded on, Crozier keeping a watchful eye for any sign of the pass up ahead. But a mile farther on he heard Doc Bo once again shout, "Just one more mile," and gave up trying to anticipate the end of the climb.

They repeated that process several more times, Doc Bo marching on, then calling back, "Just one more mile," until finally Crozier saw him stop and begin shouting and waving.

"Gokar-la!"

They had made it. There was no more up. The two Tibetan officials, oblivious to both the altitude and cold, were already at the pass, piling rocks onto a cairn and attaching a prayer flag to a line of others that were snapping in the wind like tattered kites. The pass was at a height of nearly 19,000 feet. That was an altitude at which pilots often blacked out, and certainly Crozier—his heart and head pounding—would long have had his crew on oxygen if they had been up in a plane. As it was, they stood by their mules, sucking in air and staring dully out at yet more mountains that stretched ahead as far as they could see, one or two peaks standing out even higher than the rest, their summits topped with thimbles of snow.

No one wanted to linger, exposed to the harsh wind. Doc Bo again urged them on, and this time the Americans were happy to oblige. The trail down was rougher and steeper than the one coming up, but at least it meant they quickly lost height. By the time it was dark, they had dropped nearly 2,000 feet, but still they kept going, bunched up behind

Doc Bo so their mules would not step off the trail and plunge hundreds of feet over a cliff.

They finally found shelter in Changtsu, a tiny village where they spread out their blankets and immediately collapsed into a deep and exhausted sleep. In the morning they discovered that the two Chinese had already left, riding ahead with news of the airmen's imminent arrival in Lhasa. Doc Bo had already sent a message to Sherriff—and so, too, the Americans learned later, had Ullah.

They continued their descent, finally reaching the banks of a river—the Kyi Chu—where they once more turned west, the valley around them broadening out. Their trail took them close to another village, where they skirted some well-tended fields. At one point, Ullah, who was now in the lead, led them to the top of a hill, and there he stopped. The Americans caught up, and one by one came to a halt beside him. And there in the distance, laid out below, was the capital of Tibet—the fabled, Forbidden City of Lhasa.

Flying "the Hump." Because of the mountains, and their associated weather, "the Hump" was considered one of the most treacherous routes of the Second World War.

Navigation was sometimes easy: Pilots just followed the "aluminum trail" of wrecked planes that littered the route between India and China.

In the Kunming mess hall, you were going to get "egg-es" whether you wanted them or not.

A C87. Pilots liked its super-charged engines, but were less keen on the engines' tendency to burst spontaneously into flames.

Armies of "coolies" were always at work on the crude runway, tamping it down, rolling it flat, doing everything laboriously by hand.

Frank Ludlow (left) and George Sherriff. Although the two men spent years traveling together in some of the remotest parts of the world - and their names are forever linked in the annals of Britain's horticultural hall of fame - they never quite managed to cross the threshold of intimacy that would have put them on first-name terms.

Dr. Kung Chin-tsung, head of the Resident Office of the Commission on Mongolian and Tibetan Affairs of the National Government of China in Lhasa, Tibet. Nominally an ally, he was, in fact, Ludlow's and Sherriff's rival in the on-going battle for influence over Tibetan affairs.

The 14th Dalai Lama, who was eight years old when the five American airmen reached Lhasa. He had recently received a warm letter and signed photograph from his "good friend Franklin D. Roosevelt," but the young god-king was particularly fond of the British, who gave him presents much more suited to his age.

The Potala - the Dalai Lama's winter palace; it dominated the city of Lhasa. "Suddenly in the distance, one of the most beautiful sights I have ever seen appeared before my eyes..."

Close up, the city of Lhasa held little appeal. For Spencer, its dirty streets and mud-brick houses confirmed his view that Tibet had nothing to offer that he couldn't find "twice as good" back home in Rockville Centre.

John Huffman, equipped by his Tibetan hosts, in an effort to ward off the harsh impact of a high-altitude winter.

Crossing the Tibetan plateau near the pyramid peak of Chomolhari. When it wasn't snowing, fierce dust storms would scour men and ponies alike, blasting their faces with grit and dimming the sun like an eclipse.

The Kyi Chu valley in winter. The American airmen followed this river to its confluence with the much bigger Tsangpo.

Tibet's passes could be blocked by snow that at times was as much as twenty or thirty feet deep. They hindered travel, but at the same time gave the country its near-impregnable, natural defenses.

Top, from left to right: Harold McCallum, Kenneth Spencer, Robert Crozier, John Huffman and William Perram. Below, in Tibetan clothing: William Perram, Kenneth Spencer, Harold McCallum, unknown Tibetan, Robert Crozier and John Huffman.

9

"THIS DESOLATE LHASA"

IN LHASA THAT DAY, AT THE BRITISH MISSION, George Sherriff was keenly following the Americans' progress as they made their way towards the capital, drawing on a network of informants and a surprisingly efficient, informal mail service that allowed messages to be delivered with relative speed by the herdsmen and traders who constantly plied Tibet's various trails.

Sherriff's sources were excellent. Rai Sahib Bo—Doc Bo, to the Americans—had sent him a report that he had received two days before. But even before then, Sana Ullah, the trader who had befriended the airmen in Tsetang, had sent him a separate note. So Sherriff now knew that the men were Americans. Sherriff had also learned—unofficially—that the airmen had been summoned to Lhasa. And he had been paying almost daily visits to the Tibetan Foreign Office to hear what the Tibetans were *officially* willing to say.

Sheriff soon discovered that the Tibetan government was being unusually reticent about the airmen; it willingly accepted any information that Sherriff offered, but refused to give anything back in return. He also found that the Tibetan government continued to harbor deep suspicions about the airmen, even though it, too, knew—as all Lhasa now knew—that the men were not Chinese, but Americans claiming to have lost their way. In the heavily charged atmosphere, where the city crackled with political tension, the government was still convinced that the airmen were in some way linked to the expected Chinese invasion.

Sherriff harbored suspicions of his own. He did not, of course, think the Americans heralded any kind of invasion, but he did think it was possible that they had been up to something considerably different from what they were claiming.

Ostensibly, the five Americans had been flying the Hump. But if that were the case, they had been an unusually long way off course. Could they really have strayed *that* far? By accident? In London, the British government was leaning towards the view that the Americans had been involved in some kind of "stunt"—saying one thing, but doing another.

British suspicions were partially fueled by the fact that the last time any Americans had come to Lhasa—less than a year before—they had definitely been acting under false pretenses. The Americans—Ilia Tolstoy and Brooke Dolan—had traveled under the banner of friendship, but in reality had been secretly trying to establish whether a road could be built across the southeast corner of Tibet as the much sought-after land alternative to the Hump. The two Americans had never told the Tibetan government the true nature of their mission, as, politically, the question of a road through Tibet was much too sensitive. But the British had known all about it, so it would not have surprised Sherriff if the five airmen who had crashed near Tsetang had been engaged on a similar mission—secretly scouting a possible land route, but this time from the air.

From Sherriff's point of view, the underlying problem was that the issue of a land route alternative through Tibet was hopelessly entwined with the much bigger one of Tibet's political status and its claims to be independent. The fundamental question was: Who had the right to decide if such a land route could be built? If it was Tibet, then that implied the country was independent. But if it was China, then that meant Tibet was indeed an integral part of the Chinese republic. For thirty years, Britain had been trying to sidestep the question of Tibet's political status, preferring to bury the issue under its autonomy-suzerainty form of words. But if the land route question was now going to be forced out into the open, then so, too, was the tangled mess of Tibetan claims of independence and Chinese claims of sovereign control. And for Sherriff, that could mean only one thing—trouble.

IT WAS CHINA THAT HAD FIRST PUT THE LAND route question on the table. In February 1941, nearly a year before President Roosevelt authorized the start of Hump operations, China could see it would soon need a land route to bring supplies into Kunming. The route through Haiphong had already been severed, and while the unreliable Burma Road was still in operation, it was clearly under threat from the encroaching Japanese. China therefore decided to build a road across the corner of Tibet, which would link it to India.

The British government—with its own Southeast Asian possessions under heavy pressure from the invading Japanese—was sympathetic to China's plans. But when China tried to proceed without first winning approval from Tibet, Britain objected. It was not prepared to see the autonomy-suzerainty balance tipped that far in China's favor, so it insisted that Tibetan agreement must be obtained. When that agreement was officially sought, the Tibetan government understandably said "no."

China then backed away from the road idea, pushing instead to develop one of the many pack routes that long had been used to move goods between India and China. But the Tibetans said "no" to that idea, too. However, by then—early 1942—Rangoon had fallen and the Burma Road, the Chinese army's last land link with the outside world, had been closed. The need for a land route through Tibet had become that much more pressing, so Britain shifted its ground, coming down on the side of China. It put pressure on the Lhasa government by threatening to cut off all of Tibet's wool exports—which passed mainly through India and accounted for ninety percent of the country's foreign earnings—if Tibet continued to refuse to approve the pack route. Crucially, however, Britain made clear to the Chinese that it would only follow through on that threat if China publicly guaranteed the Tibetan autonomy that Britain had tried to establish at Simla. This time, it was China that said "no." Its armies may have been facing imminent defeat by the Japanese, but it was still not prepared to weaken its claims over Tibet.

The two countries—Britain and China—then went their separate ways, each deciding to push for a pack route without the other's assistance. Britain's initial effort was simply ignored by the Tibetans, but in

May 1942—soon after Frank Ludlow arrived in Lhasa, bearing with him explicit instructions to bring the Tibetans around to the Allied way of thinking—the British decided to try again.

Ludlow called on the Kashag to present the British case for a pack route. Although still a newcomer to the capital, Ludlow wielded considerable influence; many of Tibet's more senior officials were former pupils of his, having attended the English school Ludlow had set up in Gyantse nearly twenty years before. The Kashag promised to give him an answer within ten days, but in typical Tibetan fashion, it turned its attention elsewhere to what it considered were more important matters. As a frustrated Ludlow reported to Basil Gould, his immediate superior at the British Residency in Sikkim, "The delay may have been due to arrangements connected with the annual summer migration of the Dalai Lama," during which the boy god-king moved the short distance from his winter residence, the Potala, to his summer palace, the Norbu-lingka. "All Lhasa was present in the streets," Ludlow reported, "with all state officials in gala dress, soldiers lining the road, and bands playing various tunes (including, strange to say, 'God Save the King')."

Meanwhile, the Chinese were also getting nowhere fast—in no small part because of their continuing refusal to let Kung deal with the new Tibetan Foreign Office. Furthermore, when the Tibetan government began its campaign to have Kung recalled, the Chinese became "very dependent" on the British in their "negotiations for a pack route across Tibet."

When Ludlow finally succeeded in winning the Kashag's approval for a pack route—against strong opposition from within the National Assembly—he passed the good news on to Kung, who professed himself to be "greatly pleased."

There was, however, a catch. The Kashag was happy to let goods start flowing from India into China—but only if those goods were of a non-military nature. To the Chinese, this condition must have seemed like gaining permission to borrow a car—but only if they agreed not to drive it. This restriction should have bothered the Chinese government, but apparently it did not. And that, in turn, worried the British. It appeared to the British government in London that China simply wanted a route through Tibet, and did not much care what moved along it. That raised the horrifying prospect that China might use the route, not to obtain the weapons and fuel it needed from India to fight off the Japanese, but to move its own troops into Tibet as part of the expected invasion. This was a fear that seemed confirmed when China suddenly asked to move 10,000 "refugees" along the route, and to position an unknown number of "officials" or "technicians" beside it.

It further occurred to the British that the Chinese might deploy the war materials that America was flying to them over the Hump. That prospect—where China would invade Tibet using American weapons along a route the British had helped to set up—was one that London found "intolerable." The British expressed their concerns to the American government, hoping that Washington would use its influence to rein in its Chinese ally.

In the event, the Chinese government did not invade—even though, throughout the whole of 1942, no goods of military value were allowed to reach its armies via Tibet. But then, early in 1943, the Tibetan government upped the ante when it stopped the flow of all *non*military goods, too. It insisted that a more formal contract was needed to determine what could, and what could not, be shipped along the route, and until a contract was drawn up—between Tibet, Britain, and China—no goods of any kind would be allowed to flow along it.

This time, the Chinese *were* put out, and the chances of a Chinese attack increased to an alarming degree. In London, the British government thought "this action of the Tibetans must bring things to a head, and might even cause the Chinese to take forcible measures." Sure enough, beginning in April 1943, China did begin its buildup of troops along the Tibetan border, prompting Winston Churchill to raise the question of a possible invasion of Tibet at the Pacific War Council that took place in Washington the following month.

By that time, the American government had also become involved in the land route question, and as a result had been drawn into the wider issue of Tibet's independence and true political status. Like Britain and like China, the United States wanted a land route alternative to the Hump. So soon after he made his commitment to supply China with arms by flying them into Kunming, President Roosevelt dispatched an expedition to Lhasa, hoping to establish just how feasible it was to construct a land route through Tibet.

Roosevelt placed the expedition under the command of Major General William "Wild Bill" Donovan—head of the newly created Office of Strategic Services (and forerunner of the Central Intelligence Agency)—who in turn appointed as the expedition's leader a dashing, thirty-nine-year-old, aristocratic American named Ilia Tolstoy. Tolstoy—a former cavalry officer and grandson of the Russian novelist—had the credentials to head the expedition, but he also possessed an excess of confidence that would lead him to overstep his orders to a reckless degree.

Tolstoy chose as his companion Lieutenant Brooke Dolan II, an independently wealthy, thirty-four-year-old explorer, who also looked extremely good on paper. Dolan had made two previous trips to Tibet (although not to Lhasa) and one to China, so he was able to speak both those countries' languages. Furthermore, he was familiar with the arcane complexities of Buddhist beliefs, having traveled extensively in other parts of Asia and the Far East. Dolan's single failing, which would emerge only later, was that he couldn't stand the sight of Tolstoy. In Lhasa, he confided to Ludlow that he "did not know how he was going to endure the long journey (across Tibet) to China in Tolstoy's company." Ludlow had already concluded that Tolstoy was "a man who trusted nobody but himself" and feared that when the two men left Lhasa there would, most likely, be "trouble on the road."

Long before then, the expedition had run into difficulty when the American government tried to arrange it through the Chinese. This was a grave and naive, political error. Tibet refused to allow the expedition to proceed, and only changed its mind when the American government reapplied through the British in India. The Americans should have known that in any dealings with Tibet, the issue of the country's desire to be free of China could never be completely ignored. They might have been keen to appease their Chinese ally, but not to the extent of implying that Tibet was part of China.

In spite of this shaky beginning, the expedition was well received by a Tibetan government that accepted it as the mission of friendship it purported to be. Tolstoy and Dolan arrived in Lhasa near the end of Tibet's Water Horse year—on December 12, 1942—and as Ludlow was later to acknowledge, "from the day of their arrival until the date of their departure, the Tibetan Government went out of its way to bestow upon them every courtesy and show them every consideration. They were welcomed with a guard of honour of 200 men; granted immediate audiences of the Dalai Lama and the Regent; feted by the Kashag and Foreign Office; invited to every ceremony; and permitted to visit every monastery or building they expressed a desire to see.... I cannot recall any request the Americans made which was not granted. And they were not backward in asking."

Tolstoy and Dolan were the first Americans privileged to meet a Dalai Lama—a distinction that had not been bestowed even on the well-respected Ludlow, who was forced to report on the meeting secondhand: "I understand the young Dalai Lama was greatly impressed with Captain Tolstoy, and positively beamed on him throughout the private audience." Even more surprising was that the Kashag agreed to Tolstoy's request to be allowed to cross the whole of Tibet, leaving the country by way of China, rather than returning the way he had come—and had earlier promised to go—via India. This was an unheard of concession. As Ludlow expressed it, "If Tibet had not been fearful of the future and alarmed at Chinese activities on her eastern borders, Tolstoy and Dolan would never had been permitted to proceed eastwards (to China). They would have been requested, very politely, to retrace their footsteps to India... (but) the Tibetan Government are hoping that the United States will support Tibet in her efforts to maintain her freedom and independence. Consequently, they were anxious, very anxious indeed, that the President's envoys should have no cause for complaint."

To help cement the relationship with their new American friends, both the Dalai Lama and his Regent, Taktra Rinpoche, gave Tolstoy personal letters for President Roosevelt. "These letters," Basil Gould would later note in a letter to Sherriff, "seem to be well-designed as a prelude to a request for intervention, if it should become necessary...."

Tibet, in other words, was laying the groundwork for seeking help from the American government. It knew that China derived much of its influence and most of its prestige from its close relationship with the United States. More to the point, the Chinese army owed its strength to American arms and American money. That meant the United States had the power to curb China's aggression towards Tibet, and that, in turn, made the United States an invaluable ally—but only if Tibet could dislodge China from its position as America's favorite Asian ally. That was a challenge the Tibetan government still had to face.

WHILE SHERRIFF WAITED FOR THE FIVE AIRMEN to arrive in Lhasa, he might well have been reflecting on these last Americans who had come to the capital. Certainly, it would have been natural for him to have done so, as the memory of the Americans' visit was still fresh in British minds. Not only had Tolstoy and Dolan been less than open with the Tibetans, but Tolstoy had also gone one step further by making rash promises to the Dalai Lama and his Regent, which he knew were never likely to be fulfilled. Furthermore, the Tolstoy-Dolan expedition had caused a rift between the British and the Chinese governments, with Kung in particular expressing outrage at the way it had been arranged.

And now here were five more Americans, heading along the trail to Lhasa, summoned by the Tibetan government, and claiming they had been flying the Hump—when perhaps, in reality, they had been engaged in some kind of political "stunt" that the British hadn't been made aware of. It must have seemed to Sherriff that all of a sudden Americans were popping up everywhere like weeds in his garden—pushing their way into a situation that was not just delicate, but also potentially explosive. So yes, their imminent arrival could well mean trouble.

At eleven o'clock that morning—December 15—knowing the Americans were soon to appear, Sherriff once more presented himself at the Tibetan Foreign Office. He had already suggested—even before he'd known their nationality—that the airmen should stay at Dekyi-lingka, his official home and site of the British mission in Lhasa. That was an invitation he now wanted to reaffirm.

As usual, when it came to the airmen, the Foreign Office was less than forthcoming, but it was clear to Sherriff that it thought the men would be arriving sometime later that day. Sherriff scribbled a brief note addressed to Crozier, in which he invited the Americans to join him at Dekyi-lingka, and then sent it by messenger along the route he knew the airmen were taking. The Tibetan government was also keen for the Americans to stay at Dekyi-lingka, so it, too, prepared letters ordering the airmen to go directly there, as soon as they arrived in Lhasa. By the time the Tibetan letters were ready to be sent, however, events had moved on. The airmen had reached the edge of the city—and there they had been intercepted.

WHILE SHERRIFF WAS AT THE FOREIGN OFFICE, the five Americans were little more than five or six miles away, much closer than either Sherriff or the Tibetans thought. From their vantage point on top of the hill, they sat on their mules and gazed out across the Kyi River valley. It was wide and flat, with mountains rising steeply on either side, some with a thin dusting of snow on their higher slopes and ridges. But it was not the valley that gripped their attention; instead it was the city, far in the distance—the city of Lhasa. None of the men had ever harbored any ambition to see it, but now that they were here, they could not but help to be enthralled.

It was an awe-inspiring sight, one that they would never forget, not because of the city itself, but because of its setting—12,000 feet up, yet on the floor of a valley—and, perhaps most impressive of all, because of the looming bulk of the Potala behind it. The Potala seemed to grow out of the rock on which it was perched, adding height to its already impressive dimensions. The palace's walls, rising in tiers, soared above the buildings that huddled below. They leaned inwards towards the center in such a way that they created a strange perspective, making them seem even taller than they really were. Their color was a mix of maroon and white, splashed on and carelessly broken by the long slash of a stairway that cut diagonally across them. At their highest point, the walls were topped by a row of gold pavilions—the tombs of earlier Dalai Lamas—that glittered and sparkled, catching the light.

As for the city itself, it appeared surprisingly small. But that could have been due to the width of the valley and the height of the mountains around it. In such a setting, any city would have looked small. Also, the five Americans had not yet adjusted to the sheer scale of the country. They had already discovered that distances in Tibet were often deceiving, with objects appearing, in the thin dry air, much closer than they actually were. So perhaps the city was further away than it looked, and that was why it seemed so small. The five airmen stared at the sight below them, the hardship and rigors of the past few days already fading into the past. For several moments, no one spoke, but then Ullah nudged his mule forward and the rest of the party followed him down the hill, once more wending their way alongside the river.

By coming over Gokar-la, the Americans were approaching Lhasa from the east, the opposite side from the one that travelers normally used. For about an hour, they played hide and seek with the city as they wound their way in and out of the claw-like foothills that protruded onto the plain, the city disappearing behind a spur of rock, then coming back into view as they emerged on to the open valley. They passed a few fields that looked as if they were tended in the spring or summer, and then came to a ferry— a flat-bottom boat, decorated with the hand-carved heads of gods and idols. They were rowed across by boatmen who, they were told, were Tibetan prisoners working their way through their sentences.

On the other shore, the airmen remounted and prepared to ride into the city. They expected to be met by a group of Tibetans, and as had happened in Tsetang, be taken before a panel of elders. But as they rode across the barren fields at the edge of the city, they were met instead by the two Chinese nationals who had helped escort them over the Gokar-la. The two Chinese came bearing a letter—not the one from Sherriff, but one that had been sent by Dr. Kung.

The letter was handed to Crozier, who read: "Mr. Tsao, who I sent to Tsetang, has returned [to] Lhasa, and [I] know everything about your misfortune. At the same time, I am very glad and congradulate [sic] for your safe dropping in Tsetang. Now, I again, send Mr. Tsao and representative of Chinese people in Lhasa, Mr. Chas, to present things to you.

"With Mr. Tsao," the letter continued, "I intrusted [sic] him to present you five hundred sangs (Tibetan Currency) for your miscellaneous expenses. Finally, you gentlemen, if want anything, please write to me or tell Mr. Tsao directly. Although staying in this desolate Lhasa, but we believe that we shall do our best for you."

Exactly what that "best" might be, Crozier and his crew were about to find out.

10

⊶⊷

A CHINESE WELCOME

THE TIBETAN GOVERNMENT'S INFORMATION about the five Americans and their whereabouts may have been flawed. And certainly Sherriff's was considerably better. But Dr. Kung's was the best of all. His inability to communicate officially with the Tibetans did not seem to have curbed his effectiveness. Indeed, it may have been a blessing, in that it had forced him to cultivate his own network of intelligence sources.

Kung had learned, at the same time as Sherriff had learned, that the five airmen were not Chinese. This, at least, had spared him the problem of having to explain why a Chinese plane had flown low over Lhasa—and then crashed onto Tibetan soil—without ever having attempted to obtain official permission or blessing. A lesser man—not as enterprising and not as forceful—might have been happy to leave it at that. The downed plane was not his problem, so let someone else try to solve it. But Kung could see an opportunity here—one that he was keen to exploit and turn to his country's advantage.

Kung knew almost exactly when the Americans would arrive in Lhasa, as—unknown to them—his two representatives, Mr. Tsao and Mr. Chas, had actually arrived in Tsetang *ahead* of the two Tibetan officials and Doc Bo. There, the two Chinese had spied on the airmen, collected what information they could, and returned to Lhasa to report to Kung. They reached the capital on the same day, December 11, that the two Tibetans and Doc Bo had appeared in Tsetang. By the time the two Chinese met up with the Americans on their journey over the mountains to Lhasa, Kung had developed a plan that he was able to implement with a degree of precision that neither the Tibetan government nor Sherriff could match.

The first part of that plan, which he had already put into effect, was to send the Americans a welcoming letter, along with a token amount of cash. He had also mobilized the Chinese community in Lhasa, recruiting a sizeable number of his fellow citizens and organizing a quick collection of clothing as well as some additional funds. He then set up a welcoming committee, and as his *piece de resistance* organized a reception/banquet that was fit for a party of visiting royals. When the five Americans rode their mules across the fields at the edge of the city, they were met, therefore, not by a group of Tibetans as they'd expected, but by a gathering of Chinese, bearing gifts, and expressing friendship.

THE CHINESE SWIRLED AROUND THEM, forcing the Americans to halt. Someone grabbed Crozier's mule by the reins and led the animal off the trail. A channel was cut through the crowd, and Crozier was taken into a field. The other Americans were ushered behind him, and Doc Bo also followed. But the two, maroon-robed Tibetan officials found themselves shunted off to one side, and they were last seen heading towards Lhasa.

In the field, Crozier found himself in front of a large tent, which was secured by ropes like a circus marquee. He was escorted to the entrance and helped to dismount. Kung appeared in the doorway and introduced himself, bowing politely and beckoning the Americans to enter. Crozier was all but lifted inside—and there he found a scene that might have come straight out of the *Arabian Nights*.

Plush carpets covered the floor; they were piled high, one on top of another. Soft banquettes lined the walls. And in the center stood a long, low table draped with a patterned cloth that was liberally covered with bowls of delicacies and sweetmeats as well as bottles, jugs, small china cups, and a set of large, bluish-green tumblers. Kung spread his arms, inviting the Americans to sit on the cushions that were lined up on both sides of the low table. At a signal, servants appeared, pouring a cloudy white liquid into the tumblers, which, Crozier couldn't help noticing, were made of the cheap glass with air bubbles in it, like the goblets sold at five-and-dime stores back in the States. The servants also filled the china cups, not with the same cloudy liquid, but with clear liquor that Crozier decided was the South African brandy he had already sampled on the way up to Gokar-la.

In passable English, Kung welcomed the airmen to Lhasa and told them he hoped that while in the capital they would take advantage of the hospitality the Chinese community wished to extend. He then raised his china cup in a toast, and the Americans joined in. It was apparent that they were expected to drain their brandies, and not just sip at them, and the insistent servants made sure that they did just that. No sooner had the airmen put down their cups than the servants stepped forward and filled them again—this time with a saki-like Chinese wine that had the appearance, as well as the taste, of "100-octane gasoline."

Kung offered another toast, raising one of the bluish-green tumblers that contained some of the cloudy liquid, which, Crozier now discovered, was more of the potent, white-lightning chang he'd previously tasted. The Chinese community, Kung informed them, wished to present the Americans with a selection of garments—long woolen underwear, sweaters, and socks—which they might find useful during their stay in Lhasa.

The clothes were brought out and duly presented, while much was made of the leather jacket McCallum was wearing. The Chinese paid special attention to their national flag, which was displayed on the back, and the lettering that proclaimed McCallum to be a friend of China. That declaration warranted another series of toasts, the servants running around refilling the cups and glasses.

Kung then announced that the Chinese community had also collected another sum of money the Americans might find useful, and presented them with a cash gift of 655 rupees—equivalent to about 50 British pounds or some 200 American dollars. That triggered another round of toasts that included one to Crozier and his crew, and another to Kung and the Chinese community.

Each time Kung raised his glass, the Americans felt compelled to reciprocate. When Kung proposed a toast to President Roosevelt, the Americans replied with one to Chiang Kai-shek. And when Kung drank to the United States, the Americans responded by honoring China. Each time, they drained their glasses, and each time the servants immediately filled them again.

When the Americans ran out of suitable subjects, Crozier was forced to fall back on toasting his home state of Texas. Then he toasted Coke Stevenson, the Governor of Texas. And then the Texas flag. When that line of thinking quickly played out, he appealed to the others for help, asking Spencer to offer a toast to his state's flag. But Spencer didn't know if New York even had a flag, so instead he rose to his feet and offered a toast to Rockville Centre, the Chinese all nodding and grinning and enthusiastically joining in.

By late afternoon—the airmen had arrived at the tent at about three o'clock—much of the brandy, some of the wine, and nearly all of the chang had been consumed. Kung mercifully called a halt to the toasts, and invited the Americans to join him for dinner at the Chinese mission on Barkhor Square right in the center of Lhasa. The airmen agreed and, with the tent, table, and cushions all beginning to spin, rose unsteadily to their feet, and followed Kung outside. All five were feeling distinctly unstable, and as they prepared to mount up, Spencer's mule suddenly bolted, forcing one of the Chinese to chase it down and bring it back under control. Later, Spencer couldn't recall anything about the incident; the brandy, the wine, and the chang had wiped it out of his memory.

Just before the group set off, it was joined by Sherriff's head clerk, a man by the name of Lobzang Tsering, who handed Crozier a note. It was from Sherriff, inviting the Americans to stay with him and his wife at Dekyi-lingka. In his letter, Sherriff said he hoped the airmen would go straight there, as that was what both he and the Tibetan government desired. He added, by way of an afterthought, that now the Americans were finally in Lhasa, he was sure their "troubles are almost over." But that was an assessment that proved to be premature.

AS THEY TRAILED AFTER KUNG INTO THE CITY, the five airmen were all, as they were later to describe it, in "a lovely daze" and "feeling pretty rosy," rolling from side to side on their mules as they struggled to stay in their saddles. At one point, in their happy and carefree state, they burst into a spontaneous and no doubt discordant rendition of "Home, Home on the Range," which their Chinese hosts may or may not have found to their liking.

And so it was that—at a few minutes before five o'clock on the afternoon of December 15, 1943—Robert Crozier, Harold McCallum, John Huffman, William Perram, and Kenneth Spencer, ages nineteen to twenty-seven, became, in one order or another, the seventh, eighth, ninth, tenth, and eleventh Americans ever to enter the city of Lhasa.

The airmen themselves were only dimly aware of this historic occasion. Their less-than-sober arrival was certainly in contrast to those who had gone before them. Other travelers—whether explorers, missionaries, adventurers, fortune hunters, or spies—had given their all to reach this city. To them, the Tibetan capital was the culmination of all their dreams. It was their Holy Grail—the beacon that had led them on. It was for this moment—when they could finally enter the fabled city and experience it for themselves—that they had pressed on in the face of unimaginable hardships and dangers. For those travelers, entering the city of Lhasa would become the high point of their lives, an unforgettable event. But for the five American airmen, *their* arrival was one they could barely recall, lost as it was in a numbing haze of South African brandy, Chinese wine, and Tibetan chang.

To the people of Lhasa, however, the appearance of the airmen was a significant event. Men and women came out of their houses and lined the streets, staring at the strange procession as it rode unsteadily by. Word of the Americans' arrival had rapidly spread, and as in Tsetang, a large crowd quickly gathered—first to watch the Americans go by and then to trail along in their wake. A few children skipped alongside the Americans' mules, holding on to the reins or screwing up the courage to reach up and touch one of the riders on the arm. Crozier turned in his saddle and looked back at the others, his wide grin saying, *Isn't this fun?* There was something to be said for being a celebrity, even if the constant attention might rapidly turn into an annoying intrusion.

McCallum was not so sure. The children were friendly enough, running alongside and getting under the feet of their mules. But the adults were different. He caught several of them staring at him with expressions that appeared unmistakably hostile. Of course, that's what had happened back in Tsetang. But here, the atmosphere had an additional edge. Furthermore, the people of Lhasa, unlike those in Tsetang, had seen Westerners before, so their sullen resentment could not be dismissed as merely an inappropriate expression of excessive curiosity.

The airmen, still following Kung, wound their way through a maze of narrow streets, passing a group of Muslims outside a mosque. The streets filled with people, the crowd swelling into a mob. It kept pace with the Americans, and round every corner grew even bigger as more and more people joined the throng. The five Americans stayed close together, bunched behind Kung as he led them towards the Chinese mission on Barkhor Square.

As the Americans were later to admit, Lhasa—when seen up close—proved to be a disappointment. Somehow, without having thought that much about it, the Americans had assumed the streets of the capital would be exotic, with maybe a glitter of gold or at least a shimmer of understated wealth. But the houses here were little better than those in Tsetang—mainly mud-brick, with empty windows and a piece of cloth, or sometimes paper, tacked across the tops of their frames. For Spencer, the city confirmed his already-firm belief that Tibet had nothing to offer that he couldn't find "twice as good" in Rockville Centre.

As for the streets, they were certainly not paved with anything even remotely like gold, but were instead filled with refuse and waste. Ravens pecked at the garbage, while mangy dogs sniffed through the piles for whatever scraps they could find. Spencer saw puddles he initially assumed to be water—until he remembered there had been no rain since he'd jumped out of the plane and into Tibet. Men and women were openly squatting in the streets, relieving themselves, so if the temperature had been just a few degrees higher, the smell would have been almost intolerable.

For his part, Crozier was studying the people, and—like McCallum—was beginning to sense that something was wrong. Most of the crowd wore tattered coats and ragged trousers, and many were begging by raising their thumbs as if trying to hitch a ride. To that extent, they were like the villagers that Crozier had seen in Tsetang. But there, he had been able to win over the people simply by offering them a smile. Here, the people remained sullen, continuing to glare in a way that was every bit as hostile as it was perplexing.

The first sign of real trouble came in the form of a rock, which struck Spencer a glancing blow on the head. He turned to see who might have thrown it, but couldn't spot an obvious culprit among the crowd. He moved his mule closer to the others as they entered Barkhor Square, but the mob followed, pressing around them. Kung led the way to the Chinese mission, where the Americans dismounted. But as someone led their mules around to the back, another missile came hurtling out of the crowd, this time a clod of earth that hit McCallum on the shoulder.

Kung tried to make light of the incident, and hustled the Americans inside. There they found an elaborate banquet had been laid out in their honor. They sat down to a wide selection of Chinese dishes—and yet more alcohol—and soon they were once again feeling relaxed and at ease.

AS HE SURVEYED HIS GUESTS, peering at them through his owlish glasses, Kung must have felt a similar sense of general well-being. Certainly, he had every reason to be pleased with himself and with the way he had handled the Americans' arrival. Of the various groups vying for the Americans' attention, it had been he—and the forceful Chinese community—who had managed to prevail.

Like Sherriff—and the Tibetan government—Kung was aware of the potential that the five Americans represented. Just by having them here—by bringing them to the Chinese mission—Kung had been able to make two important political points. First, he had shown that it was China that welcomed foreign nationals who visited Lhasa, whereas Tibet did not. And second, he had shown that it was China that was America's true friend, whereas—again—Tibet was not. Both points sent a powerful message that the American airmen were sure to take back and relay to their superiors at their base in India.

Even the unfortunate incident outside, when someone had thrown a rock and a clump of earth in the Americans' direction—even that could be turned to China's advantage. It could be seen as tangible proof of just how hostile the Tibetans were towards the Americans. They were not the good allies the Chinese were. They had no intention of helping America to further its war aims. So no wonder the Tibetan government had resisted American attempts to construct a land route across Tibet. They were sympathetic to the Japanese, just as China had long been saying.

KUNG'S PLANS WERE PROCEEDING WELL—certainly as well as he could reasonably have expected. But for the better part of an hour, his foreign visitors had been growing increasingly uneasy. Like polite guests professing not to hear their neighbors arguing next door, the American airmen had tried to ignore the clamor coming from the square outside. They did their best to pretend that the noise wasn't there, meanwhile attempting to enjoy a leisurely sampling of the Chinese dishes, as well as the potent drinks that Kung continued to serve. They had even managed one or two additional toasts to further the friendship between the Chinese and United States governments, rising to their feet and once again saluting President Roosevelt and Chiang Kai-shek.

But now the commotion outside had reached a level that made even their hosts appear uneasy. On several occasions, one or more of the Chinese stepped to a window, looked out, and reported to Kung. Doc Bo also went to take a look, coming back a few moments later to tell Crozier that the crowd outside had grown larger and seemed to be "working itself up into a state." At first, Crozier thought little of it. The crowd was just being rowdy. But then a rock thudded against the wall of the building. Another soon followed, and the shouts from the crowd became more insistent.

It was then Crozier's turn to have a look. He pulled back the cloth hanging in front of a window and peered out. He was astounded to see a crowd that, by his estimate, numbered in the thousands. Certainly, Barkhor Square was overflowing with a swaying, seething mass of Tibetans. And they were not merely being rowdy. Nor were they in "something of a state." They were, instead, enraged—to the point of being explosive.

As Crozier continued to look out, someone in the crowd saw him and hurled a rock his way. Then came another. Crozier ducked back inside and told the others what he had seen. The meal continued for a few minutes more, but now that the crowd knew for certain the Americans were still in the building, it kept up a steady bombardment of rocks, stones, and clods of earth that came thumping against the wall of the mission.

At a few minutes past six o'clock, Kung gave in. He sent someone out to fetch a contingent of the Lhasa police, and at the same time ordered the airmen's mules to be saddled up and brought around to the front. When the Americans stepped outside, ready to mount up and ride out of the square, the crowd surged forward. There was no mistaking its fury, or the fact that its anger and outrage were directed specifically at the Americans. More rocks were thrown—a hail of stones and some lumps of mud. A few of the Chinese who were still escorting the airmen rode their ponies into the crowd, while others drove the front lines back, using their whips.

A squad of the Tibetan police arrived—huge men armed with sticks and staves—and they, too, laid into the crowd. Among the police were several *simgas*—or monastery police—who stood as tall and wide as padded linebackers. They lashed out, attacking the crowd with their sticks and staves, beating back men, women, and children, indiscriminately knocking them on to the ground. One simga brandished a heavy metal key that was large enough to lock up a castle. He swung it round his head at the end of a leather strap, wielding it like a medieval mace, cracking heads and drawing blood from anyone unfortunate enough to get in its way.

Another hail of rocks came towards the airmen. The crowd surged forward, still in an uproar and threatening to engulf them. The Americans scrambled onto their mules, and ducking low while trying to shield their heads with their arms, charged through the gap the police had created, following Doc Bo, who was riding flat out.

As they made their escape, Crozier could not understand the crowd's sudden fury—or what he and his crew could possibly have done to inspire such obvious hatred.

II

⸞⸟⸠

GIN AND LIME?

GEORGE SHERRIFF GREETED THEM AT THE ENTRANCE of Dekyi-lingka. The Americans—led by Doc Bo—had now crossed from one side of Lhasa to the other, having entered on the east and headed out, beneath the forbidding Potala, towards the west. They followed Doc Bo as he turned south, riding towards the Kyi River on a well-worn trail that took them through thick stands of trees before ending at the British mission of Dekyi-lingka.

"Come on in and have a drink," Sherriff said.

More alcohol was hardly what the Americans needed, but they were nonetheless glad to have found a sanctuary from the mob—and to be welcomed in familiar, if somewhat clipped, English. Sherriff showed them into a courtyard, where servants helped them with their mules.

Had Crozier received his note, Sherriff wanted to know—the note advising the Americans to come directly to Dekyi-lingka. Crozier said that he had. He and his crew would have come straight to the mission, but they had been met the other side of town by a group of Chinese, and since then they had felt obliged to enjoy a (mainly liquid) rendition of Chinese hospitality. At least, they *had* been enjoying that hospitality until a crowd of Tibetans turned suddenly hostile and began hurling rocks and stones and other missiles in obvious anger about something the Americans had—or had not—done.

Sherriff nodded. "I suppose you know," he said, "that you are the first people ever to fly over Lhasa."

Crozier shook his head. He had realized, of course, that the city they had seen immediately before the bailout could not have been Tinsukia in the Assam valley, as he'd originally thought. But he had not appreciated that the city was Lhasa.

By flying over the capital, Sherriff explained, Crozier and his crew had placed themselves physically above the Dalai Lama, and no one—no Tibetan, and certainly no foreigner—was ever allowed to look down on a Dalai Lama. The Americans had given great offense, breaking a taboo in a way that was every bit as insulting as punching the President of the United States on the nose or daring to touch the person of the King or Queen of England. The Tibetan authorities had, in fact, been so incensed by the Americans' affront that they'd let it be known the gods would pluck them from the skies by way of retribution. When the airmen's plane subsequently crashed and burned near Tsetang, it was clear that the gods had taken their revenge—but even so, the people of Lhasa were still exceedingly angry and had not yet forgiven the crew.

The Americans took this piece of news with a grain of salt. Having witnessed something of the superstition and religious dogma that dominated Tibetan life, they could easily see that this explanation might make sense. But Crozier for one could not help observing that any Tibetan who climbed the slopes of the many mountains surrounding Lhasa would also be placing himself physically above the Dalai Lama.

Maybe so, Sherriff said, but that was "an observation within the realms of reason which I am sure the Tibetans would prefer to ignore."

Over the next few days, the Americans would come to understand that there was more to the stoning than Sherriff seemed willing to acknowledge. The real cause of the crowd's animosity, they would learn, was not to be found in the form of an unintended religious slight, but rather in the shape of the Chinese flag stenciled on McCallum's back, along with the Chinese lettering proclaiming him to be a friend of China who was fighting for China. The anger aroused by McCallum's blood chit had been greatly compounded by the friendship that apparently existed between the airmen and the Chinese community in Lhasa. Had not the Americans been greeted by the Chinese upon their arrival in the city? And had they not gone to the Chinese mission to enjoy still more of the Chinese hospitality? To the Tibetans, it was clear. The American airmen were aligned with the hated Chinese, and as such they needed to be driven away.

At least, Sherriff said now, the airmen would be safe here in Dekyi-lingka.

He led them inside the house, ushering them into a large reception room that was furnished in the style of an English lounge. Tibetan servants appeared from the kitchen and handed each man a gin and lime. Then Sherriff proudly introduced them to his new wife.

Betty Sherriff—"a very gracious lady"—had been born at the turn of the century in British India, high in the Himalayan foothills. She was the youngest daughter of a Scottish vicar and missionary, Dr. John Anderson Graham, who had founded the St. Andrew's Colonial Homes (now the Kalimpong Homes) on behalf of needy Indian children—the unwanted byproducts of mixed and illicit, Indian and British relationships. When Sherriff first met her, he had been a lifelong bachelor and she had again been living and working with her father, following the death of her first husband. The two of them had been married little more than a year, and during that time had become soul mates.

Like Sherriff, Betty had been educated in England, first at Cheltenham and then at Oxford. Best of all, from his point of view, she had taken a degree in botany, and shared his unbridled passion for rare and exotic Himalayan plants. She also shared Sherriff's love of wild and unknown places, so when he was appointed to his post as head of the British mission in Lhasa—just four months after the two of them were married—she was happy to give up her home in India and set out on the long and difficult trek to reach the Tibetan capital.

It was the first time the Sherriffs had been away together since their marriage, and their arduous journey could hardly have been described as a honeymoon. But Betty approached it with the British stoicism and unconscious eccentricity that allowed her to endure discomfort and hardship with the amused detachment of a well-to-do English lady traveling abroad. As she later recalled of the journey, the Sherriffs' "caravan was a mixed and fairly large one," comprising four riding mules, forty-two pack mules, five porters, four servants, two guinea fowl, a couple of ducks called Tunis and Bizerta, two ponies named King Rabden and Gallingka, and a Labrador called Jill. As it was early spring, the Sherriffs expected lots of snow, which they "experienced in full measure." Their ponies sank up to their bellies and had to be dragged over the higher passes. There were few comforts along the way, "but *Primula gracilipes, P. denticulata* and an attractive little gentian gave us great pleasure and encouragement...."

When the Sherriffs reached Lhasa, deliberately arriving on a date— April 9, 1943—that the ever-superstitious Tibetans had deemed auspicious, they were taken to see the young Dalai Lama, and on behalf of the British government, they formally presented the Tibetan leader with a set of silver dishes and a Hornby clockwork train set, complete with a large metal key to wind up the engine. They could not tell if the toy had been well received, as it was considered improper for educated Tibetans to show pleasure in any gifts they might receive. But as it turned out, the Dalai Lama was secretly thrilled with his "wind-up train," and, as they later discovered, if the engine ever fell off the tracks, the young god-king would kick up such "a rumpus" that one of his attendants would immediately "hasten to set it right again."

AT FORTY-FOUR YEARS OLD—a year younger than her husband—Betty Sherriff was just the right age to mother the Americans, and she immediately took them under her wing. She escorted them to separate rooms on the ground floor, which to the delight of the airmen contained proper beds, neatly made up with fresh cotton sheets and clean blankets. Better still, she arranged for servants to bring water—hot water—that was carried in large buckets and tipped into a metal tub. For the first time since they'd taken off from Kunming, the airmen were able to remove all their clothes and luxuriate in the soothing warmth of a bath. Sherriff then lent them some of his shirts, and when scrubbed and clean-shaven they returned to the reception room, they found a table had been laid out for dinner, the highlight of which was a double helping all round of Betty Sherriff's homemade ice cream.

During the meal, Sherriff was able to establish that his guests were just as they claimed—five young and seemingly innocent Americans who had been flying the Hump and then been blown hundreds of miles off course until they ran out of fuel and had to bail out. Crozier's openness would have made it impossible for him to maintain a false front for long. And as for the others—Spencer in particular—they all seemed much too ingenuous to be anything other than they appeared. Of course, to the so-phisticated British, all Americans seemed naive and innocent. To that extent, they were much like the Tibetans. They wore their hearts on their sleeves, and were wholly unskilled in the irony, wit, and verbal astuteness that frequently passed for understated cleverness in the many levels of British society.

Sherriff listened to their story, hearing them out and filling in the gaps in his own knowledge. The fact that the airmen had not been scouting a land route across Tibet—or indulging in any other kind of political "stunt"—did little to allay his mounting concerns. Sherriff still worried that the airmen's presence in Lhasa might yet be the cause of further disturbance. But that, he decided, was a problem that could wait until morning.

THE NEXT DAY, THE FIVE AMERICANS WOKE to an English breakfast that was reassuring in both its Western character and its size. Sherriff played the congenial host, showing them around the house, then taking them outside and starting them on what in many respects would be "the strangest part" of their Tibetan experience.

Dekyi-lingka—the name roughly translated as "Garden of Well-being and Happiness"—was a large property owned by the nearby Kundeling Monastery, which had for several years leased it to the British government. It was located a mile out of town, on the western side of Lhasa, and was surrounded by marshes and fields that ran down to the Kyi River. It was also close to the Lingkhor, or pilgrims' route, which circled more than five miles around the outer limits of the city. Pilgrims would shuffle along the Lingkhor, always moving in a clockwise direction, hoping that if they completed the circuit they would gain part of the merit they needed to escape the cycle of birth, life, and death. Many of the pilgrims would prostrate themselves, lying flat on the ground and reaching out with outstretched hands, then standing up and taking the one or two steps needed to bring them to the point their hands had reached—then repeating the process over and over. It could take them days—even weeks—to complete the entire circuit in this painstaking way.

The house itself was a fairly typical—though relatively affluent—Lhasa home, distinguished only by the Union Jack that flew above it.

Two stories high, it was built around a sizeable courtyard, with stables, servant quarters, and a separate kitchen comprising the rest of the square. The house faced west, towards Norbu-lingka, the Dalai Lama's summer palace, which was located in its own grounds further down the Kyi valley. That building could not be seen, but looking east and slightly north, it was possible to glimpse one side of the Potala, half-hidden by another large building perched on top of a rocky outcrop of its own.

The Potala remained an awesome sight, even from this angle, and the five Americans stared at it silently—until Spencer broke the spell by declaring he was glad he did not have the job of cleaning the Potala's windows. McCallum then pointed to the other large building and asked what it was.

That, Sherriff told him, was the Medical College. It sat on top of the Chak-po-ri, or Iron Mountain, and it was where monks were sent if they wanted to learn how to cure the many ills and ailments that afflicted the Tibetan people. Aspiring "doctors," or *amchi*, spent eight years at the College, learning by rote a series of long prayers, spells, and incantations. Tibetans, Sherriff said, knew a little about herbal medicine, but beyond that they were astoundingly ignorant. They had no understanding of where the main organs were in the body; nor did they know what those main organs did. This was in spite of the fact that the Tibetan dead were normally given sky burials, which involved cutting up the bodies and feeding the pieces to circling crows, vultures, and other raptors.

Societies elsewhere, which indulged in gruesome practices like human sacrifice, had learned much from the bodies they cut open. But the Tibetans, even after chopping up bodies for several centuries, had managed to acquire no knowledge at all. They still believed that women's hearts were to be found on the right side of their bodies, in spite of the clear evidence to the contrary.

On the plus side, the poor state of Tibetan medicine had handed the British an opportunity. They had opened a hospital at Dekyi-lingka, which at first had been little more than a barn—a small, square building with an open roof where birds would sit, until they were scared away to prevent their droppings falling onto the patients below. There had been no room for beds in the barn, so the sick and injured had been forced to bring their own tents and pitch them among the trees outside. Now, a new hospital had been built, and had quickly become a major factor in the overall success of the British mission. Its minimal staff could heal cuts, dress wounds, set bones, extract teeth, and fit glasses. It could also give inoculations—the work Doc Bo usually performed—primarily against syphilis and other sexually transmitted diseases.

More impressive than the hospital, however, were the extensive grounds in which Dekyi-lingka had been set. They contained large stands of willows and a magnificent garden, which the Sherriffs had worked long and hard to create. The Sherriffs had, of course, been building on the efforts of Frank Ludlow, their immediate predecessor, who had spent most of his spare time scouring the nearby hills for elusive plants he could cultivate. In the past year, the Sherriffs had doubled the size of the garden, and in the process created what Basil Gould—Sherriff's immediate superior at the British Residency in Sikkim— had described as "a scene which could not have failed to earn a gold medal at a Chelsea Flower Show."

"You should see it in the summer," Sherriff told the airmen. The garden then was full of hollyhocks, marigolds, primulae, irises, peonies, and asters. It also had one or two blossoming peach, walnut, and apple trees—although the apples, Sherriff was forced to admit, were not much bigger than the walnuts.

The Sherriffs had even managed to divert a stream—a tributary of the Kyi River—so that it flowed through part of the garden. Sherriff had constructed a dam, at the side of which he had built a water wheel from old, rusted cigarette tins and two discarded pony-trap wheels that had been brought up to Lhasa from India. The stream was alive with fish, but no one was allowed to catch them, since the Tibetans believed that water was the purest element, so any fish swimming in it must be the temporary homes of departed lamas. To catch the fish would be to bring to an end any hope the lamas might have of attaining immortality.

Nevertheless, Betty Sherriff had been thrilled with the stream. It was, she said, "very pleasant—especially for our two ducks, Tunis and Bizerta."

SHERRIFF LED THE AIRMEN BACK INDOORS and offered them tea and biscuits—in reality, cream crackers, as these were the only kind of "biscuit" it was considered proper to serve. The Americans made themselves at home in the main reception room, munching their biscuits and leafing through out-of-date copies of the *London Times, Illustrated London News* and *Life* magazine. With their second cup of tea, they were served a "special cake" the Sherriffs' Tibetan cook had baked specifically for them— either because he had taken an unusual liking to the Americans, as they were told, or because, as they suspected, he was acting under the maternal instructions of Betty Sherriff.

As they sat around, the airmen could not help feeling there was a surreal air to their new situation—an impression that was further enhanced when the only other Westerner in Lhasa arrived to greet them. This was Reginald Fox, known to the Sherriffs as "Foxy"—an affable, overweight Londoner with an acute case of rheumatoid arthritis and a shock of sandy-colored hair that made him a stand-out among the invariably dark Tibetans.

Fox had been leading an unusual life. He was fourteen years old when the First World War broke out, yet by lying about his age had managed to talk his way into the army, serving his country by riding up and down the trenches in France as a motorcycle messenger. After the war, he moved to Baghdad where he worked in communications. He then joined the Anglo-Indian railway system, before traveling to Lhasa to become part of the first permanent British mission set up by Basil Gould in 1936. After seven years in the city—and now married to a Tibetan (a woman named Nyima who came from the Chumbi valley in the southern part of the country)—Fox had every intention of staying on, serving as the mission's wireless operator.

For their outside communications, Fox said, the British used to rely on a telegraph landline they had strung all the way to Lhasa from Kalimpong in India—a distance of more than four hundred miles. The line had been laid as far as Gyantse at the time of the Younghusband invasion, and was then extended to Lhasa some twenty years later. During the invasion, the line had been a vital link to Younghusband's superiors in India. It had also been vulnerable, since at any time it could easily have been cut by the defending Tibetans. To protect the line, the British let it be known they had laid it down so they could find their way out of the country again; they planned to follow the line back to India. As a result, the Tibetans had done everything they could to preserve the line, believing that if they did not they would never see the backs of their enemy.

Until 1936, the Chinese in Lhasa had maintained a monopoly on wireless links with the outside world, and when they offered the use of their radio to the Tibetans, the Tibetans, rashly and foolishly, agreed— unaware that they were handing China a powerful weapon that would soon be turned against them. The Chinese used their monopoly to issue a stream of misinformation on what was happening inside Tibet; so when the fourteenth Dalai Lama was installed, for example, they let it be known he had been enthroned only with China's blessing, and they later claimed they had been responsible for appointing the Dalai Lama's Regent. When the Chinese press picked up these and other erroneous reports, transmitting them to the rest of the world, the lies and distortions became—for most people—accepted truths.

At that very moment, Fox said, the Tibetans were trying to discover how the Chinese had conveyed one of their more recent and important transmissions. On October 12, Taktra Rinpoche, the Tibetan Regent, had sent a message on behalf of the Dalai Lama, which was intended to offer courteous, but neutral, congratulations to Chiang Kai-shek, who had just been appointed President of the National Government of the Republic of China. Now, it seemed, the message had been radically altered—even rewritten— to make it sound as if the Dalai Lama acknowledged Tibet to be a part of the Chinese republic. And that—most certainly—was *not* what the Dalai Lama had intended to say.

The problem, Fox explained, was that the Tibetans were much too isolated—and too unworldly—to understand the extent of the damage that was being done to their cause. To the British, the Chinese deceit was not a surprise. In their view, the Tibetans had "a great regard for the truth, preferring to procrastinate or keep quiet rather than tell a lie." But the Chinese had "an addiction to make-believe" and "no objection to a useful lie"—so much so that they had managed to win "the ear of the world," as many of "their falsehoods went undenied."

FOX TOOK THE AMERICANS OUTSIDE and showed them the diesel plant that supplied his radio with power. It was strong enough to give him the ability to transmit messages directly to India, so even before the Americans had arrived, he had sent word to the outside world that they were alive. Now he offered to send word to India that the airmen had reached Lhasa and were under the protection of the British mission.

The airmen agreed to Fox's offer, and Crozier and McCallum sat down to compose a suitable message. Then, leaving Spencer to help Fox transmit it, they went with the others to rejoin Sherriff in the main reception room. They wanted to study the map there, so they could plot a possible route home.

They would all have loved to see a C-87 fly up from India and take them back to their base in a couple of hours. The Kyi valley was certainly big and flat enough for a plane to put down, but as Sherriff said, there was no chance that the Tibetan government would let a plane land, and anyway, at an altitude of 12,000 feet, the valley was too high for a plane to be able to take off again. If the airmen were going to get out of Tibet, they would have to do so under their own steam—and that meant traveling overland to India across the barren Tibetan plateau.

Assuming, Sherriff added, that the Tibetans were willing to let them leave.

12

⁓

DOUBLE BILL

THE MAP—THE LARGEST ONE OF TIBET that had ever been drafted—was a byproduct of the Survey of India, which had been chronicling the continent since the late eighteenth century. It hung on a reception room wall, almost from the floor to the ceiling, and it showed in dramatic relief Tibet's many rivers, mountain ranges, and valleys, as well as its few towns and villages. More to the point, as far as the American airmen were concerned, it showed the main pack routes joining the towns and villages together—in particular, a rough trail, trending southwest, which eventually led to the town of Gangtok in the Indian state of Sikkim.

It was the first tangible link that the Americans had seen between where they were and where they wanted to be. The rough trail had a disconcerting number of steep passes along it, and it skirted several peaks that were more than 20,000 feet high. But at least it went all the way to India.

Looking at the map, Crozier was able to grasp something of the geography of the extraordinary country in which they had landed, and to see the route that they had taken to get to Lhasa from Tsetang. The most prominent feature on the map was the Tsangpo River, slashing across the bottom of the map, almost cutting the country in two. The Kyi River, which ran through Lhasa, was a significant river in its own right, but it was still just a tributary of the Tsangpo. It flowed southwest to the confluence; the Tsangpo then flowed east to Tsetang, while the trail the

Americans had taken over Gokar-la ran to the northwest, thereby completing a triangle.

"You circled over the city here," Sherriff told them, tapping a wooden pointer on the outline of Lhasa, "then flew off towards the southeast." Their plane must then have swung round as the airmen prepared to bail out, since they had landed south of the Tsangpo but the plane had crashed on the northern bank. "You were lucky you landed where you did," Sherriff said, "as the Tsangpo valley is one of the few areas in Tibet where you could reasonably expect to find people."

"So how do we get home?" Crozier wanted to know.

"Right. Along this trail here," Sherriff said, tracing the high-level route that ran towards Gangtok. It followed the Kyi River to the confluence with the Tsangpo, then headed south, climbing steeply over a pass and dropping down to a huge lake. It skirted the lake to the west, then again headed south, before turning at a right angle west towards the town of Gyantse. From there, the trail again went south, crossing several more passes before entering a valley that dipped down into the most southerly part of the country, a wedge of land between Sikkim on the west and Bhutan on the east.

The trail was not much better than a mule track, Sherriff said, but it was relatively straightforward to follow. Of course, this was the wrong time of year to be traveling—in fact, the worst possible time, as there was bound to be snow, and the temperatures would fall a long way below zero. "I'm afraid it could be a long and difficult walk," he said.

"Walk?" Crozier asked. He had joined the Air Corps so he would *not* have to walk, and the possibility that he might have to hike all the way from Lhasa to India was not something he wanted to contemplate.

Sherriff smiled. It had long been clear the Americans were hoping to "whistle up a jeep" that would whisk them effortlessly back to their base. "Either that or ride," he said. "Hopefully, you'll have mules."

Spencer, who had joined them, was carefully studying the route they might take. "Are there no cars we can use?" he wanted to know.

"There are three in the whole of Tibet," Sherriff said. "They're at Norbu-lingka."

Two of the cars—both Baby Austins, with number plates "Tibet 1" and "Tibet 2"—had been carried to the country in pieces, as a gift for the thirteenth Dalai Lama; they were later joined by a Dodge. Unfortunately, there were no roads in Tibet, so the Dalai Lama had built a three-mile track that linked his summer palace to his Arsenal; that at least allowed him to motor along and inspect his troops. All three cars had long since run out of gas, and were now up on blocks, languishing beneath dust-sheets somewhere within the palace grounds.

Perram shook his head. He could not believe there was nothing with wheels and an engine in a country that was about the size of Western Europe.

"How long would it take," McCallum asked, "if we are forced to walk?"

"About four weeks," Sherriff said, "under normal conditions." But the airmen would have to travel much faster than that, if they wanted to avoid being trapped in Tibet for the rest of the winter. Their main obstacle—the one that was likely to prevent their escape—was the series of passes they would have to cross. There were six of them—at least, six *major* ones, some of them rising as high as 17,000 feet. And then there was the Nathu-la—the last pass they would come to, marking the border between Tibet and the Indian state of Sikkim. It was not the highest of the passes, but it was the one that received the most snow—sometimes as much as twenty or thirty feet during the course of a winter.

So did the airmen think they could handle that?

Crozier looked around at the others. McCallum was certainly fit enough, having once more resumed his daily regimen of calisthenics, including the fifty push-ups he did on his thumbs. He had also been bolstered by his religious convictions and a newfound belief—since surviving the bailout—that the Virgin Mary would take good care of him, no matter what. As for Spencer, he was reasonably healthy, and unquestionably keen to shake the dust of Tibet from his boots as soon as he could. There was no doubting his commitment to making the journey back to their base. Huffman, however, was a bit of a problem, since he was obviously still in considerable pain. But right from the beginning Huffman had shown an inner resilience that Crozier was sure would see him through. That just left Perram. His feet had recovered—at least to the extent that he could now hobble around—but if he was forced to walk even part of the way, there was a better than even chance he would not be able to make it.

The five men talked the matter over. There was some discussion of leaving Perram behind, but Perram was insistent that if the others went, he would go, too. He was not prepared to remain on his own, even if he could stay at the British mission. Crozier gave his agreement. He did not want to see his crew split up, and it seemed that Perram drew strength from the other airmen, so it would not be fair to leave him to fend for himself.

"We'll manage," Crozier said.

Sherriff nodded. Although he enjoyed the Americans' company, he was still keen to see them depart; he did not want their continuing presence to cause any more trouble.

"Are you sure you're fit enough?" he asked.

"We just want to get back to our base," Crozier said.

"And as soon as we possibly can," Spencer added.

Sherriff nodded again. The real problem, he told them, was not whether they were willing to leave, but whether the Tibetans would agree to let them go. The government in Lhasa still had not accepted that the airmen were harmless Americans who had really been blown hundreds of miles off course.

"Can you help us with that?" Crozier asked.

Sherriff said he would try, promising again to do his best.

SHERRIFF'S DOUBTS ABOUT THE TIBETANS stemmed from the way they made their decisions. They were irrational. As Kung had discovered, they often refused to make any decisions at all, and then when they did, they frequently made them for all the wrong reasons.

When Chinese troops first began to amass on their border, the Tibetans responded, not with force or even diplomacy, but with a religious ceremony that they held in the shadow of the Potala. Effigies of foreign troops were burned on a pyre, along with images of devils, a human heart, a selection of coins, and "a load each of grain, tea, cloths, and silk...." When the Chinese threat continued to mount, the Tibetan government did meet to consider the challenge—but after two days of "prolonged discussions" decided that its best course of action was to consult the state Oracle.

The Oracle—a monk by the name of Nechung Ta Lama—duly went into a trance, and then declared that the Chinese troops would not invade. That seemed to take care of the problem, but to be on the safe side, the Oracle recommended that the Tibetan government offer up additional prayers, this time to the Goddess Maha-Kali. A suitable ceremony was subsequently held, but the Chinese threat did not go away—prompting a frustrated observer, watching the buildup of troops from the safety of London, to note that "the Oracle may be right, but I wish the Tibetans would supplement their prayer by some effective defensive measures."

Instead, they went back to the Oracle, who soon began to hedge his bets. He gave the government "careful answers," and advocated still more prayers. As Sherriff later reported, "a large Tor-gyap procession was held to ward off the danger, similar to the one that was held in the time of the fifth Dalai Lama, when it was said to have been very successful. The main item in the procession was a large edifice built of small sticks, paper, and cloth, some twenty feet high, which was carried through the streets and finally burnt. Inside, was an image, made of dough, of a Chinese bound hand and foot. When the edifice was burnt, the image fell towards Chang, i.e., to the north. This, of course, was said to be a very good sign, as was a loud peel of thunder heard at the moment the edifice was set fire to...."

In spite of his doubts about the Tibetans, Sherriff immediately set off for the Foreign Office, hoping to press the airmen's case. He left the Americans in the care of his wife, who immediately challenged them to a game of table tennis, taking each one on in turn and soundly defeated them all. In her younger days, she had been a keen lawn tennis player, and while in Lhasa had tried to resurrect the "court" that had been leveled in Dekyi-lingka's grounds. At 12,000 feet above sea level, however, the air was so thin that the tennis balls flew around like rockets, so for her outdoor fun Betty had been forced to switch to the more genteel game of croquet. The Tibetans immediately took to the sport—especially the monks, who discovered that "their long robes were wonderful cover for manipulating the ball into a better position."

For his part, Sherriff had taken up basketball, teaching the Tibetans how to play, then switching in winter to the Scottish passion of curling. This latter game was played on the frozen Kyi River, using flattish stones that could easily be found along the shore. Many of the Tibetans became avid fans, and often could be seen out on the river in their robes, feverishly brooming a route for their stones as they encouraged them to slide over the ice towards the "tee."

WHEN SHERRIFF RETURNED TO DEYKI-LINGKA later that day, he brought a mixed report. The bad news, he said, was that the Tibetan government was not prepared to let the airmen leave the capital, as it still harbored too many suspicions about the Americans' intentions and the motives that had brought them into Tibet. The good news was that it had agreed to send three senior members round to the mission so they could see the airmen for themselves. If the Americans were able to convince the government officials that they were, as they said, innocent fliers who had been blown off course, then Sherriff was sure the Tibetan government would help them return to their base in India. The Tibetans were as a rule instinctively helpful, and they had every reason to want any Americans who came to Lhasa to see them that way.

The most important of the three officials, Sherriff said, would be a man named Surkhang Dzasa. He was one of the two leaders of the Tibetan Foreign Office and a powerful figure within Tibetan society. Surkhang had been dealing with foreigners for many years, and although something of an opium addict—renowned in Lhasa as a "man of moods"—he was also one of the people with whom Sherriff most frequently worked. Surkhang would be accompanied by a monk—a man named Liushahr Dzasa Lama—who also served in the Foreign Office; he was younger than Surkhang, and considerably less experienced.

The third man, Sherriff said, was a Tibetan named Kusho Chango Pa—better known by the more musical name of Ringang. He would be considerably easier for the Americans to get along with, as he was known to enjoy a cup of chang, and he spoke excellent English. As a child, Ringang had been sent to England so he could be given the supposed benefits of a British upbringing and education. He had attended Rugby, a well-known public school—a term that meant, in the arcane terminology of the British education system, that it was in fact a somewhat exclusive *private* school.

Altogether, four Tibetan boys had been shipped to England to see if a measure of "Englishness" could be drummed into their skulls. They had been part of an ongoing, cross-cultural experiment, which the British had been conducting for several centuries—one that at various times had seen North American Indians, South Pacific islanders, Tierra del Fuego stone-age tribesmen, and even the occasional African cannibal, strolling along the Strand, clutching an umbrella and dressed to the nines in whatever the latest fashion happened to be, whether beaver skin hats, sweeping tails, or glossy white spats. In most instances, the experiment had proven a dismal failure, condemning its subjects to lifelong rejection by both of the cultures they were supposed to straddle.

For three of the Tibetans sent to England, the results had not been good. But for Ringang—the youngest and brightest of the four—the strange education had proven a boon. After his formal schooling at Rugby, he had returned to Tibet, but then nine years later went back to England to train as an electrical engineer. That might have made him overqualified in a country that, upon his second return to Tibet, had no electricity and no engineering, but Ringang turned that deficiency to his advantage by designing, building, and then running a hydro-electric generating station, which, in 1935, brought the first power to parts of Lhasa.

Ringang was also able to exploit his excellent English by serving as the Tibetan government's main translator when it had to deal with Britain and other English-speaking nations. As a result, he had secured a prominent position close to the top of Tibetan society, as well as a sprawling estate outside Lhasa and two cheerful wives who were sisters.

When that afternoon the three government officials arrived at Dekyi-lingka, Sherriff showed them into the main reception room. As instructed by Sherriff, the five airmen stood up, bowed politely, and then moved from guest to guest—first to Surkhang, then to Liushahr, and finally to Ringang. In front of each one, they bowed again, then held out a silk scarf, which Sherriff draped over their outstretched arms. The scarves, or *kathaks*, were thought by the Tibetans to bring good luck. As each of the officials took a scarf, he ritually replaced it with one of his own. Everyone then sat down, while servants brought round bowls of yak-butter tea and a selection of cream-cracker biscuits.

The three Tibetans were immaculately turned out. Their rich clothes—as intricately embroidered as peacock feathers—were clean and pressed, reminding Spencer of what he imagined was the dandified finery of an eighteenth-century European court. They spoke volumes about their wearers' status and power, and they made the Americans, in their ill-fitting garments, feel like poor and slovenly country cousins.

Surkhang Dzasa—a thin, elegant man with a wispy moustache and refined cheek bones that were in sharp contrast to his boxer's broken nose—wore a yellow silk robe secured by a crimson sash, which looped around his narrow waist. His hair was long, black, and plaited, and he had a turquoise jewel dangling from the lobe of one of his prominent ears. Liushahr Dzasa Lama was dressed in a scarlet robe that was partially covered by a short, yellow jacket. He peered at the Americans through a pair of thick-framed glasses, his close-cropped hair accentuating the length of his narrow, oval face. Ringang—the most junior of the three—wore a shiny purple robe and a yellow hat, which to the Americans, seemed perched on his head like a carefully balanced bowl of custard.

The five airmen carefully told their story, making a point of explaining why McCallum had a Chinese flag pasted onto the back of his jacket. It was not intended to be a sign of unity with the Chinese, but merely an appeal for help if the airmen had been forced to bail out over Chinese—as opposed to Tibetan—territory. The airmen had made a mistake by showing the jacket in Tibet—a mistake they had only recently come to appreciate.

Unknown to the Americans, their credibility had been greatly enhanced by a report that had just reached Lhasa, saying a plane had been heard on the night of the crash, close to the spot where the Americans said they had bailed out. The report helped corroborate their story, since it confirmed the route they said they had taken.

After several hours, Sherriff showed the Tibetans out, then came back with the news the Americans had been hoping to hear.

"You mean we're free to leave?" Crozier said.

Sherriff nodded. "As soon as you're fit enough."

The airmen wanted to set out for India as soon as they could. They figured they would need two more days to recover their strength, but Sherriff suggested they wait one more. He knew the passes would soon be closed, but an extra day seemed unlikely to make the difference between reaching India and being trapped in Tibet. In fact, leaving sooner might even harm the airmen's chances of success, since, in Sherriff's opinion, they were not yet ready to make the journey. The Americans were far more depleted than they cared to admit, and they had no real idea of the dangers and hardships they still had to face. To make matters worse, Huffman, for one, seemed to be coming down with some kind of fever.

The Americans gave way and agreed to leave as Sherriff suggested, on December 19. But then they received word that the Tibetan government wanted to give them a parting gift, which would not be ready before December 20. Apparently, the Foreign Office was insisting the airmen stay at least until then—so once again the Americans gave in.

At least, Sherriff said, the added delay would give them more time to rest—and a chance to sample the best of the mission's entertainment.

THAT EVENING, SPENCER AGAIN FOUND HIMSELF in a bizarre situation that bordered on the surreal. It happened soon after dinner. The meal had been cleared away, and the five Americans were relaxing with their hosts. For the Sherriffs and Fox, the airmen's company was a welcome change. Ordinarily, as the only resident Westerners in Lhasa, they would have enjoyed a quiet meal, followed by a game of three-handed bridge. The presence of the Americans gave them a new interest—while the airmen for their part wanted to know what life in Lhasa was really like.

Sherriff told them the Tibetan capital was out of bounds, at least as far as they were concerned. They had already caused disruption enough, and anyway, he added, the airmen had seen most of Lhasa, just by riding across it.

It was a small city, he said, with a population of about twenty thousand. Its main focus was the Jokhang on Barkhor Square, the most sacred building, not just in Lhasa but in all of Tibet, as it was home to one of the Buddha's most-honored effigies. The statue had been brought to the capital in the seventh century by one of the wives of Songsten Gampo, the great leader credited with introducing the Buddhist religion into the country, and was now in an inner sanctum of the Jokhang.

"Along with an enormous number of mice," Betty said. "They quite overrun the place."

"As do the beggars," Sherriff added.

Beyond that, the main features of Lhasa were the Potala and the Medical College on Chak-po-ri, which the Americans had already seen. So perhaps, Sherriff continued, instead of exploring the town, the airmen might like to see something a little different—a secret weapon, which the British had used to gain influence with the Tibetan people.

The Americans agreed. The furniture was moved off to one side; a screen and projector were brought out, and within a matter of minutes, the main reception room had been converted into a small, but adequately functioning, movie theater.

IT WAS FRANK LUDLOW WHO HAD INTRODUCED the cinema to the Tibetans, arranging afternoon showings "with tea and drinks in the garden in the evening." At first, he merely wanted to give the Tibetans a view of the world outside, so he began with newsreels that were intended to be straightforward accounts of the way the war was progressing. Inevitably, the "shorts" had a tendency to focus on Allied successes, Allied resources, and the absolute certainty of Allied victory, so they were little better than blatant propaganda. But as such, they were highly effective.

The main problem in that regard was the Tibetans' astonishing—and seemingly willful—ignorance. "They know nothing—absolutely nothing—of the outside world or what is happening in it," Ludlow lamented. When newsreels of Allied victories in Africa were shown, their impact was greatly diminished by the fact that the Tibetans had "only the vaguest notion of what and where Africa is."

The impact of the film shorts was also reduced by the unruly behavior of the monks. At one showing, Ludlow reported, there were "numerous gate-crashers—chiefly monks—and I had to be my own policeman and expel undesirables. A few panes of glass were broken by the crowd surging in at the entrance. Finally quiet was restored when I promised to give a separate show after our guests had seen the films."

Ludlow never had trouble filling the sixty-place cinema, especially after he began mixing his newsreels with films depicting such events as the Hendon Air Pageant, Changing of the Guard at Buckingham Palace, and King George V's Jubilee Procession. Attendance took another step up after Sherriff arrived. He began screening films of the Tibetans themselves, which he had taken with his own shaky camera. The Tibetans would roar with laughter whenever they saw one of their own on the screen, gleefully drawing attention to unfortunate expressions or pointing out physical defects they never would have mentioned in real life.

But the attendance really hit a peak with the showings of films featuring Charlie Chaplin or Mickey Mouse. At such times, the cinema would be filled to overflowing, every space jammed with shaven-headed monks in purple robes, collectively exuding the musty odor of stale sweat and rancid butter that seemed to follow them around like their own shadows. The monks would sit crammed in rows or wedged in the corners, rocking with laughter at Chaplin's slapstick or Mickey's and Goofy's cartoon capers.

The Tibetans loved the movies, especially the comedies, which appealed to their childlike sense of humor. They also loved the backgrounds and settings, which appealed to their sense of wonder. They would stare open-mouthed at the city streets, at the buildings. At those skyscrapers! Those cars! The trams! Trains! And that jitterbug!

But their all-time favorite was a heart-tugging drama starring Rin-tin-tin, the loyal German Shepherd. The Tibetans took every scene to heart, and no matter how many times they had watched the film, it would reduce them to tears whenever the doggy hero suffered a temporary setback. The film's five reels lasted a total of one-and-a-half hours—and the British, who had been forced to screen it dozens of times, were heartily sick of every one.

SHERRIFF OFFERED THE AIRMEN THE RUN of his collection and they chose a comedy starring Laurel and Hardy. So that night, after dinner, Spencer found himself sitting on a comfortable sofa, a British major beside him holding hands in the dark with his wife, and an overweight Londoner perched at the far end. A projector whirred noisily behind him, and a screen in front flickered in grainy, black and white shadows, as Stan Laurel beat Oliver Hardy over the head or kicked him hard in the shins, Crozier meanwhile laughing "until he cried," and all of them thinking how appropriate it was to hear Hardy's catchphrase, "What a fine mess you've got us into."

13

———— ⊗⊗⊗ ————

R.S.V.P.

THE FOLLOWING DAY BROUGHT A NEW CRISIS. The plan called for the Americans to leave Lhasa on December 20, but before they could depart they had to comply with several diplomatic formalities. So that morning—December 17—they hosted brief visits from the representatives of Nepal and Bhutan, both of whom, besides satisfying their curiosity, offered to help the Americans in any way they could. In the afternoon, the airmen discovered that Sherriff planned a special reception in their honor, since an event such as their arrival in Lhasa could not, apparently, go unmarked—in spite of the problems it had already caused. And the only way to do that, the Americans learned, was to have a party.

Life for the average Tibetan may have been hard, brutal, and short—a basic existence scratched from a harsh and unforgiving land—but for the Tibetan elite, perched right on top of the social heap, life was rich, elegant, and relaxed. For the most part, it was centered on gargantuan meals and elaborate parties.

And the Tibetan elite did love to party. They liked to dress up in fine clothes—in richly embroidered silks, finely shaped hats, sparkling jewelry, and brightly colored sashes and scarves—and then gather together for lunch, dinner, tea, a picnic, or a party. Under Western influence, they had recently adopted ballroom dancing, although a few of the more avant-garde had taken up the Palais Glide and even the Boomps-a-Daisy—the former a lively line dance, and the latter a raucous music hall favorite, which required the participants to bump hips and bottoms.

A small party could last four or five hours—or maybe stretch to eight or nine. Larger ones could continue for days. And if the Tibetans were really in the mood, they would keep a good party going for as long as a month. That was too much for the Sherriffs, who felt compelled to restrict their social engagements to lunches only. But even the lunches could be a challenge, as they often began in mid-morning and dragged on until dark. To make matters worse, the various parties were almost always attended by the same group of people—a tight, clannish, incestuous, and ultimately claustrophobic bunch that included members of the National Assembly, Kashag, and the Foreign Office; representatives of the various foreign governments, principally the British and the Chinese; as well as the rich and the powerful in the upper strata of Lhasa society—the same group of people going round and round, sometimes amusing but often tedious, creating what the Sherriffs soon considered to be tiresome, drawn-out, time-wasting affairs.

Rarely did anything new enliven the events. The same people observed the same protocols, held the same conversations, told the same stories and anecdotes, and endlessly played the same games. And always as an undertone, there were the rumors and gossip and backbiting comments as the attendees jostled for position, trying to improve their social and political rankings while at the same time extracting the tidbits of genuine intelligence they could turn to personal advantage.

"There is singular little news this week," Ludlow had reported in one of his regular letters to his superiors, "except that there has been an epidemic of lunches and dinners. I have wasted three out of the past seven days attending these functions." Sherriff found much the same when he took over the British mission. "This has been rather a trying week of parties," he wrote, just before the airmen arrived. And a month later he again reported, "This has been a week in which nearly all our time has been taken up in attending or giving parties...."

Even the lunches to which the Sherriffs confined themselves could prove a trial. At one such event—hosted by Surkhang Dzasa in his home—the menu, in both Tibetan and English, had boasted eleven courses: "sweet peaches, fish stomach with milk, Chinese bacon and bread, sea fish, sea snake, fried chicken, dumplings stuffed with meat, sea slugs, black fish, yellow flower soup, and rice pudding"—and on the side, bowls of Gyatu noodles, along with copious quantities of chang, complemented by "Enos Fruit Salt added to the beer to make it fizz." It was a far cry from the tsampa and turnips that were the mainstays of the ordinary Tibetans' diet.

At another party the Sherriffs attended, they were invited for dinner as well as for lunch. True to their practice, they agreed to the lunch but declined the dinner—only to find that when they arrived, their hosts had decided to serve the dinner alongside the lunch. "Both meals at the same time!" Betty exclaimed. "A terrific challenge!"

In return, the Sherriffs were expected to host lunches of their own. These were held in an upstairs room at Dekyi-lingka—one that was brighter than the reception room below, with a large veranda overlooking the grounds. It could accommodate up to seventy guests. On these occasions, the Sherriffs were aided by an enthusiastic cook—a Kazak named Daud—who had built an oven in the kitchen that was large enough to roast a sheep. Daud—dressed in a chef's hat and apron, and wielding a knife as big as a machete—would serve the animal "on a kind of stretcher," while going round the room like an Austrian yodeler, slapping his thighs, chest, shoulders, and buttocks in an effort to discover "which cut the guests would like."

These meals were not entirely without their problems: "A luncheon given in honour of the Kashag passed off quite successfully," Ludlow reported, after one such event, "except the servants served the ice cream on hot dishes." The menu that day had been "hors d'oeuvres, tomato soup, mixed meats in Aspic, roast sheep *a la Simpson's in the Strand*, Turkestan pillau, American pie *a la mode*, vanilla ice, coffee and liqueurs...."

A cinema showing had followed the lunch.

To honor the airmen's arrival in Lhasa, Sherriff had organized what to the Tibetans was a small party, held outside on the Dekyi-lingka lawn. Normally, outdoor events were planned for the summer, when large tents would be set up and chairs and rugs brought out from the house for guests to sit on. But they could also be held in the middle of winter, when the sky was clear and the sun appeared, raising the temperature to a comfortable level, at least for a few hours in the early afternoon.

As usual, Sherriff had invited senior members of the Tibetan government, and as was their custom, they all arrived late. As a military man, Sherriff was never able to understand why the Tibetans could never appear anywhere on time. It was, of course, hard in Lhasa for anyone to know what time it actually was, and there was no real reason why anyone should care. But someone, apparently, had built a sundial in the Potala—or possibly it was a clock; no one seemed to really know. Either way, the Tibetans would claim that their "clock" had a tendency to "jump back suddenly," and that was why they were always late. To Sherriff it seemed an unusually lame excuse.

Along with the Tibetans, Sherriff had invited representatives of the Nepalese and Bhutanese governments whom the Americans had met that morning. He had also invited the leading members of the Chinese community. These included Dr. Kung, plus twenty other Chinese nationals, all of whom had agreed to attend.

The Chinese arrived as a group—an organized contingent that as soon as it appeared issued an invitation of its own. The Chinese wanted the five Americans—and, of course, both the Sherriffs—to join them in yet another celebration, this time a lunch followed by dinner, which they planned to hold the following day at the Chinese mission in Barkhor Square. The invitation, formally written and formally presented, was signed by all the important Chinese groups in Lhasa: "the Chinese Resident Office of the Commission on Mongolian and Tibetan affairs; the Chinese radio station; the Chinese school of Lhasa; the Chinese meteorological station; the Peking merchants of Lhasa; the Yunnan merchants in Lhasa; the Szechuan merchants in Lhasa; and the Chinese Mohammedans in Lhasa."

Sherriff had anticipated the invitation, since that was the way things were done; each event triggered another in an endless chain reaction. He felt an obligation to accept. The Americans were still planning to leave Lhasa on December 20, so a party the following day—December 18—could not easily be turned down. As soon as Sherriff agreed to attend, Kung pinned him in a corner and asked if he, Sherriff, would be so kind as to arrange with the Tibetan government for a squad of police to escort the Americans as they traveled across town to Barkhor Square—and to guard the Chinese mission while the Americans were dining inside. Sherriff, who had also anticipated *that* request, assured Kung that he had already taken the necessary steps. He did not want a repeat of the earlier trouble any more than Kung did.

Sherriff's own party then got properly under way, with the Americans once again finding themselves at the center of attention. They were forced to tell their story "over and over" to the eager Tibetans, who reacted "just like kids" in the simple, endearing way in which they listened and responded to every twist and turn.

The party was going along "with a swing" and there was a "general good feeling among all," when a letter arrived from the Tibetan Foreign Office. Sherriff read it and immediately took the Americans aside. The Tibetans, he told them, had had a change of heart. Gone was the request that the airmen stay in Lhasa until December 20 so they could receive a parting gift. The government now wanted them out of the country, and was insisting they leave no later than the following morning. If they did not, the letter stated, then the Tibetan government could not be responsible for the Americans' safety.

Sherriff knew that without the Tibetan government to protect them, the airmen could be in danger, so he advised them to leave the capital as soon as they could. The government's letter, Sherriff said, promised that Chang-ngo-pa Kusho, a member of the Tibetan Foreign Office, would arrive at Dekyi-lingka within the hour, bringing with him the passports the Americans would need to travel across Tibet, as well as the mules and a few supplies the government had earlier agreed to provide. Chang-ngo-pa would also bring a small gift to help the airmen on their way, but that should not delay their departure.

It was an unexpected reversal, and an astonishing display of efficiency from the normally prevaricating Tibetans—and that in itself spoke volumes about their newfound resolve and determination. Although it offered no explanation, Sherriff was sure that the Tibetan government—which only the previous day had been insistent that the Americans stay on in Lhasa—now wanted them to leave, because it was not prepared to see them again entertained by Dr. Kung and the hated Chinese.

Kung was livid when he heard the news. It was not the place of the Tibetan government to say when the Americans should—or should not—leave the country. If anyone told the Americans to go, it would be the

Chinese, represented by Dr. Kung. He angrily "refused to consider that either his party be put off or that the Americans should leave on December 18th." China was not prepared, under any circumstances, to back down in the face of Tibet.

Sherriff tried to calm Kung down, stressing that if he protested too strongly to the Tibetans—as he was heatedly threatening to do—then he would be committing a "folly of the worst kind."

But nothing Sherriff said would change Kung's mind, and Sherriff could see another crisis looming—one that threatened to disrupt the status quo that the British were trying so hard to preserve.

At one point, Kung insisted that he and Sherriff should, right then and there, go round to each of the Shapes' houses and demand that the Tibetan government reconsider. The Tibetans must be made to see that they had to let the Americans stay—at least until Kung's party. It was a wholly irrational and unworkable suggestion, reflecting Kung's mounting anger rather than his normally astute judgment. The Tibetan government did not operate in that way—and besides, Kung was still persona non grata as far as the Tibetans were officially concerned. Most likely, they would refuse to talk to him, heightening his rage still further.

After several hours of fierce discussion—it was now past seven o'clock in the evening. and Sherriff's own party had all but fallen apart—Kung still refused to be placated. Sherriff finally brought the argument to an end by agreeing to talk, that evening, to Surkhang Dzasa. At all costs, he wanted to avoid a complete breakdown in Tibetan-Chinese relations. He ordered a pony to be saddled up and rode across town to Surkhang's house, where for more than two hours, until nearly ten o'clock, he tried to persuade Surkhang—and Chang-ngo-pa Kusho who also joined them—to let the Americans remain in Lhasa at least for another day.

Surkhang refused. It was not China that entertained foreigners in Tibet; that was a prerogative held by the Tibetan government in Lhasa. Sherriff tried to show Surkhang just how much Tibet might be risking if it continued to provoke the Chinese. He made no progress, however, until he resorted to a mild extension of the truth. The airmen, he said, were in a generally poor state of health. Perram's feet were still frostbitten, and Huffman—who was already suffering from a broken shoulder—

had now started to run a fever. The Americans were too sick to travel the following morning. They needed to rest for at least another day.

It was that claim that won him the day. Surkhang relented—even though he had seen the airmen himself the previous day, and knew they had all attended Sherriff's party. He said he would talk to all the members of the Kashag early the next morning. But he was still not willing to let the Americans attend an event hosted by Kung.

Sherriff had a solution ready for that problem, too. He suggested that he lend the Chinese the upstairs room at Dekyi-lingka, so they could hold their party there. That way, the Americans would not have to leave the British mission, and no one in Lhasa would know who was hosting the party. It was an inspired idea, and Surkhang could see it was a clever way out. He agreed to put that proposal to the Kashag, too.

Sherriff then returned to Kung and explained the outline of the agreement he hoped he had reached. After "some grumblings," Kung conceded it was a reasonable compromise that he could accept.

The next day, Surkhang visited all four members of the Kashag, and at ten o'clock in the morning Chang-ngo-pa Kusho appeared at the British mission with "an extremely kind message." The Americans could stay one more day as Sherriff had requested. Sherriff immediately sent word to Kung, and that evening about twelve Chinese appeared at Dekyi-lingka to take part in "a long and rather tiring dinner." Everyone seemed to recover their spirits—especially Kung, who had been saved from losing too much face—and the evening ended with no further trouble.

To the bewildered Americans, caught in the center of what they could see was a political storm, the issue of the party seemed a trifling affair. But it was clear that they had become a football to be kicked from country to country, as each one tried to gain an advantage over another. It was also clear that behind the scenes, Tibet was a powder keg waiting to explode. It made sense for the Americans to get out as quickly as they could before something happened to spark it off.

14

---∽∽∽---

THE LAST WORD

AT LAST THE AIRMEN WERE READY TO LEAVE. They were grateful for the time they had spent at Dekyi-lingka and for the chance to recover from the physical hardships they had endured since their bailout. Lhasa had given them a much-needed respite. At the same time, it had revealed a deeply rooted sarcoma of political turmoil they were eager to leave behind. With each passing day, they were also becoming increasingly aware of the pressing need to get out of Tibet before the snows set in, trapping them in for the rest of the winter. It was, therefore, with a sense of release as well as urgency that they made their final preparations for a journey they knew would test them to the limit.

For his own reasons as well as theirs, Sherriff had done everything possible to get the Americans out of town as soon as he could. In record time, he had helped them secure the transportation, food, and other provisions they would need to get through to the border. At his urging, the Tibetan government had come through on its promise to give them mules to ride, and to carry their various supplies. And it had promised a guide and military escort to protect them from the numerous bandits who lurked in the hills.

Equally important, the Tibetan Foreign Office had issued the Americans with internal passports. Tibetan law required village officials to give food and shelter to foreign travelers passing through their towns—but only if those travelers had the necessary documentation. If they did not, then Tibetan law prohibited anyone from offering them help. It was a simple, yet highly effective, way of controlling the movement of undesirables around the country. For any foreigners, independent travel was out of the question, as it was seldom possible to carry everything needed on a long journey—and there was no way any traveler could live off the land, especially in the middle of winter.

As a parting gift, the Tibetan government gave the Americans 620 rupees. That, plus the 655 rupees already received from the Chinese community, gave the airmen a sizeable sum. But in Sherriff's view, it was still not enough for the airmen to complete their journey, so the night before their departure, he lent the Americans 5,000 rupees, which he gave to Crozier in a heavy wooden chest. The rupees came as silver coins, since paper money had little value outside Lhasa. Most Tibetans were unable to read the numbers on the notes, and among those who could, there were many who could not accept that a piece of paper had value—especially if that value was said to increase by a factor of ten, no less, simply by virtue of adding a zero on to the end.

Crozier's first payment out of the wooden chest was to Sana Ullah, to cover the cost of the airmen's stay in Tsetang. Ullah read out each item on the lengthy bill he had prepared, while Sherriff, after slipping a sheet of paper into his rickety typewriter, pecked out an English translation. He headed his list "Miscellaneous expenditure incurred for the American airmen" and in neat columns typed the items for which Ullah asked to be paid: hats, socks, tea, sugar, candles, potatoes, vegetables, paper, fees for the boatmen—and, right at the end, six matches the Americans had used to light their dusty cigarettes.

The total came to 1,518 sangs and 6 shos, which Sherriff equated to 506 rupees—nearly 40 British pounds or about 160 American dollars. Crozier paid that amount, then added almost the same again as a generous and meaningful tip. He not only felt that he and his crew owed Ullah their lives, but he also wanted the word to spread that helping Americans was a rewarding venture. Sherriff dated the list—"the 18th December 1943"—and gave it to Crozier as a receipt.

Crozier also set aside another 188 rupees, which Kung had told him would cover the costs that he had incurred on behalf of the airmen. Crozier left that sum with Sherriff to pass along at a later date. Both he and Sherriff were aware that the clothes the Chinese had provided were too thin and threadbare to protect them from the rigors of winter. So Crozier accepted another batch of the warm clothing, which Sherriff had collected—fur hats, long fur coats, and leather boots that were so shapeless they could fit either foot. He promised to return the hats and coats at a later date, but agreed with Sherriff to keep the boots as souvenirs.

For his part, McCallum volunteered to pack away his leather jacket.

ON THE MORNING OF DECEMBER 19—one day earlier than they had originally planned—the five Americans gathered in the courtyard of Dekyi-lingka to meet their Tibetan guide and military escort. Five mules were led from the stables for them to ride, and six more were brought out to carry their supplies. The mules were small but strong, and apparently placid. They also appeared well looked after. But under the blankets that covered their backs, the mules all had deep, white scars caused by the crude, wooden saddles they were forced to bear. The Americans chose the least-scarred animals for them to ride—not realizing that the many sacks and boxes of supplies and provisions, which were waiting to be loaded, would all be carried by just two of the other six mules. The other mules were intended for their Tibetan companions.

Then their guide stepped forward to be introduced. A wrinkled Tibetan of indeterminate years, he had traveled to India several times and was therefore able to speak a few words of English. While in India, he had visited a dentist, and there been fitted with a prominent gold tooth that gleamed whenever he flashed a smile. Spencer immediately nicknamed the man "Fort Knox," after the bullion depository in Kentucky where the United States government hoarded much of its gold.

The military escort then arrived, consisting of just two Tibetans—both soldiers, apparently—who were dressed, like the airmen, in fur hats, long fur coats, and shapeless boots. Each of the soldiers was armed with an ancient rifle and a long sword, but apart from that they were as different from each other as Mutt and Jeff. The taller one seemed active enough, but his companion—a stocky man, barely five feet tall—was considerably hampered in his movements by his sword. It dragged along the ground behind him, leaving a furrow in the dust wherever he walked.

His mule was also small, but he still had trouble getting into the saddle. He was too short to mount from the side, so had to be hoisted over the back by his stronger and taller companion. Watching the two of them mount up each morning became a daily source of much-needed amusement for the Americans.

The two soldiers—dubbed by the Americans "Rain" and "Shine" to reflect their differing personalities—were expected to ward off the bandits. Rain, the shorter of the two, and Shine did little to reassure the airmen, since in the event of an attack, their swords would have been useless and their rifles would almost certainly have jammed. The rifles were clearly pre-war—but as Spencer remarked it was difficult to tell which war. The airmen found themselves looking ahead to their journey with "a great deal of trepidation."

Their fourth and final companion was a Hindustani-speaking Tibetan who had been seconded by the Sherriffs to serve as the Americans' cook. He came complete with packets of tea and tins of cream crackers, as well as yak-skin sacks of rice and flour and a metal container of milk. He also brought butter, peas for the mules, and a live sheep that he planned to convert into mutton along the way. The cook was a jolly, "roly-poly type" with a name the Americans could not pronounce—so he became "Duncan Hines," after the restaurant critic and author, who had given his name to a line of Procter and Gamble baking goods.

THE PARTY SET OFF AT MID-MORNING, in full daylight so the people of Lhasa could see them go. Sherriff rode along with them, leading them over a bridge west of the Potala, then heading out of town through the western gate where Younghusband had entered some forty years before.

Sherriff planned to accompany the men for two or three miles and then return to Dekyi-lingka. But when he reached the point where he intended to leave them, he found an unwelcome surprise waiting in ambush. The Chinese were there. Kung had ridden out of town earlier that morning and set up another marquee. He was still determined to have the final word, and was hoping to offer the airmen one last taste of his hospitality.

Sherriff tried to hide his annoyance—as did the five Americans. They were anxious to put some miles behind them, and did not need another delay. Reluctantly, they climbed off their mules and followed Sherriff inside the tent, sitting down to what proved to be a blessedly light meal. It seemed that Kung did not want to extend the event, as he was, once again, making his point just by having the Americans there.

As soon as they could, the airmen rose to take their leave. As they prepared to mount up, Kung presented them with yet another gift—two bottles of South African brandy and another cash sum of 50 dotses, equivalent to about 830 rupees. Crozier stashed the brandy with the other supplies, and added the money to his wooden chest.

Sherriff rode a short distance with them, then warmly shook the Americans' hands. As *his* parting gift, he handed Crozier a small, folding map, which crudely outlined their intended route. After wishing the Americans a safe and uneventful journey, he then turned his pony round and headed back towards Lhasa.

Later that day, Sherriff would sit down at his rickety typewriter to compile a full report of the Americans' visit. "The whole week," he wrote, "has been taken up with matters to do with the American airmen.... The attitude of the Tibetan Government has been friendly but suspicious.... The attitude of the Chinese has been what one might perhaps expect.... They never once, from beginning to end, approached the Tibetan Government... and although Dr. Kung personally promised me any information he could gather, he never gave me any. This I did not consider too friendly, especially as I had sent a doctor to attend to what we both expected to be Chinese airmen...."

Sherriff thought the incident of the Americans' visit was over. But even as he was signing his name to his report, the Tibetan government was planning one last attempt to turn the airmen's appearance in the country to its advantage. It wanted to use the Americans' arrival to bring the United States government onto its side in the mounting struggle against the Chinese.

SHERRIFF HAD SAID HIS FAREWELLS to the Americans in sight of the monastery of Drepung. It was the largest monastery in the world, with a population that sometimes approached 10,000 monks, and as the airmen rode past it they could see its countless, whitewashed buildings, scattering the hillside off to their right like so many sprinkled rice grains. At the foot of the slope leading up to the monastery, they passed through a community of butchers, who supplied Drepung—and much of Lhasa—with fresh-slaughtered meat. The killing of animals was forbidden by the Buddhist religion, but the eating of meat was not. The Tibetans had sidestepped this contradiction by creating a lowly group of social outcasts, who handled their butchering for them.

As the Americans settled into their journey, they quickly realized how sheltered they had been while staying at Dekyi-lingka. When they had left the mission that morning, the sky had been an unfathomable blue, the air crisp and invigorating. But now a stiff wind was blowing, the sky growing dark, and they could feel the temperature beginning to fall.

Their route took them along the dusty valley of the Kyi River. Scores of streams plaited their way across the plain, leaving isolated islands of pebbles and rock. Five miles on, the airmen rode to the top of a ridge and looking back were able to see the two outcroppings of rock—one for the Potala, the other for the Medical College—which marked the site of Lhasa. It was their last view of the Forbidden City.

The trail continued to wend its way alongside the river, climbing over rocky spurs and meandering through solitary groves of trees that shook and shivered in the wind. Out in the open, drifts of sand leapt into life, performing a kind of frenzied dance, before sinking back onto the ground when the wind let go and swept on by. As the day wore on, the wind grew stronger and the air became thick and clouded with dust.

In one settlement the Americans rode through, the people lived in hovels or in caves. A few of the inhabitants emerged from their shelters to watch the airmen go by. Their dirty faces and tattered clothes were a sharp reminder that the Americans were back in another world. Crozier turned up his collar and lowered his head against the wind. He was determined to push on that day as far as he possibly could. He had set a tough schedule. The airmen had to cover some four hundred miles before they reached Gangtok, the capital of the Indian state of Sikkim. As Sherriff had said, that was a journey that normally took about four weeks. But the airmen planned to complete it in two. Two hundred miles a week meant thirty miles a day. Every day. On mules that if pushed might be able to lumber along at a pace not much faster than that of a man. That, in turn, meant a daily routine of eight, nine, even ten hours spent in the saddle.

Earlier, Crozier had been most concerned about Perram, but now he realized he was much more worried about Huffman. Huffman's shoulder was still causing him pain, and his fever—or flu—seemed to be getting worse. As he rode along—working out times and calculating distances— Crozier couldn't help thinking that he, too, was coming down with some kind of fever. For the first time since ordering his crew to bail out, he was forced to acknowledge the seriousness of the journey they were now undertaking. Perhaps, after all, it would have been better to have stayed in Lhasa, waiting out the winter in the relative comfort of Dekyi-lingka.

WITH DAYLIGHT FADING, they stopped in the village of Chushul, a collection of mud-brick huts built on a ledge of rock near the confluence of the Kyi and Tsangpo rivers. Fort Knox found them accommodation—a blackened room above the stables where they tethered their mules—and they settled in for the night. After the clean beds and crisp sheets of Dekyi-lingka, the grimy blankets spread out on the floor were less than appealing, but the airmen had ridden more than thirty miles that day and they were all saddle-sore and weary. It was a relief just to lie flat and drop off to sleep.

The next morning they left early, passing the ruins of two forts that once had helped guard the approach to Lhasa. They followed the course of the Tsangpo—heading upstream—on a trail carved into a cliff. Painted Buddhas on the rock face above impassively watched them as they rode by.

Where the river narrowed, the trail took them down to a shingle beach. A flat-bottomed boat, used as a ferry, had been pulled on to the shore, its vertical, wooden sides making it look like an open coffin. Crozier started towards it, but Fort Knox called him back, pointing instead to an oval coracle, or *kowa*, that Crozier hadn't noticed. Crozier looked at it, then at the wide sweep of the fast-running Tsangpo. Fort Knox had to be joking. There was no way the Americans were going to cross a river this size in a coracle.

But Rain, Shine, and Duncan Hines were already unloading the mules, and with the help of two boatmen, were packing the coracle with the supplies. Crozier walked over to take a closer look. The other airmen were standing around, and like Crozier were unable to believe that anyone would be crazy enough to challenge a river the size of the Tsangpo in what, in essence, was a few yak hides stitched together with leather thongs and loosely stretched over a willow frame. The stitching itself had created enough holes to sink the craft—although someone had tried to plug the holes with what looked like solidified animal fat.

When all the supplies had been placed on board—near one end, which passed for a bow—Fort Knox, Rain, and Shine scrambled in, signaling the Americans to do the same. They looked at one another, then gingerly climbed in, crouching as low as they could to keep the boat stable. Duncan Hines joined them, dragging his sheep; then came the two boatmen and a small goat that seemed to be part of the crew. The sheep and the goat huddled together, both bleating loudly, as one of the boatmen grabbed an oar and pushed off. His companion had meanwhile strung the mules onto a rope tied to their reins. He, too, climbed on board, pulling the mules into the water, forcing them to swim.

The coracle—with its load of eleven people, two animals, and the many sacks and boxes of food, money, and other supplies—rode surprisingly high on the water. It seemed relatively stable, too. It would easily tip if its load shifted, but with everyone in place and keeping still, it could be controlled by just one man. The river carried it slowly downstream, as the oarsman paddled towards the main current. But once there, the boat's motion became entirely different.

The coracle bent and twisted, causing the airmen to cling onto the sides. The oarsman appeared surprisingly relaxed, but he was unable to keep the boat moving in a straight line. It spun in circles as if caught in a vortex, tangling the rope that was holding the mules. Water slopped in, and it was easy to imagine the coracle capsizing with all on board being tossed out into the freezing water.

The Tsangpo was narrower here than at Tsetang, but that meant the current was stronger. It also meant that what had seemed like a foolhardy venture, when viewed from the shore, now appeared to be utter madness. The coracle was kicking and bucking, plunging over rocks to hit whitewater waves that curled back, swamping the boat when they broke over the sides. One of the mules started to panic and thrashed out, tearing itself free of the rope and striking out for the nearest land. Fortunately, the boat was closer to the other shore, so the mule kicked out for that. Immediately, the boatman with the rope released all the other mules, and they, too, set off for the shore, their eyes wide and their nostrils flaring, as they were forced to swim for their lives.

The coracle continued to rush downstream, rocking and twisting, and taking in water. The man with the oar managed to fight his way out of the current and paddle to the side of the river, beaching the boat at a point more than half a mile below the one at which they had started. The Americans scrambled onto dry land. To them the crossing had been a harrowing ride, but to the Tibetans it had just been part of another day's work.

Crozier dug into his box of coins and handed the two boatmen a fistful of rupees, which quickly disappeared before Crozier had a chance to change his mind. One of the boatmen then bent down, and to the Americans' astonishment swung the now-empty coracle over his head. They could not believe a boat that had carried so many people could also be so light. The other boatman packed his gear onto the back of the goat, and with the animal in tow set off with his companion back upstream. The two men would walk for a mile, before paddling across to the other bank of the river, arriving back at the spot from which they had begun.

WHEN THE AIRMEN ONCE MORE SET OFF, they rode in single file on a narrow trail parallel to the river. Before long, they entered a barren land of yellow dunes, sculpted by the wind into smooth undulations. A stiff breeze blew down the valley towards them, then without warning, it suddenly grew fierce, picking up sand and scouring their faces with grit. They could feel it between their teeth, filling their ears, blocking their noses, getting into their eyes. They leaned forward, heads bent and turned to one side. But the wind, blowing hard against them, continued to blast them with sand. The mules stopped, unable to go on. The sand swirled around, dimming the sun like an eclipse. Crozier felt as if he were being buried alive. The airmen covered their faces, shielding their eyes. But still the sand blew, filling their throats so they found it almost impossible to breathe.

Then suddenly the storm was over, the wind dying away almost as quickly as it had sprung up. The airmen dusted themselves down, and once more prodded their mules forward. Soon they were able to turn away from the river and begin the long ascent out of the valley. The trail rose in a series of switchbacks, and after several hours of steep climbing they were able to look back on the river, now several thousand feet below.

They entered a layer of mist and cloud, and soon the trail became sheeted with ice. They plodded on, still climbing higher, as the air grew colder and noticeably thinner. Finally up ahead, the Americans saw a string of brightly colored flags snapping in the wind—the prayer flags marking Nyapso-la, or Nyapso Pass.

The Americans stopped at the saddle, 16,000 feet above sea level. Behind them, through the mist and the cloud, they could just make out the shape of the Tsangpo. The next time they saw the river, it would, they hoped, be the Brahmaputra—no longer a rushing mountain torrent, but instead a muddy and somnolent flow, sliding past their base at Jorhat.

"That's one sight I want to see," Spencer said.

Ahead of them—on the other side of the pass, nearly two thousand feet below—was the glistening surface of a lake, the huge Yamdrok-tso. Filled by runoff rather than by rivers, the scorpion-shaped lake was believed by Tibetans to be home to many of their protector gods. As such, it was one of the most sacred lakes in all of Tibet. Waves ruffled its surface, and along its shore a thin line, as narrow as a thread, marked the trail the airmen soon would be taking. Not for the first time, Crozier was struck by the sheer size—the *scale*—of the country. Texas was supposed to be big; but it was nothing compared to this. The lake alone had to be fifty miles long—and maybe another fifty miles across.

For luck, the Americans laid a few stones on the pyramid cairn that marked the pass. Then they started down. They expected the air to grow thicker and warmer as they lost height, but dark clouds rolled in from the west, and before long—for the first time since they had arrived in Tibet—a light snow started to fall. It was an ominous sign, one that Fort Knox seemed to acknowledge when he urged his mule on at a slightly faster pace.

15

CHRISTMAS EVE

THE AIRMEN WERE SUPPOSED TO PICK UP fresh mounts in Pede. They reached the village later that night, turning a corner and passing beneath a darkened fort, or *dzong*, which overlooked the lake and guarded the trail that ran along its shore. A light snow was still falling, covering their shoulders and filling the crooks of their arms where they held the reins. The Americans were frozen, hungry, and—even on this, the first day of their journey—close to the point of exhaustion.

To Spencer, the village they were in looked depressingly similar to the other settlements they had seen—a tight collection of huts and hovels that were filled with people who seemed to have acquired the filth and grime of several weeks, or even months.

In the center of the village, the five airmen climbed stiffly down from their mules. They had been in the saddle for more than eight hours, but had covered fewer than twenty miles. Fort Knox presented their passports to the village elders, who found them a room and a place to cook—another mud hut, one floor above the inevitable stables below. Their hosts offered eggs to eat and milk to drink, but the Americans politely declined. For much of the time they had been in Tibet, they had been humbled by the generosity of a people who had so little yet gave so much. They had made it a point to try to accept whatever food they were offered. But Sherriff had warned them that eggs in Tibet were usually as old as the rocks they resembled. And as for the milk, it was tinged the color of blood, warning them to stay away.

The airmen did accept the tea that was offered, having finally mastered the way to drink it. The trick was to blow away the layer of grease that floated on top, before trying to take a sip.

Duncan Hines went off to buy another live sheep, and returned a few minutes later with a withered herdsman who was willing to barter. After a lengthy discussion that threatened to turn violent, the cook and the herdsman agreed on a price—fifty rupees. When Fort Knox heard the amount, he shoved his rifle into the herdsman's face, and the price promptly dropped to thirty rupees. Fort Knox grinned, flashing his gold tooth. That was better. But to his dismay, Crozier insisted on paying the agreed-upon fifty.

The herdsman appeared to know a good thing when he saw one, and hauled in a carcass that, he said, was two years old. The cold, dry air meant refrigeration was rarely needed in Tibet, so the meat was still fresh in spite of its age. Crozier agreed that that might be true, but eating a two-year-old carcass was one experience he was willing to forgo.

Duncan Hines boiled up a stew, and the airmen retired to their rolled-up blankets. They knew they were facing another cold and miserable night, but Crozier was well past caring. As he had earlier suspected, he was coming down with a kind of fever, his body aching in every joint.

ACCORDING TO THE TERMS of their Tibetan passports, the Americans were entitled to five fresh riding mules and six new pack mules every two days, and the village elders of whichever settlement they happened to be in were obliged to provide them. For now, that meant Pede. But when the Americans awoke there the following day, they could see no sign of any mules in the stables below. Fort Knox, with Rain and Shine, spent the better part of the morning prodding the elders with their rifles, trying to persuade them to comply with the rules.

On any other day, the delay would have been frustrating. Crozier had set a tight schedule that required them to leave every morning at first light. But that day he could not have cared less. He was cold and feverish, and even when wrapped in a bundle of blankets could not prevent himself from shivering. He also suffered from a deep lassitude, and noted that Huffman seemed to be feeling much the same way.

By the time they set out—with Crozier resigned to "looking at the north end of a south-bound mule"—it was close to noon. Water at the edge of the lake was still frozen, and a fresh dusting of snow covered the ground. When the wind got up that afternoon, it brought with it another fierce storm. The airmen turned up their collars and sank low in their saddles, hiding their faces from the shards of ice that blew against them, stinging their cheeks and threatening to blind them.

Crozier sat on his mule, but let his reins drop. The animal knew the way better than he did, and anyway it seemed way too much bother trying to control it. At one point, with the storm raging around them, the airmen were forced to dismount and lead their mules forward; it was the only way to keep them moving. When the trail rounded an inlet—part of the long bay that curved around, forming the tail of the scorpion-shaped lake—the snow turned into sleet that gathered and froze in the folds of their coats. Crozier began to feel light-headed. His mule picked its way over loose shale, but then refused to walk farther in the face of the gale blowing off the lake. Crozier shouted to the others, but was not able to make himself heard above the roar of the wind. Fort Knox saw him and signaled a halt. Everyone dismounted and for the better part of an hour, huddled together in the lee of their mules. When the storm moved on, they were so stiff they could barely move.

As they forced their mules on, it again started to snow, and they decided to seek shelter in the town of Nangartse. Fort Knox led them across some snowy fields, passing below another dzong perched like a castle on top of a hill. He found them a hut where they could spend the night, and they piled inside, crouching around a yak-dung fire, listening to the wind howling outside as it tried to find every fissure in the mud-brick walls.

Duncan Hines went foraging for food, and this time came back with some rice and a few potatoes, which he cooked into a makeshift stew. While the others ate, Crozier lay down. He had no interest in food. He wrapped himself up in as many blankets as he could find and tried to sleep, only to be jolted upright in a state of near panic as he felt himself unable to breathe. He sat up, but his overwhelming sense of fatigue forced him again to close his eyes—until once more he was wrenched awake by a smothering feeling of suffocation.

As he leaned back against a wall, his heart began to play tricks, losing its rhythm and beating out of time. He called for help, and when the others found him, he was propped on one elbow and violently retching in a series of dry, painful heaves. He pulled more blankets around him but continued to shiver—even when Spencer and Perram heated the blankets over a fire.

Fort Knox took one look at Crozier and issued a series of orders to Shine. Shine took off on his mule, and when he returned—an hour or so later—he had an elderly monk perched on the back. The monk, from the nearby Samding monastery, crouched beside Crozier and studied him intently. Crozier was now throwing off his blankets, even though it was cold in the room and he was still visibly shaking.

The monk spun a prayer wheel and mumbled a series of incantations, then produced a glass jar containing a reddish-brown liquid that he sprinkled over Crozier's body, adding a few extra drops to his forehead as if bestowing a blessing. He ordered Rain and Shine to bring rocks from the courtyard, which he heated by the fire and placed at Crozier's feet. From deep in his robe, he extracted a scarf, and carefully unfolding it, revealed a stash of pills the size of golf balls. He gave one to Crozier and to each of the other airmen, clearly expecting all five Americans to take the pills. McCallum looked at his, then broke it open like cracking an egg. He decided the pill was mainly flour held together by a coating of sugar. The monk was looking expectantly at him, so McCallum put the pill into his mouth and started to chew, the other airmen following his lead.

The monk nodded approval, then launched into a lengthy discussion with Fort Knox. Crozier, apparently, could only be cured if he somehow managed to increase his merit. That could be achieved either by saving a life—or by making a healthy donation. McCallum was less than convinced, but he put a stack of rupees into the monk's upturned hands. It appeared to be an adequate amount, as the next morning, Crozier—although still ashen-faced—was able to force down some food and sip at a bowl of butter-free tea. He also announced that he was willing to ride when he looked outside and saw that the storm of the previous day had finally abated.

THE AIRMEN LEFT NANGARTSE under a pale, wintry sky. High winds during the night had cleared much of the trail of snow, blowing it into high, billowing drifts. At first, the route they followed was relatively flat, as they continued to follow the shore of the lake, but then they turned west and began the climb towards Kara-la—the pass that would take them across another high range of mountains.

In the village of Langra—the most "forlorn and desolate place" Crozier had seen—they stopped to rest. Fort Knox broke through a sheeting of ice that covered a small stream and allowed their mules to drink. A few villagers gathered around, and two men, their weathered faces rubbed raw by the wind, tried to sell the Americans an earring that one of the men was wearing. At the same time, an aging woman, her skin as dry as cracked earth, attempted to take something out of their supplies.

Immediately, Rain and Shine were off their mules and laying into the woman, hitting her across the back and shoulders with their whips. Huffman moved to intervene, but the other airmen held him back—afraid that if they became involved, they might lose their soldier-escort, or worse still their guide. As it was, the woman proved to be unhurt. But to the Americans, it was another glimpse into the character of the Tibetans, who, for the most part, were open, honest, friendly and warm, but could—in the blink of an eye—turn physically violent or even cruel.

A few miles on, the airmen stopped again to eat some rice and a little cold mutton, and then they continued to climb, passing beneath the snout of a glacier. They were now above 15,000 feet, and Crozier was again beginning to feel sick. He had also developed a hacking cough, and although unaware of it, was probably suffering not from some kind of flu, but from acute mountain sickness, or AMS, brought on by his continuing exposure to the high altitudes. The danger was that the AMS could easily transmute into high-altitude pulmonary edema—a potentially fatal condition in which bodily fluids would leak into his lungs, effectively drowning him; or it could turn into high-altitude cerebral edema—an equally lethal condition in which fluids would build up inside his brain, causing the tissue to swell until it was too big to fit in his skull.

The cure for all these conditions was simple. Crozier had to lose altitude. But on the Tibetan plateau, that was not an option. From where they were, the Americans could look ahead and see a mountain rising another 8,000 or 9,000 feet above them, its flanks streaked with permanent snow that mirrored glaciers on a similar peak to the south. That was the

direction in which they were headed—to the pass that formed a saddle
between the two mountains. It was still several thousand feet above them;
there could be no question of Crozier losing height.

They ploughed on, all of them suffering from migraine-like headaches
and minor nosebleeds that were caused in part by the dry air. As they
continued to climb, Crozier began to experience a loss of awareness, as a
dreamy spaciness settled over him—one that he found was not unpleas-
ant. He was dimly aware that the glaciers he passed were not the clear,
minty blue he had somehow expected, but were, in fact, a dirty gray,
stained and streaked by rocks and other debris. But for the most part, he
just focused on following Fort Knox, again dropping his reins and letting
his mule find its own way, picking a route through frozen boulders that
were sheeted with ice.

At the pass itself, the wind blasted the airmen, driving hard into their
faces. They were now above 16,800 feet—standing where, forty years before, Francis Younghusband had fought the highest battle in British military history. The Americans did not linger. As custom demanded, their
Tibetan companions added prayer flags and stones to the poles and
cairns marking the summit, and then they started down, wending their
way through a narrow valley that was utterly barren and desolate. To
Crozier, now in a semidelusional state, the land took on a nightmare appearance, as if had been scraped clean of even the smallest hint of life.

They found shelter that night in a small village called Ralung, and
then pushed on the following day, slowly losing altitude. They came to
streams that seemed frozen solid, but when their mules started to cross
them, skittering over the hard ice, they would suddenly break through,
plunging into the water below and thrashing around, threatening to bolt
and unseat their riders. When they stopped for the night in Shuto,
Crozier was again shivering uncontrollably, his lips bleeding and his fin-
gers cracked, sliced by cuts that in the thin air refused to heal.

The airmen were now desperate to reach Gyantse, as they knew they
would find a British trade agency there. But the next morning, when
they set out, the weather had taken another turn for the worse, the temperature plunging to a new low. Their trail ran alongside the course of a
river, first on a plateau and then through a gorge, with high cliffs on one
side and a sharp drop on the other. In places, the trail had been carved

into the rock face, creating overhangs so low the airmen could barely stay in their saddles. At one point, where the trail narrowed, Crozier's mule suddenly slipped, and Crozier was thrown. He landed on the trail, but then rolled over the edge of the cliff, tumbling towards the river below, before coming to a stop when his shoulder wedged between two rocks.

The others threw him a rope, but Crozier was too weak to pull himself up, so McCallum and Spencer had to scramble down and haul him back on to the trail. Shine offered to switch mules, but Crozier stubbornly shook his head. He mounted up, determined to continue, but a short distance on, the mule threw him again. This time, Crozier was crossing a stream and the animal did not slip, but tried to buck him over its head. Again, there were offers to exchange mules, but Crozier once more refused. He climbed back into the saddle and prodded his mule forward, McCallum watching and saying to the others that "the Texan in him was finally coming out."

When they emerged from the gorge, they found themselves on a wide, open plain. The airmen started across. They were now down to 13,000 feet, the hills around them bleak and gray. In several places, the trail disappeared, but Fort Knox knew the way. The Americans were beginning to think they would need to find shelter for another night, when they saw in the distance a party of horsemen riding towards them, kicking up dust. It occurred to Crozier it might be a party of bandits that Sherriff had warned them about, but as the riders drew near, he could see they were wearing military uniforms.

The soldiers pulled to a stop in a flurry of hooves.

"You must be the Americans," their leader said. "I'm Captain Davis from the British agency. And this," he said, gesturing towards the soldier beside him, "is Lieutenant Finch. We've been expecting you. Welcome to Gyantse. You're just in time to join the festivities."

For a moment, Crozier was puzzled. The festivities? But then he remembered. It was December 24th. Christmas Eve.

GYANTSE WAS TIBET'S THIRD BIGGEST TOWN, but it still had a population of less than ten thousand people. The British had established a trade agency there, following the Younghusband invasion and the subsequent signing of the 1904 Lhasa Convention. The agency was the final stop on the little-used trade route that stretched from Sikkim into Tibet, and as such offered a tenuous link with the outer reaches of the British Empire. But Gyantse was still one of the loneliest and most isolated places a British officer could find himself stationed. To the British, the town was one that had been forgotten—or one that no one had wanted to find in the first place. In the more colorful phrase of the Americans, Gyantse was a one-horse town that even the horse had abandoned.

Captain Davis and Lieutenant Finch had been assigned there mainly to establish a British presence. There was precious little for them to do, so they spent their time endlessly drilling the small detachment of Indian soldiers who were under their command.

The troop of soldiers escorted the Americans to the agency—a cluster of mud-brick buildings about half a mile southwest of the town, close to the Nyang River. The airmen were shown to a series of rooms surrounding a courtyard, where they did their best to clean themselves up; then they joined Davis and Finch for dinner.

The two British officers were delighted to see the five airmen. Fresh blood was even rarer in Gyantse than it was in Lhasa, and to have five English-speaking people—albeit Americans—appear on their doorstep was more than they could reasonably have hoped for. Partly in their visitors' honor, and partly to celebrate Christmas Eve, Davis and Finch had laid on something of a feast. It was meant to be a celebration, but for the five airmen, it soon turned into an ordeal. Crozier was still feeling sick, with waves of nausea coursing through him. Huffman was in much the same shape. And now, so, too, was Perram. Only Spencer and—especially—McCallum were in reasonable health, but like the others they were close to the point of exhaustion.

As a result, none of the Americans were at all disappointed when Mc-Callum, unable to keep his eyes open longer, suddenly fell like the victim of a Mafia hit "face down into his soup." That brought the meal to an abrupt end, but at least it allowed the airmen to head off to bed—although as they retired, they were all too aware that they had, perhaps, broken the unwritten rules of British decorum.

THE NEXT DAY—DECEMBER 25—all five of the Americans were sick, but they managed to join the two British officers for a Christmas dinner they had prepared. About twenty Tibetans had been invited, so the Americans were expected not just to show up, but also to create an impression that would reflect favorably on their country and on their government. For Crozier, the dinner was another trial, but he managed to summon up the strength to join in the various toasts, and to hold his own in the dice-and-drinking games the Tibetans enjoyed, downing several cups of beer that were served by a bevy of Tibetan chang girls. He also sang a few verses of "I'm Dreaming of a White Christmas," and took part in a boisterous version of "Santa Claus is Coming to Town."

After dinner, Davis cracked open a prized bottle of Scotch; the chang girls were persuaded to demonstrate a selection of native dances; and McCallum kept the party going by trying to teach the Tibetans how to jive. All things considered, the dinner was viewed as a great success, with the Americans making up for McCallum's faux pas of the night before.

But Crozier still couldn't shake whatever was ailing him, and for the next few days, he was forced to remain in bed. His headaches persisted and he was finding it hard to keep any food down. The others took turns to see that he was all right, but they were not feeling that much better themselves. Perram took to his bed, and so, in time, did Huffman. Both men kept throwing up, and both began to run high fevers.

But what really nagged at the airmen was the mounting fear that it was not just their energy that was fast running out, but also their time. Their plan had called for them to stay in Gyantse only one night—two at the most. But as the days dragged on, with little sign of any improvement in their health, they began to fear they were delaying too long. The remaining passes would not stay open forever. Soon they would be trapped, forced to wait until spring. At one point, Crozier thought the others should go on without him. But as McCallum was the only one fit and able to travel, he decided against splitting the group up. Instead, they would have to wait until all of them recovered—at least to the point where they might be able to make it through to the border.

From their point of view, Davis and Finch were happy to see the Americans remain within the confines of the agency. They were aware of the trouble the airmen's presence had caused in Lhasa and did not want to see a repeat in Gyantse. In the edgy political climate, any disturbance was best avoided—as already there were signs that the political forces the Americans' arrival had helped to unleash had not yet run their full course.

EVEN BEFORE THE AMERICANS REACHED GYANTSE, the Lhasa government had taken steps to exploit their appearance in Tibet. It knew that Tibet could not stand alone against a Chinese invasion. The National Assembly may have promised to fight, but the hard truth was that Tibet did not have the military strength to repel a Chinese assault. For a long time, the Tibetan government had been depending on Britain to come to its aid. Just the previous month, Sherriff had reported to his superiors that he had "on several occasions, had remarks addressed to me that the Tibetan Government relies on the British Government for help in this question."

But how good an ally *was* Britain? It had first come to Lhasa at the head of an army, and clearly it was still an imperialist nation. The British seemed willing to let Tibet fall under the sway of China—as long as China maintained a stable Tibet and did not pose a threat to Britain's holdings in India.

America was different. Its president had sent the Dalai Lama a photograph of himself, signing it from the Dalai Lama's "good friend Franklin D. Roosevelt." And in the accompanying letter he had also sent, the President had explicitly stated that "the people of the United States" were at this moment fighting a war against "a nation bent on conquest" that was "intent upon destroying freedom of thought and of religion..." This was precisely the challenge the Tibetans were facing. They, too, were under threat from "a nation bent on conquest"—a nation that wanted to destroy "freedom of thought and of religion."

Furthermore, Ilia Tolstoy—Roosevelt's personal envoy—had made it clear that the United States was a committed defender of the world's smaller countries. In a meeting with the Tibetan Regent in March, 1943, Tolstoy had said "the American Government was in full sympathy with those weak and small nations who wished to retain their independence," citing the case of "the South American states which the United States could overthrow and swallow in a very short time, but were completely independent and free."

Taktra Rinpoche, the Tibetan Regent, had been "greatly pleased to hear of this state of affairs," telling Tolstoy that Tibet "was a religious country and wished to be free and independent like the states Tolstoy had mentioned." He had been positively delighted when Tolstoy then went on to say that he, Tolstoy, was recommending to the United States government that Tibet be represented at the international peace conference, which was going to be held at the end of the war. That proposal had been "immediately approved of by the Tibetan Government, (which) expressed a desire to be informed of the date of the conference, and when and to whom an application for representation should be made...."

The Tibetans, in short, were convinced that they could count on the American government for support. They were not to know that Tolstoy had grossly exceeded his remit. To the Tibetan government, the situation was clear. America was an ally in the struggle against China. All that was required was to bring its support out into the open.

The appearance of the five airmen seemed to offer an ideal opportunity, so in the last week of December, as the American airmen were waiting to recover their health in Gyantse, the Dalai Lama and his Regent sat at their desks in the Potala composing personal letters to the American government. The letters were typically obscure and tangential. But they were nonetheless an attempt to coax a commitment of support for Tibetan independence from their new and powerful friend.

16

———❦———

DEAD MEN WALKING

CROZIER WAS AFRAID THEY HAD LEFT it too late. They were leaving as soon as they could—their health and strength still failing—but they had spent a full week stuck in Gyantse and were, as a result, a long way behind their original schedule. And Gyantse was only halfway between Lhasa and the Tibetan border with Sikkim.

When the Americans finally rode out of town, it was December 31—New Year's Eve. They were escorted by the same squad of soldiers who had brought them into Gyantse, Davis and Finch leading the way under a gray sky that was ominously filled with low-hanging clouds. After five miles, the two British officers brought their troop to a halt and, with salutes and handshakes all round, said their goodbyes, wishing the Americans the best of luck. Then they swung their soldiers around and in a conscious display of military precision galloped back towards Gyantse.

Crozier watched them go with mixed feelings, then, looking around at the other airmen, decided that he ought to take a positive view of their situation. They still had Fort Knox to guide them, Rain and Shine to protect them, and Duncan Hines to cook for them. They also had fresh mules and a reasonable supply of food. They may have been weak and physically depleted, but they were as fit and healthy as they were likely to get, before they returned to their base. And best of all, on this, the second half of their journey, they would be able to sleep, not on the floors of Tibetan mud huts, but in the relative comfort—and hopefully warmth—of British dak bungalows.

These dak bungalows marked the staging posts, which the British had set up at strategic points along the trade route linking the Sikkimese capital of Gangtok to the agency in Gyantse. The bungalows were built soon after the signing of the Lhasa Convention and had been substantially improved since then. Many were well constructed and able to boast of several rooms. As a general rule, they were located a single day's march apart, but Crozier was hoping to double-stage, missing every other one out. It was an ambitious undertaking, and one he knew they might not be able to fulfill, but after the week lost in Gyantse he felt he had no other choice.

As they set off across the Gyantse plain, they found themselves churning up dust that hung in a cloud behind them. Soon they entered another gorge, where their progress was considerably slowed. They followed the gorge up, observed by a huge Buddha chipped into the rock, climbing steadily between towering cliffs until the trail opened out again on to another plain.

And then it began to snow. It fell in thick, heavy flakes that cut visibility to a few feet. At one point, when McCallum and Huffman took a wrong turn, they found themselves floundering around for several hours before Fort Knox, emerging out of the storm like an apparition, led them back onto the right trail. By then, the wind was howling so fiercely they were unable to make themselves heard above it, even when screaming at the tops of their voices.

They found shelter in Kangma—a small village cowering beneath a crumbling red cliff—and decided they could go no further until the storm abated. The next morning—January 1, 1944—snow was still falling, but they set out at noon, determined to push on. There had been no celebrations the night before to mark the end of one year and the beginning of the next.

Part way across the plain, the snow stopped, and for several hours they rode through a desolate land, both stark and austere—a high mountain desert that was devoid of life, intimidating in its harshness and scale. The rocks on the slopes around them were a deep, reddish brown, but occasionally they saw cliffs that were a painter's pallet of blazing color.

A late-evening wind whipped up more dust, blocking what little remained of the light. The next day, the dust clouds persisted as they rode out between two huge, shallow lakes, their waters a deep blue, shading in places to purple and green. The plain around them seemed to encourage the wind, and all that day they battled the dust storms, half-buried beneath a swirling mass of grit and sand. They made it as far as Dochen, a small village on the shore of the second lake—a disappointing distance of less than twelve miles.

The next morning, they were relieved to discover that the wind had dropped. It was a much needed, encouraging sign. They left at dawn, determined to take advantage of the change in the weather. But they still only managed a single stage—another twelve miles—before stopping for the night in the village of Tuna.

They were again heartened the following day when they saw in the distance the pyramid peak of Chomolhari—easily identifiable from their rough map, and easily recognized by the plume of snow that blew constantly from its summit, like steam coming out of the funnel of an engine. At a height of 24,000 feet, the mountain was a prominent marker on the Tibetan-Bhutanese border. Its sighting meant that the airmen were entering the arrowhead wedge—the most southerly part of Tibet—that pushed down between Bhutan on the east and Sikkim on the west. For the first time, the Americans began to feel that they might be nearing the end of their journey.

They rode on, climbing a gently rising slope, until they finally reached the summit of Tang-la—the "Level Pass." The wind howled, but they were used to that. They dropped down to the village of Chugya, then pushed on to Phari, another small town that among Western travelers to Tibet was best known as the filthiest place on earth. Mounds of garbage filled its streets, packed so deep that in places it rose to the roofs of the houses. Many of the villagers could reach their doors only by tunneling through the trash. Elsewhere, dead rats, dogs—even mules and ponies—lay where they had fallen, their bodies decaying and pecked over by crows.

That night, at the dak bungalow, the Americans sat around a fire that was fueled, not by the usual, smoldering yak dung, but by crackling logs that sent up a flurry of sparks and flames. It was another encouraging sign, as it meant they were at last coming down to the tree line, leaving the high Tibetan plateau behind.

Fort Knox quickly disillusioned them. They still had to cross one more pass—the Nathu-la—protecting the Tibetan border with Sikkim, and at this time of year, the pass could easily become blocked by snow. The airmen would have to continue forcing their pace if they hoped to escape from Tibet before the spring.

For the next two days, the Americans pushed on as hard as they could, gradually descending the long Chumbi Valley. Tall pines lined the hillsides around them, and the trail became peppered with rocks and boulders protruding from mud that was no longer frozen. They spent a night in Gotsa, then followed a trail down through a gorge that took them to the town of Yatung, on the banks of the Amo River.

Yatung was a small, dismal community, wedged so far in the cleft of a mountain that it rarely caught a glimpse of the sun. But it still qualified as Tibet's fourth biggest town. As the airmen settled in for the night, they were relieved to see that the favorable weather—which they had been enjoying for the past two days—still seemed to be holding.

TO CROZIER, PEERING OUT THE FOLLOWING MORNING, the unfairness of it all must have seemed overwhelming. The border was so close—now just twelve miles away. After the four hundred they had already come, those last twelve miles should have been easy. They still had to go over the Nathu-la, but he had been hoping that, with a bit of luck, they might make it to Sikkim that day and maybe even as far as the capital of Gangtok. There, he knew, they would be able to find a road—one they could drive a Jeep or a truck along, and one that was linked to the railway network that ran throughout the Indian subcontinent. Instead, he found himself staring out at thickly falling snow, and beginning to realize just how wrong his calculations had been.

When, later that day, the airmen left the Yatung bungalow, they were heavily wrapped in their long fur coats, their hats pulled low over their faces. The snow was coming down hard in soft, wet flakes that quickly settled into a layer as gummy as just-poured concrete. The air was cold, but far from bitter, and at first the airmen's route took them through stands of pine that offered a degree of protection from the wind. But after they forded the swift-running Amo River, they started to climb; the forests fell away, and soon they were plowing through knee-high snow with the wind battering and blowing against them.

Their pace slowed to a crawl, and they were forced to dismount and continue on foot, lifting their knees high with every step, taking so much snow with them that it felt as if their feet were lead. Dark clouds rolled down the slope towards them, and visibility was reduced to a few feet. Crozier could barely see his hand held out in front of his face. He plodded on, then in a moment of panic, realized he could no longer hear the others either plowing ahead or following behind.

"McCallum?" he called out. And was glad to hear an immediate response.

"Yeah, Chief?"

"Nothing," Crozier said. "Just checking."

They continued to climb, settling into a slow, steady trudge, the snow piling up around them. They kept going all day, but managed to cover only ten miles. With darkness pressing in, they crowded into the dak bungalow at Champitang, two miles short of the border, and still 2,000 feet below it. They took it in turns, looking out at the weather, but throughout the night snow continued to fall in thick clumps, so by morning they were not sure if they could continue.

At ten o'clock they set out, Fort Knox leading the way, forging a route through heavy snow that was now up to his waist. Every few hundred yards, he was forced to stop and let Rain or Shine take a turn in the lead, sometimes driving the mules forward, using them as a plow to flatten the snow and stomp it underfoot.

The airmen offered to help, but the Tibetans refused. They were much smaller than the five Americans, yet far stronger. To Crozier, it was an astonishing sight to see them bull their way through. By his estimate, they were well above 14,000 feet, yet the Tibetans kept going without rest or respite.

The snow continued to fall as they climbed still higher, muffling all sound, and creating an eerie, otherworld feeling. Crozier was again becoming light-headed. He felt like a dead man, the energy drained from his body. He tried to focus on putting one foot in front of the other. *Keep doing that, over and over,* he told himself—one foot in front of the other.

At one point, they crossed a snow bridge over a stream, the river below revealed only by a gurgle of water and a series of hollows scooped out of the snow. There was no longer any sign of a trail, but Fort Knox kept on pushing higher, continuing at the same steady pace. He was like a machine. Nothing seemed able to faze him.

Crozier wanted to stop and rest, to lean on his knees and suck in air. But Fort Knox kept on going. It would have been easy, Crozier thought, to have taken a superior view of the Tibetans. They were ragged and dirty, ignorant and unworldly, so it was tempting to see them as little more than overgrown children. But the Tibetans had qualities that Crozier had come to admire. As he dragged himself on, following Fort Knox, he could not help thinking that not only had he developed a deep affection for these people, but also a boundless respect.

The Tibetans he had met, with rare exception, had been generous and kind. They may have lived in an unforgiving land—and lacked even the most basic of amenities—but they had managed to create a society that was based, in part, on shared acceptance. There was little dissension, and seemingly no envy. Tibet was certainly unfair. It was also subject to abuse and corruption. But somehow, it seemed to work.

At any moment, Fort Knox could have stopped. He could have given up. He was climbing like this, pushing himself relentlessly higher, in the full knowledge that if he reached the pass, he would just have to turn around and come back down. He had been promised no reward if he got the Americans through. But he had made a commitment, and without his help and persistence, the airmen would never have stood a chance.

For Crozier, the climb had become a nightmare. But Fort Knox finally stopped, and one by one the others joined him. This was the pass—the Nathu-la—that marked the border, nearly 16,000 feet above sea level. Ahead lay Sikkim. Behind was Tibet. A string of prayer flags—shredded by the wind—stood out from a pole that was almost buried by snow. There were no barriers, no customs posts—none of the trappings that normally marked an international frontier. The pass itself was sufficient defense.

Crozier stood for several minutes, trying to regain his breath. The other Americans gathered around. With their cracked lips and frozen breath, they looked like Arctic explorers. Crozier shook hands with each man in turn, then with Fort Knox, Rain, and Shine. The three Tibetans were returning to Lhasa. Only Duncan Hines was continuing on as far as Gangtok. Crozier handed out a generous helping of silver rupees, and there was another round of lengthy goodbyes. As Fort Knox turned to go, Crozier could see he had tears stinging his eyes.

The Americans watched as the three Tibetans made their way back down the slope, following the trail they had blazed, and looking back every few hundred yards to wave. Then the airmen turned and peered into Sikkim, several thousand feet below. They started down, clouds once more beginning to drift in.

It took more than five hours for them to fight their way down the 2,000 feet from the pass, winding back and forth across the steep slope, slipping and sliding, zigzagging their way to the bottom. And there, in a wild moment of exhilaration, McCallum pulled out his pistol and fired a shot into the air. There was a loud crack and an echoing response, followed by a moment of silence. Then, to the airmen's horror, they heard a growl that grew rapidly louder, like the roar of an approaching stampede, and looking up they were appalled to see an avalanche of rocks, snow, and ice tumbling towards them. They stood transfixed as the avalanche swept past, and it was several minutes before silence was restored and any of them were able to speak.

McCallum put his pistol away. He did not know if the avalanche had been triggered by the shot he had fired or by the many traverses of an unstable slope the airmen had made on their way down. But he would not be firing any more bullets into the air.

The five airmen mounted up and, with Duncan Hines now showing them the way, began the last few miles that would take them on to Gangtok. They did not look back. But high above them—at the top of the pass—the column of prayer flags still stood out, fluttering in the wind like a row of trapped birds.

THE AIRMEN NEEDED TWELVE MORE DAYS to get back to their base at Jorhat. They could not make it to Gangtok that day, so they spent the night in the dak bungalow at Karponang, a few miles down from the Sikkimese border. The bungalow—set in the clearing of a forest—was large and spacious and far more luxurious than any they had stayed in before. Best of all, it offered them something to read—nothing more than some bound volumes of *Punch*, a copy of *Vogue*, some racy thrillers, and a series of out-of-print text-books on subjects that Crozier couldn't imagine anyone would ever want to study—but enough to confirm that they had crossed a line and were back in a familiar culture.

They continued to lose altitude the following day, on a trail that dropped steeply through thin veils of cloud. Soon they entered a dense forest that was occasionally broken by open meadows of lush, swaying grasses. It was another world. All around them, they could see trees, shrubs, birds, and—

"Did you hear that?" Crozier asked. The others stopped, then slowly nodded.

—insects. They had not seen an insect all the time they had been in Tibet, but here, there were insects all around, buzzing and whining, and for once Crozier was glad of their company.

As they neared Gangtok, they became aware of other sounds—the creak of a wheel, the thud of an axe against a tree. It was as if they were slowly awakening from a dream, recovering their senses one by one. They smelled flowers, heard birds chirping, and saw butterflies flitting among the bushes, and as they rode into town, they heard another sound they hadn't realized they had missed. It was the sound of an engine.

"Now, did you hear *that*?" Crozier said.

The others nodded. They knew what it meant. They had made it back. All of them. They could finally say they had safely come through. Crozier beamed at them. They were a wretched bunch to look at—exhausted, depleted, and as bedraggled as any group of Tibetans. But they were alive. It was a significant moment—one to celebrate, but also one that would bring another change.

Back in Tsetang, when Crozier had told the others to "forget the 'sir'," that's what they had done. It had been the five of them together, sometimes getting on one another's nerves, but also revealing their innermost thoughts, their fears and their aspirations. Now, the others would have to start calling him "sir" again. Their friendship would continue—but a bond would be broken.

IN GANGTOK, THE AMERICANS SOUGHT OUT the British Residency, which turned out to be one of the more elegant buildings any of them had seen.

They tethered their mules, and walked through carefully tended, terraced gardens before stepping onto a wide veranda that ran most of the way around the house. There, they were greeted with good-natured cheer by Basil Gould, the Political Officer in charge of the Residency and, as such, George Sherriff's immediate boss. "I trust you had a good trip?" Gould said. It was an understated welcome, even by British standards.

That evening, the Americans were treated to yet another banquet in a regal setting that left them "pop-eyed in wonderment." For entertainment, a group of dancing girls performed "intricate ballet steps," after which McCallum took to the floor with the wife of one of their British hosts. The highlight of the evening, however, came near the end, when the British produced an American dessert of pie and ice cream.

The next day, the British went one better when they gave the Americans a ride in a Model T Ford. It was another poignant reminder of home. That evening, Gould gave them the permit they would need to travel through India; Crozier paid off Duncan Hines with another generous tip, and the following morning—January 11, 1944—they left Gangtok, hitching a ride on a mail truck as far as Darjeeling, before continuing on to Siliguri on the Indian plain. By then, they were down to about four hundred feet above sea level, and the air was thick, languid, and damp.

From Siliguri, the Americans caught an overnight train to Calcutta, commandeering a first-class carriage and, since no one asked for a ticket, neglecting to pay their fares. In Calcutta, they contacted the Dum Dum Airbase, and on January 20 finally reached Jorhat. There they were greeted by a "wild and jubilant reception" and, for the next few days at least, treated as if they were long-lost, conquering heroes.

AS THE AIRMEN HAD BEEN MAKING THEIR WAY across the Tibetan plateau, the Office of the Personal Representative of the President of the United States of America to India had been wrestling with the problem of how to respond to two letters it had received from the Dalai Lama and his Regent, Taktra Rinpoche. The Tibetan Foreign Office had given the letters to Sherriff at the end of December and asked him to deliver them to the American government.

At first glance, the letters were polite and innocuous. They spoke of the "most friendly relations (that) exist between the U.S.A. and Tibet," and they stressed the help that the Tibetan government had given to the five airmen. The Tibetan government, the letters said, had "ordered an immediate search to be made for the missing airmen," and "when all the five airmen, including Lieutenant Crozier, were found safe and sound, they were asked to come to Lhasa, supplied with food, money, and transport animals, and are now being sent back to India as soon as possible...."

But the letters also drew the American government's attention to the fact that "the general public (in Lhasa) were very much perturbed and strongly resented the aeroplane coming over Tibetan territory without any previous understanding"—and then it went on to make the crucial point that the American airmen's flight over Tibet had been "contrary to all international law."

In its own circuitous way, the Tibetan government was trying to affirm its independence from China. More importantly, it was also trying to lure the United States government into giving its blessing to that independence.

The argument was simple. The American plane that had crashed in Tibet had taken off from China. It must have had permission to fly over Chinese terrain—but it had not had permission to fly over Tibet. When it did so, it was in violation of "international law"—or so the Tibetans said. This could be true, of course, only if Tibet were a separate country, and not a part of China. So if the United States government acknowledged that its plane had broken the law by flying over Tibet, then it would, at the same time, be saying that it recognized Tibet as an independent nation. In effect, the Tibetans were trying to rerun the issue of the pack route—but transferring it to the air.

The Tibetan government had had experience along these lines before. In September 1943—two months before the five Americans appeared in Tibet—a Chinese plane had circled over Chamdo, a province in the eastern part of the country. The Tibetans objected to this intrusion, sending a message of complaint to the Chinese. But the Chinese government responded by saying that the plane had flown only over Chinese territory, so there had been no need for anyone to seek permission from the Tibetans, nor to consult them about the plane's flight plans.

So did the United States government feel the same way?

Sherriff immediately saw the significance of the two letters. "In my opinion," he wrote, the two letters "showed a desire [on the part of the Tibetans] to be treated as an independent government." It was, in essence, a cry for help. But against the background roar of a global conflict, it went unheeded. The American government was still wedded to the more pressing objective of keeping China in the war against Japan. It was not willing to take on board the problems associated with Tibetan claims to be independent.

When the Office of the Personal Representative of the President of the United States of America to India responded to the two Tibetan letters, it did so merely by promising to avoid a recurrence of the unfortunate incident of the airmen. In its letter—given by Sherriff to the Tibetan Foreign Office on January 10, 1944—the American government assured the Tibetans that "American military aviators have strict orders to avoid flying over Tibetan territory, and that the incident was purely accidental [and] due to a miscalculation in aerial navigation on a return trip from China to Assam during the night time." It was recognition of a kind—but not the kind the Tibetans were seeking.

To appease its Chinese ally—and to avoid taking sides—the American military let it be known that the Americans had been attacked while in Lhasa because they had flown over the Dalai Lama—a version of events that still has currency today. This allowed the Chinese to save face, and continue to make the (false) claim that they were welcome in Tibet.

The American military also tried to ensure that the unfortunate incident would not be repeated, should any of its pilots ever be blown off course and forced to come down in Tibet again. To that end, after extensively debriefing Crozier and his crew, the United States' Air Transport Command drew up a list of recommended "Don't's and Do's for Tibet."

Don't

a. Don't wear or show the Chinese flag, as there is considerable resentment against the Chinese by the Tibetans for political reasons.

b. Don't use firearms in any way. Keep them out of sight if you have them.

c. Don't show partiality to any particular nationality that may greet you in Tibet. Treat all on the same basis.

d. Don't be frightened if they come and stare at you, as they are extremely curious.

e. Don't ridicule or scoff at their religious beliefs or the customs of the country. Remember that the Tibetans have been living their own lives for hundreds of years, and it satisfies them.

f. Don't kill any game or do any fishing unless absolutely necessary, and then only out of sight of the Tibetans.

g. Don't refuse food and gifts when they are offered to you. Eat the food even though you choke.

h. Don't cross mountain ranges. Always go down in valleys.

Do

a. Dress as warmly as possible before leaving the plane.

b. Descend mountains to the valley where there is usually a river. Follow this river downstream, as you will invariably reach a settlement.

c. Send word from whatever village you may be in to Lhasa, if possible, and remain where you are until an official party comes for you. Remain in the village even though you have to wait a considerable time, as without guides and ponies it is almost impossible to travel.

d. Save your parachute and shroud lines for warmth and gifts.

e. Get the idea across to the Tibetans that you are an American and that you are not on any war mission, but rather on one of a more humanitarian nature, such as "food dropping."

f. Learn parachute routine thoroughly.

Afterword

Tibet

+ The Tibetan government never quite believed that the five American airmen appeared in Tibet as the result of a fierce storm and navigational error. It could not let go of its suspicion that China somehow had a hand in their arrival.

+ Tibet was informed that it could not, as Tolstoy had promised, count on American government support for its attendance at the end-of-war peace conference. And Frank Ludlow, who had endorsed Tolstoy's suggestion, was reprimanded for giving the Tibetans false hope rather than sticking to official British government policy.

+ In January 1944, the Tibetan government was still trying to obtain copies from the British government in Lhasa of the messages it had supposedly sent to Chiang Kai-shek, in October of the previous year, congratulating him on his appointment as President of the National Government of the Republic of China. As the Tibetans suspected, the Chinese had radically altered the Tibetans' messages. In one message, the Chinese quoted Taktra Rinpoche, the Regent, as recognizing Chiang Kai-shek as President of "our" Republic, and had him saying that "the whole nation, including the people in this part of the country, are singing your praises. Your election to the highest office of the Republic adds glory not only to our native land but also to the universe as a whole. Henceforth our strong internal unity will surely lead to our national rejuvenation...." This was *not* what the Regent had said.

✦ The risk that Tibet was taking, by failing to set its own version of events in front of the outside world, may have been lost on the Tibetans—but not on the British. In a series of memos, the British government noted that, "Unless the Tibetan Government does something to call the attention of the outer world—including, especially, the U.S.A.—to its claims to national existence, its case will go by default. And if the Chinese in the near future carry out a military re-occupation of Lhasa, we shall not be in a position to protest, because the Chinese will have got away with their version of Tibetan 'loyalty,' and any action they may take will then be merely 'policing the border regions.'" The Tibetans, the memos said, would have fallen victim to "Chinese tricks."

✦ Both the British and the American governments knew that China planned to invade Tibet. At the Pacific War Council of May 1943, China's foreign minister, Dr. T. V. Soong, told both governments "that Tibet (was) not a separate nation, that it (was) a part of China, and that eventually China may have to take necessary action to maintain her sovereignty...." That same year, Britain thought seriously of recognizing Tibet as an independent nation, but decided against it. According to the India Office in London, the British government abandoned its plan partly because "the withdrawal of our recognition of Chinese suzerainty may precipitate a Chinese attack on Tibet..." and also because "China is bound to absorb Tibet at the end of the war, if not before, and we can do nothing effective to prevent it...." Also, in September 1943, the U.S. embassy in Chungking notified the U.S. State Department that "there have been increasing indications in recent months that the Chinese Central Government desires, and as soon as it feels in a position to, will attempt to extend its control over Tibet by force of arms. It is almost a foregone conclusion that Tibet will resist such encroachment by all means at its command, including, presumably, appeals to Great Britain and to the United States...."

✦ In 1950, after its Communist forces defeated the Nationalists, China did invade and the Tibetan government appealed for international assistance. But by then, the United States had given China "renewed assurances of our recognition of China's de jure sovereignty or suzerainty over Tibet...." And Britain had pulled out of India, so it no longer had a border it wished to protect. The United Nations later condemned the invasion on three separate occasions, but neither it nor any single country was willing to offer Tibet meaningful help.

✦ China maintained that by invading Tibet it was liberating the country from Western domination. At the time of the invasion, there were a total of five Westerners in Tibet. They were: Heinrich Harrer, author of *Seven Years in Tibet*; his companion Peter Aufschnaiter; Hugh Richardson, who had earlier been head of the British Mission in Lhasa; Reginald Fox, radio operator at the British Mission (who was still hoping to live permanently in Tibet); and Robert Ford, another radio operator, also from England, whom the Chinese held as a spy and put in prison.

✦ As has been well documented, the Chinese brutalized the Tibetans into submission, and tried to crush the Buddhist religion that lay at the heart of Tibetan society. At the time of the invasion, there were about six thousand monasteries in Tibet. All but a dozen were razed. The Chinese burned ancient Tibetan texts, destroyed libraries, smashed thousands of religious relics, and shipped hundreds of tons of crafted Tibetan metals to Beijing, where they were melted down. They also committed genocide on a scale that matched some of the worst atrocities seen in the twentieth century—the Holocaust, the purges of Stalin, and the killing fields of Cambodia. Hundreds of thousands of Tibetans were beaten, imprisoned, enslaved, tortured, shot, or starved.

◆ Today, the Chinese continue their destruction of the Tibetan culture and the Tibetan people. Tibetan children are taught a Chinese version of Tibetan history, and can only complete their education if they are fluent in the Chinese language. At the same time, an overwhelming number of Chinese people have been encouraged to move into Tibet, with the result that Tibetans now live as a persecuted minority in their own country. Many hundreds are still in prison for refusing to accept Chinese rule. Thousands more have tried to flee the country to join their spiritual leader in exile in India. The fourteenth Dalai Lama—the boy god-king to whom the Sherriffs gave a clockwork "wind-up train"—was forced to leave Tibet in 1959, along with some eighty thousand fellow Tibetans, and is now a revered international figure. Based in Dharamsala, a small town in northern India, he heads the Tibetan Government-in-Exile and helps to promote world peace and a greater awareness of human rights. In 1989, he was awarded the Nobel Peace Prize.

The Hump

◆ For three years—1942–45—the Hump was the only route by which Allied forces in China could be supplied with war materials. It later became the model for the Berlin airlift of 1948.

◆ The Hump had been launched from one base in India (at Dinjan) and one in China (Kunming), but at its height—after all the infrastructure had been put in place (more than one million men were employed in building the bases in India alone)—it operated from thirteen sites in India and six in China. By that time, as many as 650 planes were landing in China every day.

◆ Altogether, one thousand men were killed flying the Hump, and some six hundred planes were lost.

◆ The Hump was finally replaced by the Ledo Road—a more northerly version of the Burma Road—which was completed in January 1945. By then, the American government had all but abandoned any hope that China might play a significant role in the war against Japan. The Ledo Road was effectively obsolete even before it was finished.

✦ No land route across Tibet was ever built.

The Lhasa Contingent

✦ **George and Betty Sherriff.** Poor health forced the Sherriffs to leave Tibet in 1945. The high altitude aggravated the heart problem that had plagued Sherriff after he helped a porter carry a load over a pass, so he and Betty returned to Kalimpong in India, where they had been living before moving to Lhasa. The lure of wild places was still strong, however, and in 1946–47 both the Sherriffs joined Frank Ludlow on another expedition through Tibet—followed, in 1949, by one through Bhutan. During the second expedition, Betty Sherriff was thrown from her mule; she broke her arm and was forced to return to India. This marked the last of the Sherriff/Ludlow expeditions. In 1950, the Sherriffs moved back to Britain, where they bought an estate, called "Ascreavie," near Kirriemuir in Angus, Scotland. There, at an altitude of nine hundred feet, they created a successful garden full of Himalayan plants. For his services to gardening, Sherriff was awarded the Victoria Medal of Honour by the Royal Horticultural Society of London. From 1952 to 1966, he served as a member of the Angus County Council, and for a time was also the Deputy Lieutenant of Angus. In retirement, Sherriff gave lectures and showed the films he had made while in Lhasa. One of these films features the five American airmen while they were staying at Dekyi-lingka. Sherriff died on September 19, 1967, at the age of sixty-nine. Betty cared for their garden at Ascreavie until 1977. She died the following year, at seventy-eight.

✦ **Frank Ludlow.** After leaving Tibet in 1943, Ludlow went back to his job as Joint Commissioner in Ladahk. Tired of the endless parties and other social engagements, he was glad to get out of Lhasa. In 1950, Ludlow returned with the Sherriffs to England, and spent the rest of his life cataloging the Sherriff and Ludlow collection of plants and flowers in the British Museum. As a result of the two men's work, the British Museum now has the richest collection of Himalayan botanical specimens in the world. Neither Ludlow nor Sherriff did much to record the expeditions they took together. Both men kept diaries and field notes that reflected their scientific discoveries, but apart from Sherriff's films neither of them shed much light on the land and cultures through which they had passed. Ludlow confined himself to publishing a number of botanical and ornithological papers. He died on March 25, 1972, at the age of eighty-six.

✦ **Reginald Fox**. In January 1950, Fox broadcast the first radio newscast direct from Lhasa to the outside world. He was hoping to counter China's propaganda and its program of misinformation. Fox read the newscast in English, which was then followed by a Tibetan translation, broadcast by the Dalai Lama's brother-in-law. The invading Chinese forced Fox to leave Tibet. He moved to Kalimpong in India, and died there in 1953.

✦ **Sana Ullah**. He died of pneumonia in 1944, only a few months after the five American airmen left Tibet.

✦ **Dr. Kung Chin-tsung**. Kung left Lhasa in May 1944 after several futile attempts by the Tibetan government to have him recalled. To the very end, he refused to deal with Tibet's Foreign Office.

The American Airmen

✦ After their return from Tibet, there were rumors that the five airmen might be reprimanded—or even court-martialed—for having violated Tibetan airspace. But when the Tibetans failed to press any further their complaint to the U.S. government, the five airmen continued to be feted. *Collier's* magazine featured them prominently in one of its September

1944, issues; the BBC conducted a one-day interview with
them in Calcutta; and for a time there was even talk of Hollywood making a movie based on their story.

✦ **Robert Crozier.** Crozier was commended for "good leadership," which had allowed his crew to leave the plane "almost
simultaneously" and to regroup on the ground "in a short
time." He was later awarded a Distinguished Flying Cross
with Oak Leaf Cluster. After the war, he returned to Baylor
to finish his degree, and in 1946, he married Dorothy
Wilbanks, who was also at Baylor. After a miscarriage of
twins, the Croziers had three children. For many years,
Crozier worked as Executive Vice-President of the Texas Retail Grocers Association. In 1967, his wife opened a flower
shop, which the two of them later ran together. They were
then living on a small ranch near Waco, and were active in
the local Baptist Church. In his later years, Crozier suffered
from poor health, and had several heart attacks. He died of
cancer in 1984 when he was sixty-four years old.

✦ **Harold McCallum.** Soon after he returned to India from
Tibet, McCallum met an American nurse, Estelle Belnak,
and asked her to marry him (he first had to break off his engagement to a girl back home in Quincy). McCallum and his
wife had five children. When he left the Air Corps, McCallum remained true to his first love of flying, initially working
as a corporate pilot for Time Inc.'s Henry B. Luce and his
wife, Clare Boothe Luce; and then for Vincent Astor and his
wife, Mary Astor. Later, McCallum was employed—again as
a pilot—by Admiral Corporation and then by Joy Manufacturing where he remained until his retirement in 1984. Between flights, McCallum studied for a Bachelor of Law
degree from LaSalle University. He also taught himself Spanish, qualified as a locksmith and, when he was sixty-five years
old, won a black belt in karate. He continued to do fifty
push-ups a day on his thumbs, and at the age of seventy-nine
was in training to become a priest's assistant. A week before
his death—in 1998—McCallum was in the air, copiloting a

Cessna. By that time, he had logged nearly thirty thousand hours—a record that not too many pilots can match. Mc-Callum—who, like Crozier, was awarded a Distinguished Flying Cross—kept his A-2 jacket with the blood chit sewn on the back. It now hangs in a closet in the home of one of his brothers.

✦ **Kenneth Spencer**. By the time Spencer returned to Rockville Centre, he both feared and hated flying. He would not get on a plane, and had insisted on coming back to the States by ship. After a year of odd jobs, he attended college under the G.I. bill, graduating with a degree in economics. He married his childhood sweetheart, Virginia Ryder, and went to work for Western Electric in New York City. He and his wife had five children. Spencer later changed careers, becoming a business administrator for some of the public schools in Long Island. For a long time, Spencer refused to discuss his experiences in Tibet—later admitting he had been too young to appreciate what he'd experienced. He finally overcame his fear of flying—but for the rest of his life he had an aversion to mountains. In 1983, he and his wife moved to Florida, but Spencer was soon diagnosed with melanoma. He died in 1985 at the age of sixty-one.

✦ **John Huffman**. Before returning to the United States, Huffman was involved in another plane crash, this time in Europe. He was again badly injured, and was no longer able to face the prospect of flying. Like Spencer, he also refused to discuss his experiences in Tibet, except to say they were "pretty bad." After the war, Huffman moved to Seattle, Washington, where he worked as an engineer for the Boeing Airplane Company. It was there that he met his future wife. Huffman continued to be troubled by the shoulder he had broken during the bailout over Tibet. His doctor wanted to break the bone and have it reset, but Huffman maintained that he had suffered enough the first time around and did not want to go through the process again. After leaving Boeing, Huffman moved to Florida, where he became a commercial fisherman. He died there in 1989, at the age of seventy-three.

✦ **William Perram**. Perram was killed two months after arriving back at his base in Jorhat. He died on March 26, 1944, when his plane crashed into the side of a mountain eight miles east of Chengkung in China. He was buried there, but after the war his remains were brought home to Tulsa. Perram was twenty-three years, three months and thirteen days old. Huffman took it upon himself to write a series of supportive letters to Perram's parents. "I know there is nothing I can say that will lessen your sorrow," he wrote, "but I can truthfully say that he is sadly missed by all who knew him, and we will always remember him as the swell buddy and fine young man that he was... If there is anything I can do that will be of any help, please feel free to call upon me. I will count it a privilege to do what I can." The four surviving airmen made little effort to keep in touch once the war was over. Huffman thought Crozier was "a swell egg." And McCallum once went out of his way to call on Spencer. But the two pilots—Robert Crozier and Harold McCallum—did not get together for any kind of reunion.

Notes

⸺⸺⸺

Chapter One

Page 1. *Like that pilot...* This was Dick Kurzenberger, on his second attempt at a takeoff that day. The first had been aborted because of a "lack of feel on the rudders" as he taxied down the runway. Kurzenberger still remembers the storm that blew Crozier and his crew so far off course, since it was one of the worst that "Hump" pilots had experienced. Interview by authors, phone conversation, August 2001.

Page 6. *On one recent day...* This was October 13, 1943.

Page 6. *A weather alert warned...* From *China Airlift, the Hump*, Volume 1 (Hump Pilots Association, 1983).

Page 7. *"Effective immediately..."* Thomas O. Hardin was put in charge of Hump operations as Commander of the India-China Sector of Air Transport Command in August 1943. On January 21, 1944, he was promoted from Colonel to Brigadier General and put in charge of the China-India-Burma division of Air Transport Command.

Page 7. *"I was born...."* St. Patrick's Day is March 17; St. Joseph's Day is March 19. McCallum was born on March 18. He was named "Harold," after an uncle—his mother's brother. While in India, he was sometimes known by the nickname, "Blackie."

Page 8. *Ordered his landing gear up...* From *China Airlift.*

Page 8. *Half a foot shorter...* McCallum was five feet seven inches tall and weighed 160 pounds.

Page 8. *To move from Post...* The town of Post was founded in 1907 as a model community by the cereal magnate, Charles Post, using money he had made from selling Post Toasties and a coffee substitute he marketed as Postum. In 1920, the year of Crozier's birth, the town had ten stores, one doctor, one dentist, and three churches— Methodist, Presbyterian, and Baptist.

Page 9. *"He did not like to walk...."* From Crozier's wife, Dorothy. Interview by authors, phone conversation, September 2001.

Page 9. *The "first love" of his life...* From McCallum's account in *Tibet: One Second to Live* (1995). McCallum says that girls were then "an important part" of his life, but his "first love" was flying.

Page 10. *McCallum had been hooked...* From McCallum's account in *Tibet.* Coincidentally, Crozier also had an early brush with flying. When Crozier was still living in Post, Amelia Earhart, barnstorming her way across the country, flew into town and offered flights to anyone willing and able to pay. There were few takers, so the town of Post held a lottery, and Crozier's father won. Soon he was soaring high above cotton and corn fields he had only ever seen from the ground, clinging on as he buzzed and swooped over cheering crowds below. The episode did not trigger in Crozier any desire to fly, but it did give his father one of the biggest thrills of his life.

Page 10. *A propeller and wings...* McCallum also tattooed his G. I. serial number onto his arm.

Page 10. *"A guy who wouldn't have trouble..."* From Glen Marker, a Hump pilot who knew both Crozier and McCallum. Interview by authors, phone conversation, September 2001.

Page 12. *The higher the plane went...* The C-87 had a service ceiling of 28,000 feet at a takeoff weight of 56,000 pounds.

Page 12. *That morning at their base in Jorhat...* The plane left Jorhat at ten o'clock in the morning and arrived in Kunming at one o'clock that afternoon.

Page 12. *And the nacelles...* Nacelles are the outer casings of the engines.

Page 12. *Also it was Perram's job...* Perram was considered well suited to this task. In September 1943, he was described by his superior, Second Lieutenant Paul S. Silverston, as "honest, capable of any duty assigned to him, and always eager to progress." From Perram's family papers.

Page 13. *With little more than a year...* Spencer enlisted in September 1942, a few months after graduating from South Side High School in Rockville Centre.

Page 13. *The right-colored flares...* The color of the flares was changed every day.

Page 13. *Arranged through McCallum...* McCallum and Huffman were the only two members of the crew who had known each other before the flight.

Page 14. *A few minutes before four o'clock...* The plane's departure was delayed while one of the crew went to look for Dan Green, an airman who had hitched a ride over the Hump from India to China that morning. Green was not planning to return to India with Crozier, but had left his parachute on the plane, and Crozier wanted to return it before he took off for Jorhat.

Chapter Two

Page 16. *"Ceiling unlimited..."* From "Missing Air Crew Report," issued by the War Department, Washington D.C., December 1943. From the U.S. Air Force Historical Research Agency, Montgomery, Ala.

Page 20. *The wind outside...* Even under more normal conditions, winds above 20,000 feet can be incredibly strong, often blowing at 160-180 mph.

Page 21. *"Evidently wrong..."* From the secret report, now declassified (EO 11652), in which members of the crew were debriefed, after their return to India. The report, issued by the Headquarters, Western Sector, India China Wing, Air Transport Command, is dated January 14, 1944. From U.S. Air Force Historical Research Agency, Montgomery, Ala.

Page 22. *The top of a big cumulus cloud...* From McCallum's account in *Tibet.*

Page22. *"There's another. Off to the left!"* This and subsequent quotes from the *New York Times,* January 19, 1944.

Page 23. *Straight out at them...* From McCallum's account in *Tibet.* The mountains were so close that "if the gear had been down, we would have rolled it through the snow."

Page 24. *One of their superchargers...* From Huffman's account in McCallum's *Tibet.*

Page 24. *Going to have to bail out...* The airmen bailed out at 2145 or 9:45 p.m.

Page 24. *"There's the door..."* Many of the pilots and crew were given no training on bailing out, or on survival if they managed to land in one piece. One said his training amounted to being told to "Count three and pull the ripcord." Another said his training was "Here's a chute, there's the door." Interview with Hump pilots by the authors.

Page 25. *But now it was stuck...* From Huffman's account and from McCallum's account in *Tibet.*

Page 26. *"We've still got plenty of time...."* Quote and subsequent detail from Huffman's account in *Tibet.*

Page 26. *They saw Crozier go first...* It was generally expected that captains jumped last, after they made sure that all members of their crew had managed to get out. In real life, that didn't always happen. Also, the expectation was based on the assumption that the pilot was needed to keep the plane flying while the others bailed out. In Crozier's case, that didn't apply, as he and McCallum had trimmed the plane and set it on automatic pilot.

When the crash of the plane was later investigated, Air Transport Command concluded that "the abandoning of the ship by the crew indicates good leadership on the part of Lt. Crozier, and it is evident that they all left almost simultaneously, which (allowed for) regrouping of the crew in a short time." From the now-declassified secret report.

Page 26. *He was followed...* From Huffman's account in *Tibet.* Huffman saw Crozier bail out first, with Spencer right behind. When Huffman then jumped, McCallum and Perram were still in the plane. But Perram must have jumped last, given his position on landing, relative to the others.

Page 26. *Less than forty-five seconds...* This and subsequent detail comes from the now-declassified secret report.

Page 27. *He was shaking with cold...* Crozier estimated the temperature was twenty degrees below zero. McCallum says it was twenty-six degrees below zero.

Chapter Three

Page 29. *Sew the cut closed...* From Dorothy Crozier, interview by authors, September 2001.

Page 29. *Still in China...* At this point, the airmen had no idea they were in Tibet. They were, in fact, on the south side of the Tsangpo river, about fifteen to twenty miles west of the village of Tsetang. Their plane crashed on the north side of the river.

Page 30. *Every day for the rest of his life...* From McCallum's daughter, Mary. Interview by authors, phone conversation, August 2001.

Page 31. *Thought he could hear...* From Huffman's account in McCallum's *Tibet,* in which he says he could actually see "one of the fellows" above him.

Page 32. *"Like long-lost brothers..."* From McCallum's account in *Tibet.*

Page 33. *A few extra bullets...* Both Crozier and Spencer had a magazine with seven bullets in each one.

Page 33. *They rested until one o'clock...* From declassified report.

Page 34. *An irate father...* Huffman's mother may have been almost as rough. In a letter he wrote to Perram's parents, dated November 10, 1944, Huffman says, "I can sure remember when she'd get me down to scrub my ears and neck, before I took off for school. I'd put up a howl that if she wanted to dig in my ears, to go get a spade." From Perram's family papers.

Page 34. *"Poor, poor, poor..."* From Huffman's sister, Norma. Interview by authors, phone conversation, November 2001.

Page 35. *"Another miserable night..."* From Huffman's account in McCallum's *Tibet.*

Page 36. *"Tire, auto, and accessory business..."* From Perram's father's application to become an American citizen. From Perram's family papers.

Page 36. *He was sent overseas...* Perram qualified as an aircraft maintenance specialist on May 13, 1943.

Page 36. *"A man with a character..."* In a letter written "To Whom it May Concern," dated December 7, 1942, a neighbor in Tulsa, Oklahoma, described Perram "as a good boy, never in any trouble of any kind." He was, the neighbor said, "a man with character above reproach—honest, dependable, and trustworthy." Perram's Personnel Officer, First Lieutenant Lanham B. Thomas, also said Perram was "trustworthy," and someone who could "be depended on to do the job to the best of his ability." From Perram's family papers.

Page 37. *Firing a shot at a bird...* From McCallum's account in *Tibet.* "The .45 was not a very accurate pistol."

Page 37. *"Like buffalo, but with a lot more hair..."* From McCallum's account.

Chapter Four

Page 39. *An enthusiastic round of applause...* From Dr. Pemba's *Young Days in Tibet* (Jonathan Cape, 1957). "The villagers had never seen such queer people as the Americans before. They all turned out in a crowd, and, as the Americans shuffled into the village, began a thunderous clapping in order to drive out these devils from another world...."

Page 41. *This was no Shangri-La...* From *Long Island Daily Press,* Saturday, September 10, 1955. "Most of the natives looked old and withered—no eternal youth as in the Shangri-la of James Hilton's *Lost Horizon.*"

Page 42. *A dozen or more villagers...* McCallum estimated about fifty.

Page 44. *"A gentle cluck of the tongue..."* From Huffman's account in McCallum's *Tibet.*

Page 45. *"All saddled up and ready to go..."* From Huffman's account.

Page 45. *"A kind of broken English..."* From Huffman's account.

Page 46. *He was taken straight to Ullah's house...* This was on December 5. Both Perram and Huffman arrived in Tsetang that day. The other three airmen had arrived on December 2.

Page 46. *"The happiest bunch of guys..."* From Huffman's account in *Tibet.*

Chapter Five

Page 47. *A population of about two-and-a-half million...* Estimate from *Tibetan Precis,* by Hugh Richardson. London: British Library L/PS/20/D222.

Page 48. *But with rare exceptions...* Probably the first Westerners to reach Lhasa were two Jesuits, an Austrian and a Belgian, who arrived in 1661 and spent a month there.

Page 52. *He was keen to let people know he was alive...* Telegrams had been sent to the airmen's families, saying that they were missing. On December 7, 1943, McCallum's mother was told, "The Secretary of War desires me to express his deep regret that your son Flight Officer Harold J. McCallum has been reported missing in flight since Thirty November in the Asiatic area. If further details or other information are received you will be promptly notified." By that time, McCallum's basha had already been cleared of his possessions on the assumption that he would not be returning. From McCallum's family papers.

Page 55. *They decided they must all be "sissies."* From *CBI Roundup*, an Army newspaper published in India, dated February 3, 1944.

Page 56. *Who tried to tuck him in at night...* From *Collier's* magazine, September 23, 1944.

Chapter Six

Page 57. *The Tibetan capital was already on edge...* From Sherriff weekly letter of December 5, 1943. London: British Library and Public Record Office. "There is some anxiety in Lhasa lately owing to the reported behaviour of one of the water gods in the Cathedral... The appearance of the aeroplane over Lhasa on 30th November has not made things any easier...."

Page 57. *There was widespread agreement...* From Sherriff letter, December 5, 1943. "The official view is that it was a Chinese plane... In some parts of Tibet there seems to be considerable fear of an aerial attack...."

Page 58. *Exhibited many of the qualities...* The Dalai Lama was selected after a long search that saw the elimination of two other worthy candidates.

Page 58. *Like the Kashag, the National Assembly...* Structure of government comes from *Tibetan Precis*.

Page 58. *A Regent named Reting Rinpoche...* Reting played a major role in the search for the fourteenth Dalai Lama. This greatly boosted his status.

Page 59. *A much-shortened life...* Reting was later charged with treason; he had become too close to the Chinese. He died shortly afterward, in prison.

Page 59. *Reting was replaced...* Reting had an agreement with his successor to return to his post in two years' time, but the arrangement fell apart and led to a long and bitter period of infighting.

Page 59. *The even-then-ancient Buddhist religion...* Although Buddhism was introduced to Tibet in the seventh century, it took a long time to gain a foothold. Initially, it had to displace, or be integrated with, the religion of Bon, so it encountered considerable resistance.

Page 60. *One particular order...* These were the Yellow Hats.

Page 61. *When the Great Fifth died...* A Regent concealed the Great Fifth's death for fourteen years.

Page 61. *During the long period of Tibet's isolation...* Tibet's isolation was largely designed to keep out the British, who were thought to have colluded in the Gurkha invasion from Nepal, which took place in 1788.

Page 61. *Their authority declined...* Ambans were in Tibet from 1728 to 1911.

Page 63. *"Which one of you blighters...."* From Hopkirk's *Trespassers on the Roof of the World* (Oxford University Press, 1982).

Page 63. *In article 2 of the initialed Convention...* From Richardson's *Tibet and its History* (Shambhala Publications, 1984).

Page 64. *At the Pacific War Council...* Quotations come from White House memorandum dated May 20, 1943. New York: Franklin D. Roosevelt Presidential Library and Museum.

Page 64. *"The Chinese continue to increase their forces..."* From Sherriff weekly letter, October 3, 1943.

Page 65. *The plane's crew had to be working for the Chinese...* From Sherriff letter, December 19, 1943. "The Tibetan Government were therefore sure that the American plane was really a Chinese one... One officer had on his back a Chinese flag and notice in Chinese..." Also from Betty Sherriff writing in *A Quest of Flowers* by Harold Fletcher, Frank Ludlow and George Sherriff (Edinburgh University Press, 1975). "Reports came to the Tibetan Government that the airmen had Chinese writing on their backs and this led the Government to believe that they were Chinese and not American...."

Page 65. *Bringing them back for interrogation...* From Sherriff weekly letter, December 12, 1943. "George Tsarong... told me privately that the airmen had asked... to go direct to India, but that the Kashag had sent instructions that they should come to Lhasa. Presumably the Tibetan Government wish to know why the aeroplane came over Lhasa."

Chapter Seven

Page 68. *Asking China to have him recalled...* Kung did not leave Lhasa until May 1944.

Page 69. *That basically meant Britain, as well as Nepal...* Bhutan also had a representative in Lhasa.

Page 69. *One of the four members of the Kashag...* When the five American airmen arrived in Lhasa, Surkhang Dzasa was head of the Foreign Office, but, unusually, he was not at the time also a member of the Kashag.

Page 70. *"An excellent illustration of passing the baby..."* From Ludlow weekly letter, August 24, 1942. London: British Library and Public Record Office.

Page 70. *So independently of the Tibetans...* From Sherriff letter, December 19, 1943. "The attitude of the Chinese in the whole case (of the airmen) has been what one might perhaps expect. They never once, from beginning to end, approached the Tibetan Government. They sent their men out and got reports back, admittedly quicker and more accurate than the Tibetan Government's reports...."

Page 71. *Frederick Williamson...* Williamson was the British Consul General in Kashgar who introduced Sherriff and Ludlow. Before then, he had been the British Trade Agent in Gyantse, when Ludlow had been headmaster of the English school there.

Page 71. *"Our interests in Tibet..."* From the British government's "Political Department." London: British Library and Public Record Office. FO/371/46121.

Page 72. *Eden had sent his Chinese counterpart...* Memorandum from Anthony Eden dated August 5, 1943. London: British Library and Public Record Office. FO/371/93001.

Page 75. *He, too, assumed that it was Chinese...* From Sherriff letter, December 19, 1943. "On 6th December, when I still thought the plane must be Chinese... I called on Dr. Kung and told him what I had done... He was very pleased, doubly so, as I have little doubt he thought the plane was Chinese...."

Chapter Eight

Page 80. *The following morning...* This was December 12, 1943.

Page 81. *Introduced them to "the Western handshake"...* From McCallum's account in *Tibet.* "The whole village turned out... I guess we shook hands with about 2,000 people before we left Tsetang...."

Page 83. *At this altitude was invariably served cold...* At high altitude, because of the lower pressure, water boils at a lower temperature than it does at sea level.

Page 85. *Long have had his crew on oxygen...* Many crews went on oxygen above 12,000 feet, although others preferred to wait until they were above 15,000 feet.

Chapter Nine

Page 87. *He had received two days before...* This was on December 13. From Sherriff letter, December 19, 1943.

Page 87. *Had sent him a separate note...* This was on December 11.

Page 87. *Sherriff had also learned—unofficially...* This was on December 9.

Page 87. *Almost daily visits...* From Sherriff letter, December 19, 1943. London: British Library. "I asked on each occasion I saw the Foreign

Office for any official news, but they gave me none. This at the time was curious and I could not understand what was being done by the Tibetan government. I saw the Foreign Office nearly every day and gave what information I could, but was given none in return. I had however heard through a friend that the airmen had been called to Lhasa."

Page 88. *Some kind of "stunt"*... Annotation to a British government memo. London: British Library. "It now seems to be established that the aeroplane reported in the east diary as having flown over Lhasa was flown by Americans, and crashed south of Lhasa. One wonders whether the flight was influenced by American love for stunts, since they were a good way off Indian or Chinese territory, whichever way they came...."

Page 89. *Britain shifted its ground...* In an internal report headed "Chinese Threats to Tibet," the British government noted that "the project for a pack supply route from India to China through Tibet revived in an acute form the political dissensions over Tibetan relations with China and Great Britain. The Chinese regard Tibet as an integral part of the Chinese Republic. The Tibetans claim complete independence as from the fall of the Manchu Empire. His Majesty's Government recognise Tibetan autonomy and are committed through the Government of India to giving it diplomatic support against Chinese encroachment. They have, however, been willing hitherto to recognise Chinese 'suzerainty' over Tibet, and have in the past offered to say so in a tripartite agreement regulating Anglo-Chinese relations with Tibet and defining the frontiers on an acceptable basis. The Chinese have refused to conclude such an agreement.

"When the pack supply route was mooted, we offered to try to overcome Tibetan reluctance by the use of economic pressure, provided the Chinese Government on their side would make a public statement guaranteeing Tibetan autonomy. The Chinese refused and took the line that they would arrange matters directly with the Tibetan authorities, would appoint supervisors along the route, and would give the necessary instructions to the Tibetans." London: British Library and Public Record Office. FO/371/35755.

Page 90. *"The delay may have been due to..."* From Ludlow weekly letter, May 17, 1942. The summer migration took place on May 14.

Page 90. *Their refusal to let Kung deal...* From Ludlow weekly letter, August 24, 1942. Kung "would be unable to represent matters to the Tibetan Government, so a rather unfortunate 'impasse' has been reached between Dr. Kung and the Tibetan Government."

Page 90. *Made the Chinese government "very dependent"...* From Ludlow weekly letter of November 8, 1942.

Page 91. *China suddenly asked...* Tibet wisely said "no" to both requests.

Page 91. *One that London found "intolerable"...* From file on China's insistence on treating Tibet as a vassal state. London: Public Record Office. PREM 3/90/5B.

Page 91. *"This action of the Tibetans..."* Comment from the British government dated April 8, 1943. "It seems a pity that the Tibetans gave orders that all goods destined for China shall be held up pending a settlement of the Trans-Tibet pack route question. We had rather hoped that Chinese face might be saved by their utilising ordinary trade channels much more extensively, and so avoiding the necessity for any special contract. But this action of the Tibetans must bring things to a head and might even cause the Chinese to take forcible measures." FO/371/35754.

Page 91. *To construct a land route...* From *Tibetan Precis.* The object of the expedition was to examine the possibility of building "a motor road from India to China, but this was not disclosed to the Tibetans."

Page 92. *"Trouble on the road..."* From Ludlow weekly letter, April 4, 1943. "Tolstoy struck me as a man who trusted nobody but himself. He did not even trust Dolan, his companion, and the two were not on good terms with each other. Dolan confided to me on more than one occasion that he did not know how he was going to endure the long journey (across Tibet) to China in Tolstoy's company, and I am afraid there will be trouble on the road...."

Page 93. *"Not backward in asking..."* From Ludlow letter, April 4, 1943.

Page 93. *"No cause for complaint..."* From Ludlow letter, April 4, 1943.

Page 93. *Personal letters for President Roosevelt...* In one of the letters, the Regent wrote: "Tibet, which has been free and independent from her earliest history, devotes her entire resources to the cause of religion, and being the great seat of Buddhism, we are striving to maintain and strengthen our national and religious status...." Dated the 11th day of the first month of the Tibetan Water Sheep year—i.e., February 15, 1943. FO/371/35759.

In the other letter, the Dalai Lama wrote: "We are happy to learn that you and the people of the United States of America take great interest in our country and it is of special significance that the people of the United States of America, in association with those of twenty-seven other countries, are now engaged in a war for the preservation of freedom, which has been thrust upon them by nations bent on conquest who are intent upon destroying freedom of thought, of religion, and of action everywhere. "Tibet also values her freedom and independence enjoyed from time immemorial and being the great seat of the Buddhist Religion I am endeavouring, in spite of my tender age, to uphold and propagate our religious precepts and thereby emulate the pious work of my predecessors. I earnestly hope and pray for a speedy termination of hostilities so that the nations of the world may enjoy a lasting and righteous peace, based on the principles of freedom and goodwill..." Dated the 19th day of the first month of the Tibetan Water Sheep Year—i.e., February 24, 1943. FO/371/335739.

Page 93. *"Well designed as a prelude..."* From telegram sent by Basil Gould to George Sherriff, dated April 21, 1943. FO/371/35759.

Page 94–95. *Events had moved on...* From Sherriff letter dated December 19, 1943. The Foreign Office moved "very quickly and sent letters by special messenger to tell the airmen to go direct to the British Mission. By the time these were sent off, however, the Chinese community had met the airmen outside Lhasa and escorted them to Dr. Kung's house...."

Page 95. *They would never forget...* From McCallum's account in *Tibet*. "Suddenly in the distance, one of the most beautiful sights I have ever seen appeared before my eyes. It was Lhasa, the original Shangri-la. It was a scene so beautiful that I can hardly describe it...."

Page 96. *Was handed to Crozier...* Text of letter comes from declassified report.

Chapter Ten

Page 102. *Tibet had nothing to offer...* Quoted in the *Long Island Daily Press*, Saturday, September 10, 1955. "There's nothing in Tibet that you wouldn't find twice as good in Rockville Centre."

Page 104. *At a few minutes past six o'clock...* From declassified report and Sherriff letter, December 19, 1943.

Chapter Eleven

Page 108. *"I suppose you know...."* From Crozier's account in Sinclair's *Jump to the Land of God* (The Caxton Printers Ltd., 1965).

Page 108. *The gods would pluck them...* From Betty Sherriff, writing in *A Quest of Flowers* (among other sources). The Tibetans "had been told by their monks that no plane could fly over Lhasa and look down on the Dalai Lama and escape disaster. So, of course, no one was surprised at the news that the 'object' had dropped out of the skies near the little town of Tsetang and had crashed on the banks of the Tsangpo. Later the 'object' was identified as an American plane...."

Page 108. *"Within the realms of reason..."* From Crozier's account in *Jump to the Land of God*.

Page 108. *There was more to the stoning...* From declassified report. "The fact that we were friendly to the Chinese caused great resentment and friction on the part of the Tibetan citizens; that is, the common people...." Also from McCallum's account in *Tibet*. "There was a lot of feeling against us because we seemed to be siding with the Chinese..." There was also a precedent to the attack on the airmen. In 1904, some of Younghusband's soldiers were stoned in Lhasa because they had a Chinese escort.

Page 109. *"A very gracious lady..."* From McCallum's account in *Tibet*.

Page 109. *As she later recalled...* From Betty Sherriff, writing in *A Quest of Flowers.*

Page 110. *A Hornby clockwork train set...* The Sherriffs also gave the Dalai Lama a clockwork speedboat. British presents were very different from those offered by the Chinese. China gave the Dalai Lama traditional gifts like carpets and vases. Britain gave him toys. The young god-king was always pleased to receive the British.

Page 110. *Such "a rumpus"...* From Goodman's *The Last Dalai Lama* (Shambhala, 1986). "Kundun preferred to play with a wind-up train he had received as a gift from the British Mission. Whenever it went off the tracks, the rumpus he raised ensured that one of the attendants would hasten to set it right again."

Page 111. *"The strangest part" of their Tibetan experience...* From *Collier's* magazine, September 23, 1944.

Page 115. *A stream of misinformation...* From *Tibetan Precis.* "Much of the Chinese propaganda, treating hopes as facts, is directed at the foreign press. Here the Chinese have the field to themselves and they have taken advantage of Tibetan inarticulateness to present to the world a stream of tendentious wish-projections in the guise of facts. Their publications speak of Tibetan affairs as a Chinese domestic concern, and claim a control over events in Tibet which is quite at variance with the truth... In matters of this sort the Tibetan Government do not appear to be aware of the importance of world opinion or the power of the press...."

Page 115. *Tibetans were trying to discover...* From Sherriff's weekly letter, November 9, 1943. "The Kashag asked me through the Foreign Office if I could give them a copy of their message of congratulation to Generalissimo Chiang Kai Shek on his assumption of the office of President of the Republic of China...."

Page 115. *Deceit was not a surprise...* From *Tibetan Precis.* "Tibetans have a great regard for the truth. They prefer to procrastinate or to keep quiet rather than to tell a lie. Chinese standards appear to be more flexible. They have no objection to a useful lie, and their flights of imagination make it difficult to define the border between wish and fact. This tendency is wholly absent from the Tibetan mind.... Another deeply seated tendency of the Chinese mind is to believe, without regarding what other people would call facts, that things are as Chinese theory decrees that they ought to be. The reiteration that the Chinese are treating the Tibetans with every considera-tion and benevolence, and that the Tibetans really want only to be united to China means to the great majority of Chinese that those are the facts."

Page 116. *Now he offered to send word to India...* As a result of Fox's mes-sage, McCallum's mother received a second telegram saying, "Am pleased to inform you your son Flight Officer Harold J. McCallum who was pre-viously reported missing is now safe and accounted for. Undoubtedly he will communicate with you at an early date concerning his welfare and whereabouts." From McCallum's family papers.

Chapter Twelve

Page 118. *"Whistle up a jeep..."* From Betty Sherriff, writing in *A Quest of Flowers*. "(We) were very amused at (the Americans') surprise and dis-may when they found they could not just 'whistle up a jeep' but had to ride and walk... to reach the nearest railhead...."

Page 119. *Nothing with wheels and an engine...* From *CBI Roundup*, Feb-ruary 3, 1944.

Page 120. *"A load each of grain, tea, cloths, and silk..."* From Ludlow weekly letter, August 17, 1942. When signs of Chinese hostility were first detected, "the Tibetan Government performed a big-scale religious cere-mony below the Potala to prevent the spread of war into Tibet. Effigies of foreign troops and devils, along with a human heart, coins (and) a load each of grain, tea, cloths and silk were burnt in a huge pyre...."

Page 120. *Consult the state Oracle...* From Ludlow weekly letter, March 22, 1943. "The Kashag met to discuss the situation on the Sino-Tibetan frontier, and after prolonged discussions lasting for two days, it was de-cided that the state Oracle should be consulted...."

Page 121. *"A large Tor-gyap procession..."* From Sherriff letter of June 6, 1943.

Page 121. *Set off for the Foreign Office...* From Sherriff letter, December 19, 1943. "On December 16th I asked the Foreign Office to come and see the Americans and hear the whole story."

Page 126. *Blatant propaganda...* From Ludlow weekly letter, November 2, 1942. "The cinema is the most potent of all propaganda weapons in Tibet."

Chapter Thirteen

Page 129. *Offered to help the Americans...* From Sherriff weekly letter, December 19, 1943. "While in Lhasa, official visits were paid on the airmen by the Bhutanese representative and by a representative of the Nepalese Legation, both of whom offered all help."

Page 129. *Palais Glide and even the Boomps-a-Daisy...* From Dr. Pemba's *Young Days in Tibet* (Jonathan Cape, 1957).

Page 130. *"Singular little news this week..."* From Ludlow weekly letter, September 6, 1942.

Page 130. *"A trying week of parties..."* From Sherriff weekly letter, July 25, 1943.

Page 131. *"Which cut the guests would like..."* From Betty Sherriff, writing in *A Quest of Flowers.*

Page 132. *"Jump back suddenly..."* From McKay's *Tibet and the British Raj: the Frontier Cadre 1904-1947* (Curzon Press, 1997).

Page 133. *Tell their story "over and over..."* From McCallum's account in *Tibet.*

Page 133. *"General good feeling among all..."* From Sherriff letter dated December 19, 1943.

Page 133. *Could not be responsible...* From McCallum's account in *Tibet.* "All of a sudden they told us we had to get out of there in a hurry. If we didn't get out of Tibet pretty soon they would not be responsible for what happened to us.... We were advised by Major Sherriff that we were to get out of the Forbidden City as soon as possible. We couldn't say this in official reports before, but now it makes no difference...."

Page 134. *He angrily "refused to consider..."* From Sherriff letter, December 19, 1943.

Page 134. *"Folly of the worst kind..."* From Sherriff letter, December 19, 1943.

Chapter Fourteen

Page 137. *Sherriff had done everything possible...* From declassified report. "The Major and his wife made complete arrangements for the journey... and furnished us with a cook, food, and clothing."

Page 140. *To ward off the bandits...* From declassified report. "The reason for the escort is that bandits are prevalent in that territory."

Chapter Fifteen

Page 149. *Another fierce storm...* From McCallum's account in *Tibet*. "For days we made our way through blinding snow storms which at times blew so fiercely that we had to get off our mounts and lead the donkeys along by their reins. One of the storms was so bad that we had to stop and pitch camp while the blizzard howled through the mountains with such intensity that we couldn't hear each other talk, even when we yelled at the top of our voices."

Page 149. *Shelter in the town of Nangartse...* Nangartse is about 85 miles from Lhasa so the airmen were averaging nearly 30 miles per day.

Page 150. *Nearby Samding monastery...* The monastery was headed by the "Thunderbolt Sow," or Dorje Phagmo, the only female incarnation in Tibet.

Page 151. *Look ahead and see a mountain...* This was probably Nodzinkangsa, which is 23,800 feet high.

Page 154. *And now, so, too, was Perram...* From declassified report.

Page 154. *"Face down into his soup..."* From McCallum's account in *Tibet*. "My eyes were beginning to close and all of a sudden the next thing I knew, boom, down I went with my face right in the soup."

Page 156. *In the accompanying letter...* Roosevelt wrote that "the people of
the United States, in association with those of twenty-seven other countries, are now engaged in a war which has been thrust upon the world by
a nation bent on conquest, who are intent upon destroying freedom of
thought, of religion, and of action everywhere. The United Nations are
fighting today in defense of and for the preservation of freedom...." Letter to the Dalai Lama in Lhasa, dated July 3, 1942. It was in response to
this letter that the Dalai Lama and his Regent wrote personal letters for
President Roosevelt. See note for page 93, above, under Chapter Nine.
These letters were seen as an appeal for United States help, should the
Chinese invade Tibet.

Page 156. *A committed defender...* From *Tibetan Precis.* Americans were
seen as the "proclaimed champions of self-determination for small nations."

Page 156. *In a meeting with the Tibetan Regent...* From Ludlow weekly
letter, March 23, 1943. "Subsequently, Tolstoy told the Regent that the
American Government was in full sympathy with those weak and small
nations who wished to retain their independence. He instanced the case
of the South American states whom the United States of America could
overthrow and swallow in a very short time, but were completely independent and free. The Regent said he was greatly pleased to hear of this
state of affairs, and remarked that Tibet was a religious country and
wished to be free and independent like the states Tolstoy had mentioned."

Page 157. *Recommending to the United States government...* From Ludlow
letter, April 4, 1943. "One act of Tolstoy's in particular appealed very
strongly to the imagination of the Tibetan Government. It was this. Tolstoy mentioned one day to the Tibetan Foreign Office that he had recommended to his Government that Tibet should be represented at the
Peace Conference at the end of the war. The Foreign Office passed his
suggestion on to the Kashag and Regent. This proposal was immediately
approved of by the Tibetan Government who expressed a desire to be informed of the date of the Conference, and when and to whom an application for representation should be made...."

From Ludlow weekly letter, March 23, 1943. "When I lunched with the Regent on February 25th, Tolstoy, Dolan and I had a private interview with him. At this interview, the Regent remarked that the Foreign Office had informed him of Tolstoy's views that Tibet should be represented at the coming Peace Conference. The Regent added that he was carefully considering the matter, and that he would acquaint the Kashag and Foreign Office with his view in due course."

Chapter Sixteen

Page 160. *They entered another gorge...* This would have been the Red Idol Gorge.

Page 161. *Two huge, shallow lakes...* These were Kala tso and Rham tso.

Page 162. *Quickly disillusioned them...* From McCallum's account in *Tibet.* "We were told we would have to increase our traveling speed if we wanted to make the next mountain pass before a real snow storm set in and blocked our passage, which meant we would have to stay there for three months if we didn't make it... This was enough to spur us on at an increased pace."

Page 165. *Tears stinging his eyes...* From McCallum's account. "The Tibetan guide had tears in his eyes as we finally shook hands in our own style."

Page 165. *Fired a shot into the air...* From McCallum's account. "We have no firecrackers to celebrate with, so here goes!" He pointed his gun into the air and pulled the trigger.

Page 165. *To the airmen's horror...* From McCallum's account. It was "the most awful noise I had ever heard... an avalanche of rocks, dirt and snow heading directly towards us... It roared through the stillness.... We all had a pretty good scare...."

Page 167. *At the end of December...* From Sherriff weekly letter, January 2, 1944. "On December 29th the Foreign Office sent me a second message regarding the aeroplane which crashed on November 30th, for transmission to the American Mission in New Delhi. (My telegram No. 1206 dated December 29th refers.) In this the Tibetan Government asked the American authorities to issue orders that their planes should not fly over Tibet and asked for a reply...."

Page 167. *Polite and innocuous...* From letter sent by the Tibetan government to the American Mission in New Delhi. "On the evening of November 30th, 1943, an unknown aeroplane flew over Tibetan territory from the east and eventually crashed to the ground at Do, near Nedong, and upon enquiry it was found to be an American aircraft. Although the general public were very much perturbed and strongly resented the aeroplane coming over Tibetan territory without any previous understanding and contrary to all international law, as most friendly relations exist between the U.S.A. and Tibet, we ordered an immediate search to be made for the missing airmen. When all the five airmen, including Lieutenant Crozier, were found safe and sound they were asked to come to Lhasa, supplied with food, money and transport animals and are now being sent back to India as soon as possible...." FO/371/41585.

Page 168. *Experience along these lines...* From Sherriff letter, December 19, 1943. "As reported in the Lhasa letter of October 3rd, 1943, a Chinese plane circled over Chamdo in eastern Tibet... The Tibetan Government complained to the Chinese Government regarding this, and asked that it should not occur again... The Chinese Government had replied that this plane had flown over Chinese territory which it had every right to do...."

Page 169. *An independent government...* From Sherriff weekly letter, January 2, 1944. "In my opinion (the two letters)... showed a desire to be treated as an independent government."

Page 169. *Not willing to take on board...* In 1943, the U.S. State Department had told the British that it was aware that "the Chinese Government has long claimed suzerainty over Tibet, and that the Chinese constitution lists Tibet among areas constituting the territory of the Republic of China. This Government... has at no time raised a question regarding either of these claims. The Government of the United States does not believe that a useful purpose would be served by opening at this time a detailed discussion of the status of Tibet...." From Aide-Memoir dated

May 15, 1943, sent by the U.S. State Department to the British Embassy in Washington, and published in *Foreign Relations of the U.S., Diplomatic Papers, 1943, China, Washington.*

Page 169. *To avoid a recurrence...* From Sherriff weekly letter, January 16, 1944. "On January 10th I handed (Ringang) a note containing the message from the American Mission in Delhi regarding the plane which crashed on November 30th, vide Foreign's telegram No. 239 dated 8th January, 1944...." The note said: "In reply to your recent message transmitted through the British Mission at Lhasa regarding the unfortunate crash landing of an American military plane on Tibetan territory on November 30, 1943, I am requested by the American Military Headquarters here (in Delhi) to convey to you an expression of profound gratitude for the assistance and extremely kind treatment rendered the personnel involved. I am authorised at the same time to explain that American military aviators have strict orders to avoid flying over Tibetan territory and that the incident was purely accidental due to a miscalculation in aerial navigation on a return trip from China to Assam during the night time. I am assured that every effort will be made that such an incident does not recur. Please also accept my own sincere thanks for the Tibetan Government's benevolent consideration of the incident and the magnanimous treatment and hospitality accorded the personnel." FO/371/41585.

Page 169. *"Don'ts and Do's for Tibet"...* From declassified report.

Afterword

Page 171. *It could not let go of its suspicion...* From Sherriff weekly letter, January 16, 1944. "On January 20th I called on the Foreign Office and handed them a private letter which the American airmen had written to the Tibetan Government thanking the latter for their help and kind treatment. Even now many officials do not believe that the plane came over Lhasa due to navigational errors. The belief is still strong that the Chinese had a hand in the business and that it was just bad luck that the plane crashed and did not get back safely to China...."

Page 171. *Was reprimanded for giving the Tibetans false hope...* From letter to Basil Gould from H. Weightman, Joint Secretary to the Government of India. "The Government of India disapprove of Ludlow's action
in associating himself with the suggestion made by Tolstoy that Tibet
should be represented at the Peace Conference... Such a suggestion was
clearly ill-conceived... Ludlow's support of the proposal was therefore un-
wise and little in consonance with his admirable handling of the other
problems with which he has dealt in so satisfactory a manner while he
was in charge of the mission in Lhasa... We should be glad to have your
views as to the best means of repairing the damage done by Ludlow's
statement without unduly alarming the Tibetan Government...."
FO/371/35759.

Page 171. *In one message...* The Chinese rewrote the message sent by the
Regent on behalf of the Dalai Lama so that, directly counter to the Tibetans' intentions, the message said, "I am happy to learn that the people of the whole of China, who hold Your Excellency in great esteem,
have elected you as the President of our Republic and Commander-in-
Chief of the Naval, Military, and Air Forces. Your great virtues and
achievements are truly unprecedented and unrivalled in China. The
whole nation, including the people in this part of the country, are singing
your praises. Your election to the highest office of the Republic adds
glory not only to our native land but also to the universe as a whole.
Henceforth our strong internal unity will surely lead to our national rejuvenation and all people, both in this country and abroad, are eagerly
looking forward to the early realization of international peace and goodwill. I hereby pay Your Excellency my highest respect and pray for your
personal welfare." FO/371/35760.

Page 172. *Fallen victim to "Chinese tricks..."* From memo dated March
20, 1944. "The Chinese are certainly doing well at persuading the world
that the Tibetans wish to be subject to China ..." FO/371/41585.

Page 172. *Take necessary action...* From White House memorandum
dated May 20, 1943. New York: Franklin D. Roosevelt Presidential Library and Museum.

Page 172. *Notified the U.S. State Department...* From a "strictly confidential" note sent to the U.S. State Department by George Atcheson, Jr., Charge d'Affaires at the United States Embassy in Chungking, dated September 20, 1943.

Page 173. *"Renewed assurances..."* In 1948, the United States gave the Chinese "renewed assurances of our recognition of China's de jure sovereignty or suzerainty over Tibet..." It also determined that "any decided change in our policy might give China cause for complaint." From *Foreign Relations of the United States, 1949, Volume IX, The Far East: China.*

Page 173. *Pulled out of India...* "The UK no longer has an abiding interest in the future of Tibet since British control was withdrawn from India, our Embassy in London reports in August, 1947 on the basis of discussions with a British Foreign Office official." From *Foreign Relations of the United States, 1949, Volume IX.*

Page 173. *A total of five Westerners in Tibet...* From *The Last Dalai Lama.*

Page 173. *As has been well documented...* A personal account of Tibetan life under Chinese rule is given in *Fire Under the Snow* by Palden Gyatso, published by The Harvill Press, London, 1997. For a more general history, see *Tears of Blood: A Cry for Tibet* by Mary Craig, published by Counterpoint, Washington, D.C., 1999.

Page 177. *"Good leadership..."* From declassified report.

Page 179. *"I know there is nothing I can say...."* From Huffman letter to Perram's parents dated March 28, 1944. From Perram's family papers.

BIBLIOGRAPHY

Bell, Sir Charles. *Tibet Past and Present.* Oxford at the Clarendon Press, 1924.

———. *The People of Tibet.* Oxford at the Clarendon Press, 1928.

Bernard, Theos. *Penthouse of the Gods.* New York: Charles Scribner's Sons, 1939.

Berzin, Alexander, and N.S. Kuleshov. *Russia's Tibet File.* Dharamsala, India: Library of Tibetan Works and Archives, 1996.

Bhanja, Dr. K. C. *Mystic Tibet and The Himalaya.* Delhi: Gian Publishing House, 1987. First published in 1948.

Bird, Isabella. *Among the Tibetans.* New York: F.H. Revell, 1894.

Brackenbury, Wade. *Yak Butter and Black Tea.* Chapel Hill, N.C.: Algonquin Books of Chapel Hill, 1997.

Chan, Victor. *Tibet Handbook,* Chico, Calif.: Moon Publications, 1994.

Chapman, F. Spencer. *Lhasa the Holy City.* London: Harper & Brothers, 1939.

———. *Memoirs of a Mountaineer.* London: Chatto & Windus, 1951.

Chodag, Tiley. *Tibet: The Land and the People.* Beijing, China: New World Press, 1998.

Chophel, Norbu. *Folk Culture of Tibet.* Dharamsala, India: Library of Tibetan Works and Archives, 1983.

Coleman, Graham. *A Handbook of Tibetan Culture.* Boston: Shambhala, 1994.

Constein, Dr. Carl Frey. *Born to Fly the Hump.* 1st Books Library, 2001.

Dargyay, Eva. *Tibetan Village Communities.* Warminster, England: Aris & Phillips, 1982.

Das, Sarat Chandra. *Journey to Lhasa and Central Tibet.* New Delhi: Manjurst Publishing House, 1970. First published in 1902.

David-Neel, Alexandra. *My Journey to Lhasa.* Boston: Beacon Press, 1986.

de Riencourt, Amaury. *Roof of the World.* New York: Rinehart & Co., 1950.

Downie, Don, and Jeff Ethell. *Flying the Hump.* Osceola, Wisc.: Motor-books International, 1995.

Duncan Date, Marion. *Customs and Superstitions of Tibet.* 1964.

Feigon, Lee. *Demystifying Tibet.* Chicago: Ivan R. Dee, 1996.

Fletcher, Harold, Frank Ludlow and George Sherriff. *A Quest of Flowers.* Edinburgh, Scotland: Edinburgh University Press, 1975.

Ford, Corey. *Donovan of the OSS.* Boston: Little Brown and Company, 1970.

Ford, Robert. *Captured in Tibet.* London: George Harrap and Co., 1957.

————. *Wind Between the World.* New York: David McKay Co., 1957.

Forman, Harrison. *Through Forbidden Tibet.* Delhi, India: Cosmo Publications, 1996.

Foster, Barbara M. *Forbidden Journey: the Life of Alexandra David-Neel.* San Francisco: Harper and Row, 1987.

Goldstein, Melvyn. *History of Modern Tibet 1913–1951: The Demise of the Lamaist State.* Berkeley: University of California Press, 1989.

Goodman, Michael Harris. *The Last Dalai Lama.* Boston: Shambhala, 1986.

Gould, B. J. *The Jewel in the Lotus.* London: Chatto & Windus, 1957

Hedin, Sven. *Trans-Himalaya: Discoveries and Adventures in Tibet.* London: Macmillan, vols. 1 and 2, 1909; vol. 3, 1913.

Hopkirk, Peter. *Trespassers on the Roof of the World: the Race for Lhasa.* Oxford: Oxford University Press, 1982.

Jones Tung, Rosemary. *A Portrait of Lost Tibet.* Reprint ed., Berkeley: University of California Press, 1996.

Kingdon Ward, F. *A Plant Hunter in Tibet.* London: Jonathan Cape, 1934.

Knaus, John Kenneth. *Orphans of the Cold War.* New York: Public Affairs, 1999.

Lamb, Alastair. *Tibet, China and India 1914–1950: a History of Imperial Diplomacy.* London: Roxford Books, 1989.

Landor, Henry Savage. *An Explorer's Adventures in Tibet.* La Crescenta, Calif.: Mountain N'Air Books, 2000.

Larsen, Knud, and Amund Sinding-Larsen. *The Lhasa Atlas.* Boston: Shambhala, 2001.

Li, Tieh-Tseng. *Tibet Today and Yesterday.* New York: Bookman Associates, 1960.

Maraini, Fosco. *Secret Tibet.* Reprint ed., London: The Harvill Press, 2000. First published in 1952.

McCallum, H. J. (Mac). *Tibet - One Second to Live.* Self-published, 1995.

McGovern, William Montgomery. *To Lhasa in Disguise.* New York and London: The Century Co., 1924.

McKay, Alex. *Tibet and the British Raj: the Frontier Cadre 1904–1947.* Richmond, Surrey, England: Curzon Press, 1997.

Normanton, Simon. *Tibet: The Lost Civilisation.* Viking Penguin Inc., 1989.

Pemba, Dr. Tsewang W. *Young Days in Tibet.* London: Jonathan Cape, 1957.

Quinn, Chick Marrs. *The Aluminum Trail.* Self-published, 1989.

Richardson, Hugh. *Tibet and its History.* 2nd ed., revised and updated. London: Shambhala Publications, 1984.

Rockhill, William Woodville. *The Land of the Lamas.* New York: Century Co., 1891.

Roosevelt, Kermit, and Theodore Roosevelt. *East of the Sun and West of the Moon.* New York: Charles Scribner's Sons, 1926.

Shakabpa, Tsepon W. D. *Tibet - A Political History.* New Haven: Yale University Press, 1967.

Shen, Tsung-Lien. *Tibet and the Tibetans.* Stanford, Calif: Stanford University Press, 1953.

Sinclair, William Boyd. *Jump to the Land of God.* Caldwell, Idaho: The Caxton Printers Ltd., 1965.

Smith, Richard Harris. *OSS: The Secret History of America's First Central Intelligence Agency.* Berkeley: University of California Press, 1972.

Spencer, Otha C. *Flying the Hump: Memories of an Air War.* College Station: Texas A&M University Press, 1994.

Thies, Jan (ed.). *China Airlift, the Hump*. Poplar Bluff, Mo.: Hump Pilots Association, 1983.

Tucci, Giuseppe. *To Lhasa and Beyond*. Ithaca, N.Y.: Snow Lion Publications, 1987.

Turnbull, Colin, and Thubten Jigme Norbu. *Tibet*. New York: Simon and Schuster, 1968.

Williamson, Margaret, and John Snelling. *Memoirs of a Political Officer's Wife in Tibet, Sikkim and Bhutan*. Dorset, England: Wisdom Publications, 1987.

About the Author

RICHARD STARKS IS AN AWARD-WINNING JOURNALIST, former editor, publisher, and author of four other books. Miriam Murcutt is a former magazine writer and editor, and publishing industry marketing executive. Both authors have traveled extensively throughout the more mountainous regions of the world, and they have made many trips to the Himalayas. They have also walked with pilgrims around the *koras* of some of Tibet's greatest monasteries. And they have crossed the Tibetan plateau to follow, as closely as possible, the route taken by the five airmen whose story is told in this book. The authors may be contacted at starksmurcutt@msn.com.

IN PRAISE OF *LOST IN TIBET*

"A well-written and interesting tale . . . A good story that's an interesting footnote to world history."

—Associated Press

"An intriguing tale . . . that keeps the reader riveted to the story. A 'must read' for WWII enthusiasts."

—American Legion Observer

"Starks and Murcutt have crafted a nonfiction adventure that would make a good action film. *Lost in Tibet* vividly weaves contemporary political intrigue with five American airmen's mission to return to base, one making the other more vivid, even as it provides insights into a once secret world."

—Daily Camera

"The authors tell this engaging tale clearly, skillfully keeping its different elements in balance while keeping a focus on the plight of the airmen. From their travels to mountainous areas in Asia, they bring a special sense of the five airmen's struggles to survive in the Tibetan terrain at the beginning, and again at the end, of their incredible story."

—Midwest Book Review

"A page-turner for readers enamored of true-life adventure tales. China's 1950 invasion of Tibet is a major sub-current of the book, and its seeming inevitability provides the sense of doom hanging over Tibet throughout the story."

—Climbing magazine

"A gripping, detailed account of a time and place (pre-Chinese Tibet) that most Americans have never glimpsed."

—Joint Forces Journal

"An entertaining and well-written book . . . The authors tell this story with an exemplary understanding of the issues, and prove themselves masters of the Himalayan terrain . . . An amazing story, still remarkably fresh sixty years after the fact."

—National Geographic Adventure